DOES EDUCATION MATTER?

D0625848

DOES EDUCATION MATTER?

BRIAN SIMON

LAWRENCE AND WISHART

London

Lawrence and Wishart Limited
39 Museum Street
London WC1A 1LQ

First published 1985
© Brian Simon, 1985

Photoset in North Wales by
Derek Doyle & Associates, Mold, Clwyd.
Printed in Great Britain by
Oxford University Press

Contents

Foreword

In a long and distinguished career Brian Simon has never hesitated, when the occasion arose, to break a lance in favour of educational advance. In 1953 he published his first challenging book, *Intelligence Testing and the Comprehensive School*, as a young lecturer in education. In the 1980s, as Emeritus Professor of the University of Leicester, his writing on education and its history continues, supplemented by travel as a guest professor, and it is mainly his more recent lectures and writings in this capacity that make up this volume, with its challenging title.

In the late 1950s, when I was senior history master in a London comprehensive school, I was privileged to be invited to contribute a chapter on 'the common history syllabus' to a symposium entitled *New Trends in Education*, edited by Brian Simon and published by MacGibbon and Kee in 1957. In succeeding years further lances were broken with advocates of 'streaming' and the notorious IQ, most conspicuously with the late Cyril Burt, whose failure to convince by argument led him to fake the evidence with disastrous results both for his own reputation and for the theories he had long proclaimed. There is a return to this episode in a chapter of the present book. But since these comparatively early days Brian has widened his range. He has written a three-volume (soon to become a four-volume) series of *Studies in the History of Education*, published papers on the local history of education, and co-edited the symposium *The Victorian Public School*.

The first President of the International Standing Conference for the History of Education, and Chairman of the History of Education Society in this country, Brian Simon also served a term as President of the British Education Research Association. He has recently taken part in a large scale funded project on primary classrooms and what goes on in them, known as ORACLE (Observational Research and Classroom

Learning Evaluation), the results of which have been published in four volumes which have aroused much interest among teachers. He has been awarded honorary degrees by the Catholic University of Louvain in Belgium and by the Open University, and been a visiting lecturer at Universities in Canada, Sweden, Australia and West Germany. His most recent concerns have been with educational theory in, for instance, 'Why No Pedagogy in England?', included here, and with the politics of education in 'Education and the Right Offensive' and 'Breaking School Rules'. These are all items in a collection which, I have no doubt, will meet an enthusiastic response.

George Rudé
January 1985

Introduction

The essays, articles and lectures collected in this volume, several of which make the case that education does matter, and matters very much in terms of human development and social change, are all concerned with contemporary issues in education and its relations with society. Their composition, over the last five or six years, has been motivated by a variety of factors. An invitation to deliver the annual Fink lecture at the University of Melbourne early in 1981 gave the opportunity to focus on the difficult issue of the relation between theory and practice in education. Another, to the University of British Columbia, tangles with the crucial question of the relation between educational and social change. Both these issues are approached historically, as indeed are others in this volume, for I remain firmly convinced that historical study is essential to understanding.

Other questions discussed also arose from invitations – the three Memorial lectures, for instance, permitted concentration on relevant issues in each case: on the neglected topic of the part played by local government and teachers in the development of the publicly provided system of education (the Lady Simon of Wythenshawe Memorial lecture, 'To Whom Do Schools Belong?'); on the development of the concept and practice of comprehensive education over the last forty years (the Raymond King Memorial lecture, 'Secondary Education for All in the 1980s'), and, in the case of the Marx Memorial lecture, on a contemporary assessment of Karl Marx's many-sided contribution ('Marx and the Crisis in Education').

Over thirty years ago I had the temerity to write a short book critical of the theory and technology of mental testing, *Intelligence Testing and the Comprehensive School* (1953). This, it seems, was hardly appreciated by Cyril Burt who, according to his biographer, was determined to re-present his case with the whole armoury of weapons at his command. The world now

9

knows the outcome. The paper on this, also highly
controversial topic was requested by the Vancouver Institute –
a successful 'town and gown' organisation at Vancouver which
attracts 500 or more consistently to its lecture series. 'The IQ
Controversy: the case of Cyril Burt' is, therefore, based on
what might be called a 'popular' lecture, but attempts to
explicate the key educational issues raised by this extraordinary
case.

Other papers deal with closely related questions of
psychology and education. The profound (and historical)
disdain for pedagogy in England has for long seemed a
phenomenon worth investigating, and if possible, interpretation. This forms the subject matter of 'Why No Pedagogy in
England?' A further paper tackles a very specific question, if of
a different order. Why did Samuel Taylor Coleridge, who
named his first son Hartley to celebrate the work of the first
systematic psychologist whose outlook underpinned the
Enlightenment concept of the perfectibility of man, several
years later devote four chapters of his remarkable *Biographia
Literaria* to demolishing the whole (or most of) Hartleian
theory? And what was the significance for *education* of
Coleridge's transition? These are fascinating issues, having I
believe considerable relevance for education today.

The collection finishes with two papers analysing the
contemporary scene – specifically the policy, ideology and
actions of the Thatcher governments since 1979. The first,
'Education and the Right Offensive', was written only some six
months after the election of that year; the second, 'Breaking
School Rules', in the summer of 1984. This is based on an
invited lecture to the secondary school section of the National
Union of Teachers, given at its annual conference at Blackpool
in April 1984.

It will be evident that certain issues predominate. First, a
deep concern about the implications of the powerful
centralising thrust which has been apparent from the
mid-1970s (and even earlier), now sharply accelerated. And
second, a series of specifically educational issues relating to the
form and content of educational systems and their social
relations. The interpretations offered will, hopefully, contribute to clarifying some at least of the issues at stake.

These papers could not have been written without the support of many friends and institutions. My thanks are due to the Universities of Melbourne and of British Columbia for their invitations, and particularly to Gwyneth Dow and William Bruneau for their kindness and stimulation during these visits. They are due also to the City of Manchester Education Committee, to the New Education Fellowship and to the Marx Memorial Library for inviting me to give the three Memorial lectures reprinted here; and to the Vancouver Institute for motivating me to write once more on IQs and for providing one of the liveliest and largest audiences it has been my privilege to address on what some might regard as an abstruse psychological matter. My thanks are also due to Martin Jacques, editor of *Marxism Today*, for demanding that I focus my attention from time to time on the contemporary politics of education. I should like also to thank my publishers, Lawrence and Wishart, and their manager, Jeff Skelley. In more than 30 years of working with this firm I have experienced nothing but kindness and encouragement, together with constructive criticism and advice. I am grateful also to George Rudé, teacher at one of London's first comprehensive schools in the 1950s and now a distinguished historian, for contributing a foreword to this book.

Finally I must add that every topic that features in this book has been discussed thoroughly with Joan Simon. Our partnership extends now to some 45 years, and it is impossible adequately to acknowledge what I owe to her consistent support and, above all, to the stimulation of what has been a lifelong dialogue (or seminar) on all the issues discussed here and, of course, many others as well.

Brian Simon
Leicester
January 1985

Acknowledgements

Thanks are due to the Centre for the Study of Curriculum and Instruction, University of British Columbia, for permission to reprint the paper, 'Can Education Change Society?' from J. Donald Wilson (ed.), *An Imperfect Past: Education and Society in Canadian History* (1984); to Melbourne University Press for permission to reprint 'Education in Theory, Schooling in Practice: the experience of the last hundred years' from Stephen Murray-Smith (ed.), *Melbourne Studies in Education, 1982* (1983); to the City of Manchester Education Committee for permission to reprint 'To Whom Do Schools Belong?', from *Problems and Perspectives in Education* (the Lady Simon of Wythenshawe Memorial Lectures 1974-1978); to Batsford Academic and Educational Ltd (and to my editorial colleague, Dr William Taylor) for permission to reprint 'Why No Pedagogy in England?', from Brian Simon and William Taylor (eds.), *Education in the Eighties, the Central Issues* (1981); to Malcolm Skilbeck, editor of the *New Era*, for permission to reprint 'Secondary Education for All in the 1980s: the Challenge to the Comprehensive School' (the Raymond King Memorial Lecture); to Martin Jacques, editor of *Marxism Today*, for permission to reprint 'Marx and the Crisis in Education' (the Marx Memorial Lecture 1977), 'Education and the Right Offensive' and 'Breaking School Rules'.

These articles and papers are reproduced as they were published except for the elimination of some unnecessary repetition and the correction of minor errors.

Brian Simon
Leicester
January 1985

1

Can Education Change Society?

The best laid plans of mice and men, wrote Robbie Burns, gang oft agley. Much the same thought, if in a different context, was expressed by Karl Marx. However carefully planned particularly social policies may be, he wrote, the outcomes will not be those desired by any one of the groupings concerned. Unexpected outcomes, in fact, are the rule, rather than the exception.

When the Russian monarchy in the early nineteenth century was concerned to ensure in an economical and tested way the production of administrators and bureaucrats to administer that vast and ramshackle domain, not unreasonably (in the context of the times) they took Prussia as their model, and established in the main cities the equivalent of the German classical gymnasia and, in St Petersburg and Moscow, both universities and higher professional schools (for instance, the famous Medical Academy and others, which reflected the French Grandes Ecoles). The outcome of this policy was, however, hardly that desired. Certainly these institutions did produce the officials and bureaucrats, the doctors, lawyers and military experts that were required. What was clearly not intended was the massive alienation and radicalisation of a large proportion of the students, leading to the great student strikes and related actions of the 1860s.

In *Training the Nihilists*, Daniel Brower analyses this striking social phenomenon, showing clearly that the radicalised students came roughly equally from all the privileged social classes, including the nobles.[1] Brower also describes the social forms and philosophic and social/political outlook of these

Lecture delivered at the University of British Columbia, Vancouver, October 1983.

students, the literature that they used for their own self-education (the French socialists, Saint-Simon, Fourier, and the English political economists in particular), and the way this student movement linked with the democratic thinking of the leading group of advanced radicals of the 1860s – Dobrolubov, Belinsky, Chernyshevsky and, in exile, of Herzen. Nihilism does not describe the outlook of the students of the 1860s, who were really children of the Enlightenment, deeply concerned with clarifying the nature of moral behaviour, especially as it concerns relations between the sexes, and whose social policies related to such matters as the establishment of small co-operative producer societies, seen as an alternative 'system' in much the same way as the early Owenites established co-operative communities in England some thirty years earlier. All this forms the subject matter of Chernyshevsky's *What is to be Done?*, a seminal and profoundly influential book which delineated the ideal type – the new man and woman – of the Russian democrats of that time. Later, in an effort to link up with 'the people', these students turned to mass literacy campaigns among workers and peasants (a movement with which Tolstoy was closely connected in his old age). The terrorist policies which followed the failure of all these initiatives were policies of despair. But it is worth recalling that Lenin's brother, who participated actively in student affairs in the 1880s, was in fact executed as a result of activities in which he was closely involved shortly after leaving university.

Is there not a direct line of connection between the alienated students of the 1840s, 50s and 60s and the events of February and October, 1917? If the relations between education and society are now generally interpreted, by neo-Marxists and by sociologists, as ensuring social reproduction, and therefore the stability and perpetuation of existing social relations, does this mean that unintended outcomes no longer occur in this field? That policies of social control always achieve their objectives?

1

What is of particular interest to the historian is not so much what the consensus views are at any given moment in time, as *how and why these views change*. Views often stated with the utmost authority and certainty, and accepted without question in one period, are totally contradicted in another, the new interpretation now finding equally widespread acceptance, again being presented with authority and certainty. In 1961, for instance, there appeared a well known reader in the sociology of education, *Education, Economy and Society*, edited by A.H. Halsey, Jean Floud, and C. Arnold Anderson; a popular and massive textbook for students at least in the English-speaking countries.[2] The many contributors here unanimously expressed the view not only that education could be, but also that it certainly was, a major factor in bringing about social change. Specifically oriented to capitalist societies in the West, it argued that, through planned expansion of education, an egalitarian society could and was being constructed in Britain and the United States in particular.

The ideological basis of this outlook lay in human capital theory, then widely accepted. Investment in human capital – that is, in education – was the key to economic, and so to social advance. Wealth creation through this means gave the opportunity for a relatively painless redistribution, and so for the construction of a more equal society in which class and other social divisions might be overcome. Education, in this interpretation, was *the* tool for social change, though, it should be noted, without disturbing basic structural features of the economy. This view was widely accepted by policy makers in the West, and provided the ideological support or legitimisation for relatively massive educational advances, particularly in the tertiary sector, but also within the school system, leading to support for experimental 'compensatory' measures such as Headstart and Follow Through in the United States, and for such positive discriminatory policies as the Education Priority Areas initiatives in Britain – master-minded, incidentally by Dr Halsey, one of the editors and compilers of the 1961 reader.

But here again there were unexpected outcomes – specifically the coincidence with this policy of another student movement which took its most radical form, perhaps, in the United States, though Britain, Canada, and in particular

France and West Germany were profoundly affected. This is
not the place to discuss this new alienation, or student
disaffection, which certainly deeply affected the subjective
experience of two or more generations of students, because I
don't want to lose sight of my argument, which concerns shifts
in consensus interpretations of the relations between education
and society. Reverting, then, to the sociologists – the discipline
which is most directly involved in offering an interpretation of
this issue – there appeared, in 1977 (that is, only sixteen years
after the volume just mentioned), another reader, more up to
date and modern in style, with a very contemporary title, *Power
and Ideology in Education*, this time edited and compiled again
by A.H. Halsey, but with a young American partner, Jerome
Karabel (not a mainstream sociologist, but a product of the
New Left – and of the 1960s student movement as we are
editorially informed).[3] And what now is the consensus view?
That education can do nothing of any significance; that it must
inevitably reflect the society which creates it, that, as mentioned
earlier, its function is that of ensuring social reproduction.
This tergiversation, and of course it is one (though nothing is
said about this aspect in the book nor any reference made to
the earlier reader), is also now reflected in the attitude of policy
makers and in government actions. What is heard of human
capital theory now? And what Western government pursues a
policy based on this ideology?

The sixteen years between the publication of the two readers,
of course, also saw the publication of several important
empirical studies and of much theorising on this crucial issue.
In the United States first Coleman and then Jencks produced
their Reports, both analysing a mass of contemporary (that is,
non-historical) data using modern social science techniques.[4]
Both reached the conclusion, as is well known, popularly
encapsulated in the phrase 'Schools make no difference'. That
is, schooling was shown to have no significant effect either on
the pattern of income distribution or on life chances; these
depended very specifically on parental status and income
(though Jencks included a factor which he called 'luck', and for
this was sharply criticised by the sociologist, Jean Floud).[5]
Nothing on quite this scale was attempted in England, but the
Coleman/Jencks thesis was influential here and elsewhere.

Both studies chimed with the times, in that, appearing in 1966 and 1972 respectively, they coincided with the beginning of a traditionalist (and populist) backlash against educational change (the first of the series of so-called Black Papers appeared in England in 1969), and with the onset of what turned out to be a world economic recession.

Perhaps more important in the long run were the many new contributions in the field of theory. In 1970 the French Marxist, Louis Althusser, published his well known essay entitled, 'Ideology and Ideological State Apparatuses', used as a set reading text by the Open University in England and so widely influential.[6] Althusser advanced a highly abstract theory as to the inevitable dominance of 'established' ideology through the education system which, he argued, had in modern times taken the place of the Church as the chief means by which the dominant ideology of a class society was perpetuated, and so that society itself. Teachers and other workers within the field of education were inevitably subsumed as agents of ideological domination, and nothing they could do could have any significant effect. Those who took a radical stance, holding that their actions as teachers could have some effect on the nature of society, and even bring about social change, were, said Althusser, 'a kind of hero', but one can only pity the futility of their efforts.[7] Some would say that it is ironic that so fatalistic and mechanistic an interpretation should be contributed by a Marxist, since Marxism surely stresses the flexibility and the complexity of the interrelations between education and society, particularly when analysed historically.

Other important theoretical contributions were made in this decade. Samuel Bowles and Herbert Gintis, best described, perhaps, as neo-Marxists, contributed their close analysis. *Schooling in Capitalist America* in 1976, arguing very ingeniously what has come to be described as the 'correspondence theory'; that the educational structure and ethos 'corresponds' to the structure and ethos of the institutions of monopoly capitalism – the factory and the modern corporation.[8] For their historical support and evidence, Bowles and Gintis rely on the works of the revisionist historians in the United States, and this foundation may be regarded as a little shaky; however that may be, in essence Bowles and Gintis reached the conclusion that, as far as the United States is concerned, this relationship was fixed and inevitable. Many critics, of which I am one, hold that their final chapter entitled 'Education, Socialism and Revolution', which, in contradiction to the book's whole thesis, sets out a programme for social as well as educational change, carries little conviction.

Schooling in Capitalist America was another of the set books of the Open University, whose antennae are, no doubt rightly, beamed to pick up the most contemporary, or modern interpretations, and therefore are widely influential. But of course the most powerful intellect to have been involved in this issue is another Frenchman, the sociologist Paul Bourdieu. In his *Reproduction in Education, Society and Culture* and in other writings, Bourdieu has advanced a tightly argued set of logically related propositions which lead to the conclusion that the educational structure, together with the pedagogical processes embodied within it, operates to ensure the reproduction of existing social categories, classes or groups.[9] Nothing is said in Bourdieu's work of unintended consequences, in the sense I outlined earlier, nor of what Antonio Gramsci defines as 'counter-hegemonic' activities and influences arising from social forces resistant to the status quo; nor is attention given to the coincidence of educational and social change as experienced historically – though both of course have continuously occurred. Instead we have a highly stimulating analysis explaining with great precision why everything must remain exactly as it is – in terms of social relations; 'The School as a Conservative Force', to quote the title of one of Bourdieu's most influential articles.[10] Bourdieu's motivation for these studies, it appears, arose from disillusion following the May 1968 events in France, as that of Bowles and Gintis followed the decline of the radical student movement in the United States.

So, both the empirical researches of social scientists, and the theoretical work of sociologists and neo-Marxists occurring between the publication of the two readers pointed in the same direction: put crudely and briefly, that education reflects society, and is certainly not a force for social change. The fact that, through the 1970s and early 1980s, the Western world has experienced a growing economic crisis, with massive cuts in public expenditure including education, has provided a context in which such theories, even if advanced by Marxists, neo-Marxists and sociologists, provide no direct challenge to the social order or to education. These are interpretative theories. Their implications are that, if social change is what is aimed at in terms of greater egalitarianism, then it is necessary first to change the 'deep structures' of society and the economy; that is, to work for a socialist transformation of society. This is, in fact, overtly stated at the conclusion of the Jencks study, but no strategy for its achievement is advanced. In essence these studies, both theoretical and empirical, project a kind of frigid or pallid fatalism concerning the role of education and of the teacher.

Enough has been said, perhaps, to clarify my thesis, which is that interpretations of the relations between education and society are themselves subject to change, and that the degree of optimism or pessimism expressed, if one may use these value laden terms, appears to vary with the economic situation: an expansionist phase appears sympathetic to concepts stressing the importance of the role of education, a recessionary phase the opposite. That, at least, might appear to cover the succession of contradictory theories over the past two decades. But if we extend our analysis historically, other strands in the argument may be elucidated or defined, extending the complexity of the situation beyond the simplistic conclusion just presented.

2

It was my contention, in the first of my historical studies covering the period 1780 to 1870, that many of the educational measures undertaken and supported by the industrial and commercial middle class in England in the early nineteenth century should primarily be regarded as a response, and a considered one, to the rapidly growing and perhaps increasingly threatening independent political and educational activity of working people at that time.[11] I am not suggesting that this was a deliberate exercise of social control as I do not find that this concept has serious explanatory power. But I am suggesting that the Mechanics' Institute movement of the

1820s and 30s, for instance, the formation of the Society for the Diffusion of Useful Knowledge with its *Penny Magazine* and avalanche of cheap literature, the reluctant provision of Treasury support for elementary education and later for teacher training, and like measures, were, in the circumstances, seen by those in authority, both nationally and locally, as necessary or desirable in view of the widespread movement both towards independent political activity (especially after 1832), and towards strictly independent forms of education. I refer here to the whole radical tradition and movement starting with the Corresponding Societies in the 1790s, through the activities of the Hampden Clubs, the Political Protestants, and others (especially in the north of England), culminating in the Owenite Socialist and the Chartist movements in the late 1830s and 40s.[12] If we ask the question, 'can education change society?' then we should ask this question not only in relation to formalised and state or local authority controlled *systems* of education, as we have them today, but also in relation to informal, if you like independent networks (to use Illich's phrase) whereby, as in the case just mentioned, whole generations of working people (or at least their leading representatives) educated themselves, in many cases consciously, in order the more effectively to transform society – the outer world – to their desires.

It would be rash to deny that this experience had no effect in bringing about social change, because these were mass, popular activities which brought thousands, and, in the case of the Chartist movement in Britain, hundreds of thousand of people into new forms of social and political activity and were themselves educative and profoundly so. How do we explain the extraordinary deep and widespread change in the consciousness of large sections of the British people between, say, the early 1790s – when Church and King mobs could rampage around Birmingham destroying the Unitarian chapel and ransacking its Minister's (Joseph Priestley's) house, scientific equipment and personal belongings, forcing him and his family to flee the city – and, let's say, the events at Peterloo in Manchester in 1819 where a huge popular demonstration swelled by representatives from all the villages round about demanded the extension of the franchise and an end to the

Corn Laws? Edward Thompson has, of course, chronicled and interpreted this change in consciousness in his well-known book, *The Making of the English Working Class*,[13] and this points to an issue that needs stressing in this context.

What do we mean by *education*? Are we to reduce the term only to the systems of schooling – at different levels – which, even in advanced industrial societies, are a product, generally speaking, only of the last century, or, at the most, a century and a half? This situation today profoundly affects our thinking, so that education is taken to consist solely in what goes on within these systems. And, because of their nature and social function, the *process* of education is ordinarily conceived (and certainly historically) as essentially didactic. I am reminded of the illustration in the preface to one of the earlier editions of Comenius's *Orbis Pictus*, which represents a grave and learned teacher and a child or pupil with the slogan, 'the teacher teaches, the child learns'. Within modern educational systems in general, teaching and learning is conceived of as a one-way process, and normally this is precisely what it is. This was strikingly confirmed in the ORACLE studies into primary education in England based on systematic classroom observation with which I was closely concerned.[14] Even when the teaching was maximally individualised, and indeed especially in this case, the teacher-pupil interactions were found to be overwhelmingly didactic.

But it is arguable, at least, that it is through their *activity* that human beings learn, and learn best; that the unity of consciousness and activity, mediated through language, is what differentiates human beings from the rest of the animal species and underlies the development of the higher mental processes peculiar to man. Education, as Joan Simon has put it, is *the mode of development of human beings in society*,[15] and, seen in this light, the *process* of education involves all those formative influences including the family, peer groups, the Church, apprenticeship and the village or civic relations with which all are involved from the earliest times; relationships growing in complexity, of course, as society itself becomes more complex. Within these sets of inter-relations, organised schooling, of course, plays a part, but one which only affected a small, even tiny, proportion of the population until very recently.

Reverting then, to the situation in Britain between 1790 and 1819 and beyond, was it not the case that a changed consciousness, resulting from new circumstances and new forms of activity, profoundly influenced social development? In his fascinating study of nineteenth-century autobiographies by working men, many of them not yet in print, Vincent shows that, as a result of bitter and deeply felt experiences, a profound effort at independent self-education was made, particularly by men who became leaders of the Chartist and later movements – best epitomised, perhaps, in the title of one of the best known of these: *The Life and Struggles of William Lovett in the Search for Bread, Knowledge and Freedom* (1876).[16] In his recent study of the Corresponding Societies of the 1790s, Professor Goodwin draws particular attention to the educational implications of this movement, and of the forms of activity associated with it – the intensive discussions, debates, and readings as well as the mass demonstrations and similar forms of activity.[17] From all this there developed a self-conscious and deliberate movement for political and social change; in particular for the extension of the franchise; for full and genuine citizenship; for the right to leisure – the ten hour and later the eight hour bill; for the right to education. The measures that resulted, though never gained in their pure form as originally demanded, certainly effected social change – and on a massive scale; nor was there anything inevitable about it. Further, those measures that were achieved, once gained, acted as spring-boards for further demands, for new perspectives.

3

We started by examining recent analyses of the relation between education and society, and found quite opposite interpretations within a very short time-span, sixteen years to be exact. We then broadened the concept of education and looked at the subjective experiences of working people in Britain over a longer time-span, and found (or posited) a long term but clear relationship between educational and social and political change. Can we now attempt a longer view?

It was the distinguished archaeologist, Gordon Childe, who gave to one of his influential books the striking title *Man Makes*

Himself. This embodies the concept I am tangling with, and trying to unravel in terms of the role of education. Human beings, Childe argues, make themselves – have made themselves through their growing understanding of, control and so transformation of nature; people's actions on nature being the product of socialised labour on the one hand (the determining form of activity), and their growing knowledge, or what slowly came to be science, on the other. The crucial aspect of human activity in this context is that it increasingly takes place in a humanised world; a world in which people's knowledge, and abilities, as they develop, are crystallised, as it were, in a transformed external world, existing independently of them and so forming for him or her a humanised environment. The modern computer is a good example, but, as Childe showed, the earlier and crudest of tools in their time played the same formative role. So, through new forms of activity, the senses themselves are refined, new skills and new abilities are developed. In an important sense, the whole long transition from savagery to civilisation (another title in a series Childe edited),[18] and the process of human and social change involved is a result of this development in which language, closely related to consciousness, plays a vital part. Through language, culture and knowledge are, as it were, crystallised and may be handed on, or made available to each new generation. 'Language, mathematics, or other theoretical ways of structuring knowledge,' writes Jerome Bruner, 'capitalise upon innate capacities. But these skills, though they depend on innate capacities, originate *outside* the organism and memorialise generations of encounters by members of the culture.'[19]

Insofar as man transforms his external world, and by changing it changes himself, the whole historical process must be accounted essentially educative – and indeed this is why it is illuminating to refer to education as the mode of development of human beings in society.

But if this argument carries conviction, how is it that today the consensus appears to be fatalistic – allowing no scope for education to effect social, or for that matter, human change? Here we may, perhaps, remind ourselves of one of Marx's aphorisms when tangling with this precise issue. It was not, he thought, through the imposition from above of changed circumstances that human change was brought about (Robert Owen was his example). The coincidence of human and social change, he argued, can only be understood in terms of what he called 'revolutionising practice'. In changing his circumstances, man changes himself. The educator, he concluded, must himself be educated. The key to both sets of changes lay in human activity – or self-change.[20]

These are overall philosophic propositions but I think highly relevant to our problem. Marx was here concerned with a critique of the mechanistic materialism of the late eighteenth century which fuelled the Enlightenment, and to re-emphasise the importance of subjective experience, the contribution of contemporary German idealism – and to fuse the two in a new world outlook. Mechanistic materialism saw human beings as the simple product of external circumstances; their role was seen as purely passive, as the recipients of innumerable external stimuli which determined their disposition and development, intellectual, moral and aesthetic. So much is attested by all the literature of that period relating to education and human formation. This strand was later developed into the consistent schemata known as behaviourism, which denied the role of consciousness and so of all subjective experience.

But behaviourism has had a long life, based partly on a misunderstanding of the significance of Pavlov's seminal studies early in this century, and a failure to grasp the profound implications of his later work on language – what he called 'the second signalling system' – and its role in the formation of the higher mental properties. It was on the basis of this work in particular that Pavlov laid the greatest stress on the flexibility and adaptability of the higher nervous system. Summarizing a lifetime of research, he wrote:

> the *chief, strongest* and *most permanent impression* we get from the study of higher nervous activity by our methods, is the extraordinary plasticity of this activity, its immense potentialities; nothing is immoveable or intractable, and everything may always be achieved, changed for the better, provided only that the proper conditions are created.[21]

It is my contention that the current critiques that I have

referred to adopt as an unexamined assumption what amounts to a crude behaviourist interpretation of the relations between man and the external world, and that it is this that underlies their pessimism and, indeed, fatalism. The subjective experiences of those being educated within the modern systems, not only within schools, but in the whole course of life itself, is nowhere examined. Instead we are presented with analyses which simply *assume* that the intentions of the architects of these systems are inevitably achieved. But we saw in the case of the Russian universities and higher professional schools that these intentions, in that case, were at the most only partially achieved, and that, in some senses, the outcomes were diametrically opposed to the original intentions. Can we look a little more closely at all this?

4

There is no doubt that in Western Europe, and in a modified sense in North America, highly structured and hierarchic systems of education have been established; full systematis-ation, in Europe at least, being a feature of developments in the last three or four decades of the nineteenth century. The historian, Geoffrey Best, characterises mid-Victorian edu-cation in England as not only reflecting class differences, but as deliberately erected to perpetuate them. 'Educational systems', he writes, 'can hardly help mirroring the ideas about the social relationships of the societies that produce them.' Education became, at that time, a 'trump card' in what he called 'this great class competition'. The result was that 'the schools of Britain not only mirrored the hierarchical social structure ... but were made more and more to magnify its structuring in detail.'[22] Institutionalised education, in this view, acted to reinforce and exacerbate class differences. This view is widely held among British historians; Harold Perkin, for instance, describes developments in the 1860s as intended 'to put education in a strait-jacket of social class.'[23]

Such was certainly the intention – but how can we assess the outcome? Once the whole population was brought into the systems of schooling – and this was not really so long ago –

new contradictions, new perspectives, inevitably arose. Among those relegated to the lowest rung in the elementary schools, new aspirations developed. These systems acquired a certain autonomy; in England local school boards, several of which developed very progressive policies, took a pride in their schools; a skilled and devoted teaching force, increasingly professional, was created, its material and spiritual interests bound up with its advancement. Parental support gradually developed. In England it was a mere thirty years after the establishment of universal elementary education that a political and social crisis arose closely related to the upward thrust of a system which had been intended (and, indeed, carefully designed) to preserve the social structure inviolate.

That crisis was dealt with by a fundamental restructuring and in particular by the belated establishment of secondary schooling as a *system* around the turn of the century. But no sooner was this achieved than new struggles arose, related particularly to the issue of access to this new system; and so new crises, new forms of legitimisation, new concessions. The conclusion of all this, in Britain, was the swing to comprehensive secondary education together with the revulsion from forms of early streaming and/or tracking which had fastened on the schools in the inter-war and immediate post-war years. This potentially radical move swept away (at least in theory if not altogether in practice) what was left of the divisions between elementary and secondary education, and between segregated and differentiated forms of secondary education. Today in Britain over 90 per cent of all pupils in the maintained, or state, secondary schools are in comprehensive schools. This experience has been reflected in other countries in Western Europe, in France, Italy, Scandinavia.

Of course these schools are now subjected to a great deal of criticism – it would be surprising if it were not so. And equally of course, the intentions of the pioneers who established them are not being realised in their pure form. It is worth noting, as significant for our thesis, that comprehensive secondary education was originally a grass roots movement in Britain, the first schools being established in the late 1940s or early 1950s by certain advanced local authorities in opposition to government policy and advice, whether that government was

Labour (as it was from 1945 to 1951) or Tory (1951 to 1964).[24]
This movement arose, in this sense, from the experience of
those subjected to the harsh, and apparently arbitrary,
decisions about the future of children taken at an early age in
order to fit them into the mould of a system erected to preserve
what Geoffrey Best called 'the hierarchical social structure'.
Experience shows that the establishment of a new system of this
kind, which certainly embodies changed values and changed
objectives, holding out the prospect of universal secondary
education for the first time, is inevitably a hard and difficult
process, disturbing deeply engrained vested interests and, for
some, quite traumatic. Further, as is to be expected, a new
system has to contend with practices and attitudes both deeply
entrenched and reflecting the values and outlook of the
obsolescent systems of the past. Here the role of examination
systems is particularly important in that even today, in
England, a threefold level of examination or non-examination
still dominates the internal structures of schooling, placing
severe restraints on the degree of transformation that may be
achieved.[25]

These are all areas of conflict, as are, for instance, the
Thatcher government's measures designed to shore up the
private sector (still important in Britain) at the expense of the
publicly maintained system of schools. Modern education
systems, it seems to me, are an area where the interests and
objectives of different social classes, strata and even groups
meets and very often clash. Hence contradictions develop
within these systems which have a degree, as is now generally
accepted, of relative autonomy. In this situation, as the
historical record surely makes clear, there is scope for a variety
of solutions; which of these will be successful depending on the
balance of forces at any particular time.

5

I want to suggest that the crucial feature we need to take into
account is the subjective experience of the educand – his or her
activity and its effect on consciousness; and this in the large
historical sense. I would not myself expect education systems,

deriving from (or embedded in) societies with sharp class divisions reflecting, if you like, the distribution of wealth in modern capitalist societies, to act directly and immediately to transform that society – say in a socialist direction. And while some degree of social mobility is necessary for the health and continued stability of such societies, a moderate increase or decrease in its degree seems to me of little significance in terms of social change; nor do I regard the degree to which, for instance, comprehensive secondary education in England (or similar measures elsewhere) may marginally affect this as a chief criterion by which the success, or other, of such a change may be judged or evaluated; though this is the measure commonly appealed to by those who espoused the egalitarian objectives of the sixties.

It is, in any case, far too early to arrive at any such conclusion in the case of the transformation referred to; and one of the very real problems in tackling an issue of this kind is precisely that outcomes take a long period to manifest themselves, and then of course, they are only one of the factors determining social change. But it is, I suggest, the long term outcomes to which we should devote attention. Here the evaluation of the significance of what he called 'the old primary school' by the Italian Marxist Antonio Gramsci seems relevant. In his essay on education, far from criticising the narrowness and inadequacy of the system, Gramsci points to its long term positive implications.[26] In this school system, he says, there were two elements in the educational formation of the children. 'They were taught the rudiments of natural science, and the idea of civic rights and duties.' 'The scientific ideas the children learnt,' he writes, 'conflicted with the magical conception of the world and nature which they absorbed from an environment steeped in folklore; while the idea of civic rights and duties conflicted with tendencies towards individualistic and localistic barbarism – another dimension of folklore.' The school, then, in Gramsci's view, was not a prison for children, nor a simple measure of social control. In combating folklore and 'every residue of traditional conceptions of the world,' as he put it, it taught a modern outlook relating to what he calls the 'objective intractable natural laws to which man must adapt himself if he is to master them in his turn'. The pupils also learn that there exist 'social and state laws which are the product of human activity, which are established by men and can be altered by men in the interest of their collective development'. All this, he writes, 'creates the first elements of an intuition of the world free from all magic and superstition,' providing a basis for a new, realistic conception of the world, one 'which understands movement and change ... which conceives the contemporary world as a synthesis of the past ... and which projects itself into the future'. This, says Gramsci, writing around 1930 in Mussolini's prison in Southern Italy, 'was the real basis of the primary school,' though whether all this was achieved in practice, he adds, is another question.

I have quoted Gramsci at some length both because his evaluation was based very much on his own experience, in that it was through his own education in childhood that he was able to throw off the folklorist and magical interpretation which surrounded him in Sardinia, and because, in view of current trends, it is perhaps salutary to quote a Marxist who in fact made so positive an assessment of the imposition of mass primary or elementary education, so often profoundly denigrated by radical critics. And I wonder whether it is not in terms of criteria of a similar order that historians of the future will evaluate the great leap forward in education, specifically secondary and tertiary, of the 1960s and 70s, in spite of the crises and conflicts this gave rise to, and of the subsequent backlash? There cannot, of course, be any guarantee that education may not be misused, to reinforce mythical and mystical interpretations on the basis of nationalist ambitions, as was certainly the case in Germany from 1933 to 1945 and in other countries later; in this sense the struggle for education in its true sense is and must be continuous.

6

So we return now to the initial question – Can education change society? And with the broader definition that I cited earlier. It must be clear by now that my own answer to this question is in the affirmative – especially if one takes the long view, as I attempted to earlier. We will not, I think, find our answer from the techniques of contemporary social science since these studies, with their heavy reliance on statistical analysis, necessarily leave out of account, or lose sight of, the crucial human factor – subjective experience; and it is this which determines outcomes – not whether it can be shown statistically that schooling, and/or a particular innovation, has a marginally positive or negative effect on the distribution of income, or life opportunities, however measured, or on social mobility.

I started by stressing unintended outcomes – with the Russian example. And were the outcomes of primary education in Italy all those intended? I then looked at the long-term, though in a sense quite sudden and certainly unexpected, change in the consciousness of important sections of the British people early in the nineteenth century and subsequent social and political action bringing social change; as well as at developments in the late nineteenth century with its restructuring, new contradictions, struggles, culminating in Britain in the movement to comprehensive education. Certainly, it seems to me, contemporary theorising and empirical studies on this issue – that is, on the relation between educational and social change – are both seriously misleading and, in many ways, shortsighted. They ignore human subjective experience – people's capacity for movement, for acting on the environment, transforming it, and so for self-change. It is this process which is educative, and profoundly so. And it is this which we need to take into account when seeking an answer to our question. There is no joy here for the fatalists who claim that all such action is futile. On the contrary the future is open and undecided; and it is, I suggest, of supreme importance that those closely involved in education recognise, and struggle consistently to realise, its potential.

Notes

1. Daniel Brower, *Training the Nihilists. Education and Radicalism in Tzarist Russia*, Ithaca, 1975.
2. A.H. Halsey, Jean Floud and C. Arnold Anderson (eds.), *Education, Economy and Society*, New York, 1961.
3. A.H. Halsey and Jerome Karabel (eds.), *Power and Ideology in Education*, New York, 1977.

4. Christopher Jencks *et al., Inequality: A Reassessment of the Effect of Family and Schooling in America*, New York, 1972; James Coleman *et al., Equality of Education Opportunity*, Washington, 1966.

5. Jean Floud, 'Making Adults More Equal: The Scope and Limitations of Public Educational Policy' in Peter R. Cox, H.B. Miles and John Peel (eds.), *Equality and Inequality in Education*, New York, 1975, pp. 37–51.

6. Louis Althusser, 'Ideology and Ideological State Apparatuses' in *Lenin and Philosophy and Other Essays*, London, 1971, pp. 121–173.

7. Ibid., p. 148.

8. S. Bowles and H. Gintis, *Schooling in Capitalist America*, London, 1976.

9. Paul Bourdieu and Jean-Claude Passeron, *Reproduction in Education, Society and Culture*, London, 1977.

10. Pierre Bourdieu, 'The School as a Conservative Force: Scholastic and Cultural Inequalities' in Roger Dale, *et al.* (eds.), *Schooling and Capitalism*, London, 1976, pp. 110–17.

11. Brian Simon, *The Two Nations and the Educational Structure, 1780–1870*, London, 1960, first published under the title *Studies in the History of Education*.

12. Ibid., chapters 4 and 5.

13. Edward Thompson, *The Making of the English Working Class*, London, 1963.

14. See Maurice Galton, Brian Simon and Paul Croll, *Inside the Primary Classroom*, London, 1980, especially chapters 4 and 5. Observational Research and Classroom Learning Evaluation – ORACLE – was a Social Science Research Council research study into primary education in England.

15. Joan Simon, 'The History of Education in *Past and Present*,' *Oxford Review of Education*, Vol. 3, No. 1, 1977.

16. David Vincent, *Bread, Knowledge and Freedom: A Study of Nineteenth-Century Working Class Autobiography*, London, 1981.

17. Albert Goodwin, *The Friends of Liberty: The English Democratic Movement in the Age of the French Revolution*, London, 1979.

18. Graham Clark, *From Savagery to Civilization*, London, 1946.

19. Jerome S. Bruner, *The Relevance of Education*, London, 1972, pp. 119.

20. Karl Marx, 'Theses on Feuerbach' in Karl Marx and Frederick Engels, *Collected Works*, Volume 5, London, 1976, pp. 3–8.

21. I.P. Pavlov, 'A Physiologist's Reply to Pyschologists' (1932), In *Selected Works*, Moscow 1955, pp. 446–7.

22. Geoffrey Best, *Mid-Victorian Britain, 1851–1875*, London, 1973, p. 170.

23. Harold Perkin, *The Origins of Modern English Society*, 1780–1880, London, 1969.

24. David Rubinstein and Brian Simon, *The Evolution of the Comprehensive School*, 1926–1972, London, 1973, chapter 3–5.

25. For more recent developments in this area see pp. 225ff.

26. Essay 'On Education' in Quintin Hoare and Geoffrey Nowell-Smith (eds.), *Antonio Gramsci, Selections From the Prison Notebooks*, London, 1971, see especially pp. 33–5.

2

Education in Theory, Schooling in Practice: The Experience of the Last Hundred Years

My topic is the relation between theory and practice in education – a central issue which requires elucidation if significant advances are to be made in the practice of schooling. Concern with this topic has been fuelled over the past few years by participation in a carefully designed observational research project into what actually goes on in primary school classrooms in England – an issue that, perhaps surprisingly, became highly politicised during the last ten years. One thing that emerged very clearly from our findings was the wide gap between what one might call prescriptive theory as defined and formulated in the Plowden Report of 1967 (*Children and Their Primary Schools*), and actual classroom practice itself as implemented by teachers in the schools. So extreme a dissonance seems, to put it mildly, hardly helpful to the teachers, the children, or to educational outcomes generally.[1]

One characteristic of the present, or recent, phase is a proliferation of theories about education which often derive from the different disciplines now embedded in the educational arena in a new way. Psychology has, of course, always been present, but not in so many guises, some contradictory, as today; historical studies have for long made their own contribution to understanding; but both of these have been somewhat pressed into the background by two newcomers. One is philosophy, in what its proponents describe as a 'revolutionary' guise; not at all revolutionary in relation to education – it should be added – only at odds with earlier philosophical propositions. The other acquisition,

The Fink lecture, delivered at the University of Melbourne, April 1981.

barely present before the war, has been sociology. Born of several founding fathers, seeking to attain all the attributes of a science, sociology has mushroomed of late into a fluster of contending 'schools', each ready to pronounce on key educational issues in one way or another.

The resulting surveys, research findings, theses, publications, disputations, represent a proliferation of discussion about education which may often be more directly related to the concerns of the particular discipline involved than to actualities and problems in the educational arena. It is clear enough that it would today be out of the question to conduct a social survey which excludes education altogether, as an American author recently did of Britain between the wars, on the grounds that there is nothing to be said about it. On the contrary, in Britain, the United States and elsewhere education has been recognised as a very arrow-point of social policy and practice, not only by theoreticians of various kinds but also by politicians of all colours.

As for the average educationist or teacher, hard at work in a tough, demanding and exacting field, he or she has an embarrassment of riches on which to draw in terms of theory – anyway, if sheer bulk and variety is at issue. Coming from such different quarters, the analyses, interpretations, advice offered can hardly be other than contradictory. But apparently it is up to those practising education to set aside large tracts of time, first to absorb the offerings, then to perform the onerous task of co-ordination and extraction of the relevant kernel for use on the everyday plane. It is an odd supposition, to say the least, especially when it is held that all this theorising casts a disciplined, if not rigorously scientific, light on education for the first time. Science and spawning verbiage do not easily go together. Elegance is more usually the accepted characteristic.

In tackling this topic I intend to adopt an historical approach, and to look in turn at several moments during my chosen century. First, I will turn back to the two opening decades when measures to establish a universal, compulsory system of elementary schooling were well in train – that is, to the 1880s and 1890s. What was the relation between theory and developing practice as the first national system of schools was brought into action?

Then I will look at the decades between the two world wars which punctuated the first half of the twentieth century. By this time the elementary school system in Britain had been battened down below stairs, as it were, a separate and parallel, publicly-maintained, secondary system having been launched in 1902 on the traditional pattern – which has yet to be altogether outgrown. Moreover, advance was continually arrested by heavy cuts in expenditure mistakenly dubbed 'economies' – a custom recently revived, in Britain at least. Nevertheless, the schools remained at work and there was much discussion of education – its proper aims, suitable methods and so on. What were the specific characteristics of this period, and what new influences were operating?

My third period, once more twenty years on, is that from which we have just emerged, 1960 to 1980, when there have certainly been important developments on the ground and a great deal of theorising about education – but when the relation between the two is by no means easy to define. Concentration on the details of classroom practice in the research project mentioned earlier has led me to see quite a number of topics in a new way, and to appreciate more fully why teachers so often look askance at the research results thrust under their noses, let alone the merely verbal logic of some theoreticians. And, as indicated earlier, this is largely responsible for suggesting my present theme.

The Late Nineteenth Century

We may start in 1880, the initial year of the century under review: in effect the year when schooling in England first became compulsory up to the age of ten. Developments in the wake of legislation, enabling the direct election of local school boards to supervise and administer the building up of a national system of elementary schooling, made this step possible. In 1870 there had been just over one million children in school. By 1896 there were four and a half million and the board schools had come to the forefront, *vis-à-vis* those run by the Church. In particular, the industrial cities of the Midlands and North took a pride in the new buildings provided – large, many-storied, spacious, now providing (for the first time) separate rooms for the new system of class teaching; and moreover incorporating a new standard of ventilation and ancillary provision in terms · of cloakrooms, equipment, playgrounds, giving them a character all their own. This was the material context within which the battle for attendance was won; school life was to be twice lengthened in the 1890s – the leaving age being raised to 11 in 1893 and to 12 in 1899.

Once a high proportion of children aged 5 to 13 were squarely within the school system, a new perspective opened. With the schooling of a whole generation actively in progress, a new body of teachers came into being required to act in rapidly changing conditions – a growing core of whom were specially trained. What were the ideas to the fore at this period, or brought to bear on those at work in, or for, the new national system?

Perhaps the most striking feature, to the modern eye, was the ready supposition that the ordinary child was capable of intellectual development, and that this could be brought about by sound and thorough teaching in school. In later years, as we know to our cost, this conception was by no means generally accepted. Rather the opposite. What prompted or underlay it in the 1880s?

At a time when hundreds of teachers were facing a multitude of new tasks, as elementary schools developed rapidly, it was possible to depend on a generally accepted psychological theory of learning – associationism. Foreshadowed by John Locke, spelt out in 1749 in David Hartley's *Observations on Man*, popularized by Joseph Priestley, then in due course by James Mill and later John Stuart Mill, it was also taken up by the early socialists, particularly Robert Owen. In 1879 this theoretical approach found expression, in modified form, in a specifically educational context when Alexander Bain, professor at one of the four Scottish universities, published *Education as a Science*. In the circumstances this was bound to exercise an extensive influence, and it is no surprise to find the views there set out faithfully echoed in the many teaching manuals of the time. Indeed, Bain's book was frequently reprinted in the next ten or twenty years. In particular Bain emphasized the physiological basis of mental functions; as he put it, 'the plastic or acquisitive functions of the brain – the property of cementing the nervous connections that underlie memory, habit and acquired power', in a way that looks forward to present-day findings of neuropsychology. Consider also his definition of education as 'the means of building up the acquired powers of human beings'. This is an uncompromising statement which points to teaching and learning as the means of enhancing human capacity. It is a text very different from that to which a later age has become accustomed – the insistence that a child is born all that he or she may become; that the most teaching can do is bring to light a given, inborn quota of 'Intelligence'.

In the circumstances it is understandable enough that there should have been a firm intention, on the part of the central authorities at least, to keep schooling for the majority short, in order not to outrun the intended limits of popular education. But, in the event, this is just what the elementary system did, as what were called higher grade schools and 'higher tops' were established by advanced school boards to take their pupils still further, and as systems for training teachers in colleges and one the job evolved. As a consequence there was resort to legislative and administrative means of control but, meanwhile, for a couple of decades or more, a bracing, optimistic outlook held sway which can be traced in the many manuals on the conduct of teaching, particularly those published in the 1890s.

What was the positive core of the pedagogy that sustained and promoted the experience, and extension, of elementary schooling? Central to Bain's approach, as has been seen, is the concept of development, of growth. Moreover although Bain recognises differences in educability (or what he calls 'facility of acquirement') it is the foundation of his thought that human beings are essentially educable. 'Every impression made upon us,' he writes, 'if sufficient to awaken consciousness at the time, has a certain permanence,' persisting after the original ceases to work and open to restoration as a 'remembered impression'. Such impressions, or ideas, can be 'fixed' by practice or exercise. The art of education consists in 'economising the plastic power of the human system'. We need to search out 'all the known conditions that favour or impede the plastic growth of the system'. It is in this context that particular attention is paid to memory, or what is called 'the retentive faculty' and its cultivation. For on it rests the possibility of mental growth, or the acquirement of what Bain calls 'capabilities not given by nature'.

As presented by Bain, the classic theory of associationism extended beyond formation of the intellect and acquisition of knowledge to the formation of character and the acquisition of attitudes and habits: as indeed it had done throughout the period of the Enlightenment and in the work, for instance, of Richard Lovell Edgeworth, who had sought to put into practice with individual children his own development of effective pedagogical means in the early nineteenth century. Now these conceptions were to be generally applied, and one thing that strikes the modern reader is the extent to which responsibility accrues to the teacher for apparent failures or inadequacies on the part of the child. This follows logically from what is essentially a positive, optimistic theory in its appreciation of the powers of teaching and learning.

Some examples may be given from the teachers' manuals already referred to which were published in a constant stream and which passed these ideas on to students in training. Thus Joseph Landon, Vice Principal and former 'master of method' (as he described) at Saltley Training College, published in 1894 *The Principles and Practice of Teaching and Class Management*. This was also the subject of one of the 'Royal Handbooks for Pupil-Teachers' published by Nelson of Edinburgh in 1895, by a former assistant at the Edinburgh Normal School, J. Gunn. In 1896 *A New Manual of Method* appeared by A.H. Garlick, head of the Woolwich Pupil-Teacher Centre, which reached a fifth edition in 1901 – a guide aspiring to be 'comprehensive in its range, practical in its nature, and modern in its methods'. Another popular manual was *The Art of Teaching*, published in 1898 by David Salmon, Principal of Swansea Training College. Although it seems that Australia did not experience turbulent advances as in England in the 1890s, these years saw the publication, for instance, of F.J. Gladman's *School Method*, which reflected this outlook. Headmaster of the Model and Practising Schools at Borough Road, later 'normal master' at the Borough Road Training College in London, Gladman then moved to the Central Training Institution at Melbourne. All

these manuals depend in large part on the precepts advanced
by Bain as the spine of an ordered system of pedagogy.

Garlick, for instance, presents a whole list of characteristic
behaviours as remediable, provided that the teacher
understands how to tackle the problem – whether it be
inattention, laziness, stupidity, truancy, or whatever else. Such
forms of behaviour may be the result of ineffective action or
understanding on the part of the teacher. Thus, it is said, 'To
fix and maintain the attention there are certain laws of the
mind which must be obeyed, and any violation of these laws is
sure to be followed by more or less inattention.' Similarly
ignorance or indifference to the elementary principles of child
life is likely to generate laziness. Should the task set make little
demand on 'child activity' then 'there is a tendency to despise
and reject it', and sit back. Likewise stupidity, if sometimes a
gift from parents, may also be 'bestowed by the teacher' if he is
'unmethodical or not properly acquainted with his subject',
careless or inaccurate in describing or informing, a poor
questioner, or harsh or cruel in his manner so as to 'chill or
freeze the efforts of the timid, the weak, or the shy.'

More specifically, associationist theory provides an explanation of habit formation which was seen as the key to discipline
and character formation, no less than intellectual acquirement,
and underlay much methodological advice. Joseph Landon, of
Saltley Training College, attributes to the science of education
'the foundation truths' on which all practice must rest, and
goes on to deal with oral teaching and lesson procedures
before turning to the detailed of questioning, illustrations, the
lecture, problems of class management and, finally, the
teaching of specific subjects; that is, in particular, reading,
spelling, writing, arithmetic, but also the secondary or
so-called 'class' subjects of history and geography, English and
elementary science.

It is germane to note here how much attention is paid to the
matter of class management – in a systematic way which has
long passed out of fashion so far as theory is concerned. Yet the
problems of managing a class remain, for all teachers (as we
certainly found on the primary school research project
mentioned); and to ignore them, or sweep them under the
carpet, is to make a false assessment of the teaching and

learning situation which may well be one of the most potent causes of the gulf between theory and practice.

I have provided no more than a brief and partial excursion into the closing years of the nineteenth century when, with the aid of a long-standing psychological approach – deriving it might be said, from the 'Enlightenment' years, but later brought specifically into relation with educational tasks – the emergent teaching profession built up a coherent system of pedagogy, even if the word was rarely used in Britain. This was constructed at a time when there were no effective brakes to prevent the upthrust of the elementary schools, however hard the system of payment by results might weigh on and distort teaching. In all the circumstances, advance was much faster and went much further than had been envisaged.

During these twenty years it was not on advice from universities – bar those in Scotland with an atmosphere all their own – nor by following the example of old established grammar schools, that the national elementary school system was constructed. Practical guidance had come from the training colleges for teachers and pupil-teacher centres specifically serving the elementary system. There was an optimistic theory of learning on which to draw, to build up a serviceable system of pedagogy, while in practice the keynote of the period was expansion, development – more and more children in school, a rising leaving age, a firm push to provide higher classes, the growth of the teacher-training element. True, these features were characteristic of the industrial towns and other centres of population. There was a large gap between the best of the new board schools and relics of the old in slums or all-age village schools still under the aegis of the Church. Nevertheless a new base had been laid for educational developments.

When one is making a case, in the attempt to amend the balance of interpretation, it is easy to go too far. But it is germane to note that a current history of psychology virtually dismisses Bain's *Education as a Science* – whose detailed coverage conveyed to innumerable readers what they most needed – describing it as 'particularly long-winded and tedious'.

Ironically enough this assessment is by L.S. Hearnshaw, whose latest book is a biography of Cyril Burt which is forced, in the face of inescapable evidence, to write off as tainted the work of a most highly-regarded psychologist who, in practice, led teachers in the wrong direction for most of the twentieth century. It is hardly necessary to add that the intervening guide in the 1920s and 1930s, *Education, its Data and First Principles*, by Percy Nunn, widely disseminated to propagate the 'New Education', fails even to mention, let alone recognise, the value of Alexander Bain in the ideas he promoted.

It is not part of my intention to deny the immense difficulties faced by teachers in the closing years of the nineteenth century. Classes could be enormous, premises overcrowded, resources often meagre in an enterprise conducted cheaply enough. Many teachers were unqualified, if not little more than children learning on the job, and over all hung the restrictive influence of a system whereby salary level was dependent on the number of passes obtained by pupils on precisely defined 'standards' in the basic subjects. The system of 'payment by results', though phased out in the 1890s, necessarily confined the curriculum, and led to drill, drudgery, and a strong emphasis on rote learning – which indeed persisted long after the current cause had been removed. All this has frequently been emphasised as the hallmark of the period, quite often in surveys written from the standpoint of the 'New Education'.

But such accounts by no means cover a scene which was informed by a positive pedagogy stressing educability, the 'plasticity' of the human brain, the power of education, systematically conducted in the light of psychological understanding, to *develop* capacity. One swallow does not make a summer, but Stuart Macintyre, historian at the University of Melbourne, in *A Proletarian Science* cites the case of T.A. Jackson, a well-known autodidact and popular socialist lecturer in Britain throughout the first half of this century.[2] Jackson was the son of a compositor of radical views, and was educated at a local elementary or board school in London. Macintyre particularly mentions the encouragement given to the boy by his teachers, especially in his extra-curricular interests in a range of subjects, notably in science and Greek mythology. Jackson was born in 1879; he would have been at school from 1884 (aged 5) to 1893 (if he stayed to 14). He therefore spans this period. I have seen audiences ranging from high-level theoretical physicists to ordinary workers listening open-mouthed to Tommy Jackson, as he used to be known. We should not, perhaps, underestimate what was achieved in the elementary school at that period.

That students in training were advised to pay close attention to discipline, to maintaining their authority as teachers leaving nothing 'to the caprice of the children' – as Salmon put it in the 1890s – is understandable in the circumstances, especially if one takes into account that the system itself had been introduced, in part at least, as a social-disciplinary measure shot through with a class morality. All the more remarkable, it might seem, that it was from within precisely such a system that a positive pedagogic pattern emerged, one which took intellectual development seriously and sought to further it by promoting systematic teaching and learning to that end.

Before the nineteenth century was out, steps had been taken to halt the resulting upthrust of the elementary schools which, it must be remembered, were designed explicitly for the working class, as laid down in the 1870 Act. Indeed Draconian measures were taken from 1899 to 1904 which destroyed the school boards, introduced a new administrative discipline and pattern and emphasized the lower status of the elementary schools. No more higher classes reaching up beyond the leaving age to the secondary level were permitted. Instead there was interpolated a separate system of schools giving what we now term a 'secondary' education, charging fees, and taking children from 5 or 7 in parallel with the elementary system. Into these a small percentage of children from the elementary system were allowed to step, sideways, at the age of 11. So opened a new phase. But whatever changes were to supervene, the basic classroom situation remained constant and the core of the pedagogy, consolidated at a time when the first national system of schools was born and teaching became a profession in the modern sense, persisted as an important element of school practice.

The Inter-War Decades

If we turn to the second period – the inter-war decades of 1920 to 1940 – we have a very different picture, at least as far as educational theory is concerned. In place of the optimism of the 1890s we find on the one hand a pervading fatalism – a stress on the limitation of human powers based on what I have characterised elsewhere as the 'iron laws of psychometry'; on the other hand, seemingly by contrast, the rhetoric of the 'New Education' – or, as it came to be known, 'progressivism' – which operated, as Professor R.J.W. Selleck has pointed out, as a kind of persistent obbligato, above and beyond the actual practice embodied in the system of mass schooling. The scene has certainly changed – and rather fundamentally.

The various strands which made up the 'New Education', which began to make an impact at or around the turn of the century, have been extensively analysed by Selleck in his book of that title.[3] There he brings to light the wide variety of approaches subsumed under this heading – classifying the different groupings as the practical educationists, the social reformers, the naturalists, the Herbartians, the scientific educationists and the moral educationists. In tracing the origin of ideas he points specifically to a genesis not from practice in Britain but from overseas. 'The naturalists', he writes, took their two main deities, Pestalozzi and Froebel, from Germany, while lesser gods, such as Montessori and Dewey, came from Italy and the United States. From Germany, too, though via the United States, came the Herbartians. From the United States for the most part, though originally from Germany, came the 'scientific educationists'. Nor is Sweden to be forgotten as the source of that approach to manual training known as 'Sloyd', and of Ling's gymnastics.

It is clearly not possible here to do more than point to this eruption of ideas at this specific time. Duly modified, or transmuted for conveyance to an English audience by English disciples, these ideas were sometimes mingled and amalgamated and no doubt to some extent affected practice. But, says Selleck, 'they were never submitted to a searching analysis', so that contradictions and ambiguities prevailed within what passed as the New Education movement. This left space for practising teachers to manoeuvre, to select relevant aspects from the spectrum on offer to fill out gaps or expand aspects of the workaday pedagogy evolved for the elementary school.

Here, then, is a certain relation between theory and practice – a certain give and take characteristic of that period when the initial explosive development of elementary education had simmered down. Then came the First World War, with its unprecedented horrors and, too, the promises of reconstruction at a new level, promises unfulfilled during the next twenty years when retrenchment supervened, together with the depression and that attendant mortgaging of the future inflicted on society when educational expenditure is heavily cut. Interestingly, it was during this black period that a 'progressivism' emerged to occupy the centre of the picture by 1939.

This process is generally held to have begun with the publication in 1911 of Edmund Holmes's book *What Is and What Might Be*. Insisting that the child could be at the centre of attention, Holmes held up to obloquy the whole tradition of what he called 'Western education', as something imposed upon children requiring 'blind, passive, literal, unintelligent obedience'. This denunciation applied to the traditional secondary school no less than to the mass schools so organised as to drum the elements of literacy and the ruling morality into the prospective adult workers and voters of the twentieth century. By contrast Holmes described the free, joyful activity of individual children, allowed to be themselves, prevailing in a small 'progressive' school in Sussex run by an understanding 'Egeria', which Holmes aptly dubbed Utopia.

Here progressivism was held up as the ideal and, by definition, an ideal is unattainable – something to be striven towards but never reached or realized. There had been danger to the established order and institutions in the power and force of the upthrust from the elementary system up to 1900. There was no danger at all in the possibility that the inter-war elementary school might turn 'progressive'. In any case, any such suggestion was likely to be met with strong opposition from teachers, immersed in quite another order of activity in the daily affairs of the nation's elementary schools.

In sum, there was something more than an element of unreality in proposals for educational change which presupposed small classes, plenty of equipment, gardens surrounding classrooms, not to mention freedom from the pressure of the 'scholarship' exam at eleven which in England now virtually determined the core of the elementary curriculum. Nevertheless, whenever reforming advice was proferred (as for instance in the various consultative committee reports of these years) it tended to juxtapose 'progressivism' to current practice, to the detriment of the latter. Thus the former was held out as the only desirable way forward. In effect, given that the approved way was out of the question, this was to deprive the elementary school of a perspective.

In fact, practical predominance was achieved during this period by the so-called 'scientific educationists' (whose concepts of a science of education contrasted sharply with Bain's). The emergence on to the stage of mental testing can be traced in one of the manuals produced in the first decade of the century, in this case by a professor at one of the new education departments rising to prominence at modern universities, J.W. Adamson of King's College, London. Entitled *The Practice of Instruction*, this was first published in 1906. Re-issued in 1912, it now carried a largely rewritten section on 'experimental pedagogy' which marked the eruption of a new brand of psychologists into the field. This new section on measuring 'intelligence' incorporated references to works by Spearman, Brown, Burt and other psychometrists. This was, of course, the period when the Eugenics Society, founded in 1907, got under way, propagating the theory (then taken as axiomatic) that heredity is the dominant influence in determining human characteristics, including intellectual powers; an idea which earlier had had little or no impact on educational thinking, and scarcely finds mention in the manuals of the 1890s.

The significance of mental testing, from our point of view, lies in its implicit denial of the power of education to bring about human change – at least in what was defined as the primary mental characteristic, intelligence. This was a fundamental re-orientation of psychological theory, and it operated to place learning theory on the shelf, literally for decades. In Britain this was of profound importance, since it was here, above all, that the theory and practice of mental testing became closely intertwined with the whole system of schooling, as it developed in the inter-war period and beyond.

The processes of streaming and selection, which dominated the period, were both operated and legitimated by theories derived from mental testing. There was, in this sense during this period, a close link between theory and practice – but at what a cost!

'By intelligence', wrote Cyril Burt in 1933, the 'official' psychologist who most closely influenced developments in Britain at this period,

> By intelligence, the psychologist understands *inborn, all-round intellectual ability*. It is inherited, or at least innate, not due to teaching or training; it is intellectual, not emotional or moral, and remains uninfluenced by industry or zeal; it is general, not specific, i.e., it is not limited to any particular kind of work, but enters into all we do or say or think. Of all our mental qualities, it is the most far-reaching; fortunately, it can be measured with accuracy and ease.[4]

And, related to this, what was the function of the school system? As late as 1950 Burt spelt out the role of education in what he described as the 'ideal community' as follows:

> Obviously, in an ideal community, our aim should be to discover what ration of intelligence nature has given to each individual child at birth, then to provide him with an appropriate education, and finally to guide him into the career for which he seems to have been marked out.[5]

So, in the name of tailoring education to the needs of the 'individual', as diagnosed by mental testing, children were allocated to specific streams from the age of seven or even earlier, and to different and parallel types of post-primary schools where, in fact, they were still treated (inevitably) in the mass. The key words were concentration and classification, each differentiated group of children to be treated according to predictions about mental development derived from testing – predictions which placed clear limits on what might be achieved. Whereas in the late nineteenth century the stress had been on what children have in common, on the possibility of developing human potential, on the enlarging of the intellect through the acquisition of knowledge and on devising teaching to this end, as the twentieth century gathered way, all the emphasis came to be put on the limitation of human powers, the low or mediocre level of intelligence with which most were endowed, and on the impossibility of improving this. By definition, one half of the child population was, and was bound to be, 'below average' – according to the precepts of the psychometrists. Once it had been the proposition that failure to advance on the part of the pupil reflected adversely on the teacher's technique and command of learning theory. Now the stress was well and truly on pupil deficiency. With the basic elementary school no longer on the upgrade, but battened down below hatches so that it was impossible for the majority to advance beyond a certain point, a theoretical outlook came to the fore to prove that this was just as it should be. That, by nature, most children cannot achieve much academically (or intellectually), so that marking time in school with no perspective up to the age of fourteen is all that is required.

How do we account for the coincidence of the hegemony of mental testing on the one hand, and of the ideas of the 'New Education' – or 'progressivism' – on the other? For these ideas intertwined and reinforced each other in the period under review, and are, for instance, clearly fused in the outlook of Susan Isaacs, an influential educationist in the 1930s, who combined hard-line psychometry with pioneering work in what might be called 'liberationist' theory and practice, both at the famous Malting House School at Cambridge and in her well-known books on the social and intellectual development of children. Evidently both sets of ideas and practices stem from the same source – belief in inherent, given or inborn qualities of the child as determining development. Is it not this kind of reductionist biologism which lies behind both the belief in the determining character of inborn mental powers, and the idea that the function of education must be restricted to the flowering (or maturation) of inborn qualities as the Froebelians claimed – a process which, it came to be held, requires that the teacher stand away from the child in order not to interfere, or distort, his or her natural spontaneous development? Is it any wonder, then, that given the economic and social circumstances of the time, a watered down 'progressivism', as Selleck concludes from another study of the

period, 'became the orthodoxy'. 'Most of those who wrote
books on education,' he writes, 'spoke at conferences,
produced official reports or sat on important committees,
trained teachers, or contributed to the educational journals
came to accept progressive views as a basis for their own
thinking', adding that 'as the twenties and thirties progressed it
became clear that the progressives were dictating the terms of
the debate'. By 1939, says Selleck, it could almost be said, and
particularly in relation to the primary school, that they
constituted the 'intellectual orthodoxy'.[6]

If so, it was an intellectual orthodoxy perfected over and
above the school system, where the pedagogy of mass
schooling perforce held sway, though now, as compared with
the 1890s, having very different perspectives. It was during this
period, and as a result of this experience, that the forces
matured that were to force a new transformation in the years to
come.

The Proliferation of Theory

Turning now to my last period – 1960 to 1980 – we find,
perhaps not surprisingly, an entirely different scene. Even if
some of the deficiencies in the last period I have discussed seem
now to have been, at least partially, overcome, the increasing
sophistication of educational theory meant that it was now in
danger of taking off far away from the practice of the schools
themselves; indeed much of it must appear unintelligible to
practitioners.

It is not difficult to account for the proliferation of theory
since 1945, or more particularly, since the 1960s. It is a direct
result of the expansion of higher education and, with this, of
the advent of the new areas of study or the mushrooming of
areas barely established in the 1930s, such as philosophy and
sociology. This is the context in which it was decided, back in
the 1960s, that a viable theory of education is only to be
attained by bringing to bear established disciplines in the
academic field. Those in favour of the move, initially the 'new
philosophers', had little difficulty in exposing the educational
theory prevalent in colleges of education – which, at the time,

were undergoing an enormous expansion – as a mishmash of ambiguity and contradiction. Thus the 'progressivist' invasion, so apparently successful down to 1939 and ready to take over after 1945 had its quietus – up to a point; at the theoretical level, shall we say.

I have already referred to the contemporary scene deriving from these developments, at the start of this paper, so there is no need to elaborate on it now. The main conclusion was that what is now being produced in this field too often bears little relation to the actual practice of schooling – on the ground, as it were. Of recent years a main focus has been on overarching theories concerned with the relations between education and society – the work of Bourdieu, for instance, or of such social analysts as Bowles and Gintis.[7] A main conclusion appears to be that education inevitably reflects the interests of one or other of the dominant power groups or classes in society as defined variously by these authors; it is either concerned with the reproduction of the direct needs of capitalist industry or with those existing class and group relations necessary for the maintenance of the status quo. Education as a whole is allotted little or no autonomous power or scope for activity. In either case the educator's task is defined, and indeed determined by, inexorable forces quite outside his control. Such analyses tell us little about the process of education and indeed, in some respects, exhibit a fatalism rather similar to that embraced by the psychometrists of the 1930s, if on different grounds.

One difficulty with sociological – or socio-economic – surveys of this kind is that they seem somewhat naïvely to reflect the prevailing socio-economic atmosphere, so that in this sense they hardly contribute to elucidating what one may refer to as strictly educational issues. For instance, a well known text in the sociology of education published in 1961 – *Education, Economy and Society* – reads now as a paean on the crucial importance of educational development and growth as the essential ground both to achieve more rapid economic and technological advance, and to produce a more 'egalitarian' or 'meritocratic' society. Its successor, significantly now entitled *Power and Ideology in Education*, appearing in 1977, is basically a set of papers highlighting the ineffectiveness of education to effect any social change – a transposition of view closely paralleled by fluctuations in the world economy.[8] For the historian all this provides interesting data on the movement of ideas and their relations to social change. But for the classroom practitioner little of significance remains. In particular, such approaches appear profoundly hostile to learning theory and its educational implications – that is, to areas of concern which must constitute the heart of any theory of education.

Education as a Process

What can we conclude from all this? In two of my three periods, at least, there seems to have been a close relation between theory and practice. The first of these, 1880–1900, was a period of impressive educational advance. For a whole concatenation of reasons, and from a variety of motives, it was thought that the masses should be educated, or at least schooled – and they were. This whole enterprise was, as it were, powered by an ideology – or theoretical stance – which emphasized the educability of the normal child, a view underpinned by advances in the fields of psychology and physiology relating to human learning. Indeed these views still reflected those of the English philosopher, John Locke, who held that nine parts in ten of what a person becomes is due to his or her education and upbringing. In this period, then, the view of education as powerfully formative was predominant – an outlook that accorded well with the role of the teacher as then defined, and with classroom practice which is and must be primarily concerned with promoting learning in students, with developing particular skills and abilities, with intellectual, no less than moral and aesthetic development.

If the 1880s and 1890s stressed the power of education, and hence of environment, in human development, the opposite was the case in the period 1920–40, and later. Now it was the power of hereditary endowment that was claimed as all important; a theory or ideology that tied in closely with what had now become a stratified, rigidly controlled and hierarchical school system that seemed closely to reflect the economic, social and even political stagnation of the period. Once again, theory and practice seemed closely related – but in a determination to prevent advance and change; in an entirely opposite sense to the 1890s.

This prompts the thought as to whether the time has come when we should break out, once and for all, from the heredity/environment dichotomy which has bedevilled educational thinking – and theory – for so long. One positive feature of the last twenty years has been the increasing understanding of education as a *process*, or series of processes, in the course of which specific abilities and skills are developed in the child through his or her own activity with the guidance and held of adults. This I conceive to be the main significance of the work of Jerome Bruner in the United States, of Jean Piaget, of the late Professors Luria and Leontiev in the Soviet Union – both pupils of the remarkable Lev Vygotski who died young in 1934, but who stressed the formative power of the children's life experiences (and especially schooling) in the development of the higher mental processes, and in particular the role of language in their formation. What is ignored in the mechanistic heredity/environment model is precisely the child's own self-activity through which he or she masters and transforms the surrounding world, and in so doing transforms himself – in short, learns, develops, acquires skills, abilities, an outlook, character, attitudes, autonomy – and all the better with systematic aid from adults, in the family, the school and elsewhere. It is on this *process*, I suggest, that we need to concentrate and focus our attention if we are to bring theory once again into close relation with practice, but now on a new level – with the aim of achieving a new, purposive educational advance, now an urgent necessity (as many think) in view of the implications for education and life styles generally of the micro-electronic revolution, automation and robotics.

The focus, then, for study and research must, I suggest, be on education conceived of as a process. It is agreed that education is not and cannot be an autonomous discipline; that it must rely for its theory on psychology, sociology, philosophy and advances in related areas – and in the 1960s to 1980s this has been the dominant approach. While recognizing the importance of the contributions made in these fields, let us recall that education is in fact a mass social activity and as such is clearly open to investigation; as the Bryce Commission on secondary education noted in the 1890s, in a sense every lesson, or joint activity involving teachers and pupils, partakes of the nature of an experiment founded on certain hypotheses. What is needed is a new kind of operational research, involving both teachers and researchers, which seeks directly to penetrate into, illuminate, and so improve the process of education – above all to increase its productivity across the board. Encouragement of school-based curriculum development may well prove a good 'way in' to such an approach which itself can generate theory closely related to practice.

What we now need to aim at has, I think, been well expressed by the sociologist, Bourdieu, in a passage analysing how it is that the mass of the children, particularly from the working class, fail to survive a school system whose ethos and procedures are alien to them. What is needed, he says, echoing the great seventeenth-century Moravian educationist Comenius, is 'a rational and really universal pedagogy', which takes 'nothing for granted initially', and is organised 'with the explicit arm of providing all with the means of *acquiring* that which, although appearing as a natural gift, is only *given* to the children of the educated classes ...' We need to develop, he goes on, 'the most effective method of transmitting to all the knowledge and the know-how which it demands of all'. Such a pedagogy, he adds, must be 'explicitly and technologically methodological'.[9]

Such a perspective may be controversial, but I suggest it provides an objective which could and should be embraced by any society calling itself democratic that has a concern to maximise the development, intellectual and otherwise, of all its citizens. But there is a further implication. To achieve this we need, I suggest, to shift the emphasis, both in theoretical work and in our practice, from concentration on the *differentiation* of children one from another to focus on what children have in common, their shared characteristics. The former emphasis rose into prominence when the selective function of school systems was dominant, as in the 1930s and later. Today the challenge is to raise educational sights right across the board, and modern psychological thinking stresses that all, except those with pathological disorders, are capable of learning, and that for all, the process of learning is broadly similar. It should, therefore, be possible to winnow out general principles of teaching underlying practice and appropriate for all (though modifying these if necessary to meet specific individual idiosyncracies); and to develop genuinely unified school systems which are a condition for minimising early differentiation. Contemporary concern for a common or core curriculum underlines this necessity.

If we can find the way, and gain the resources necessary, to implement modern knowledge relating to learning and teaching (and that is quite a challenge in the present climate), then we may be on the edge of a new period which historians of the future will assess if not as a golden age, then at least as one when theory and practice were again unified, on a new level, to the advantage of human development and social change. But no doubt hard battles lie ahead. The historical record clearly shows that there is nothing inevitable about educational advance. Far from progress being linear, advances are more often met by setbacks, by new crises, by ideological and political struggles of all kinds. Our present age is no exception. The chances of success will be the greater, I suggest, the more clearly we recognise the obstacles that must be overcome if we are to turn existing potentialities into reality.

Notes

1. Maurice Galton, Brian Simon and Paul Croll, *Inside the Primary Classroom*, London, 1980. See especially chapters 4 and 5.
2. Stuart Macintyre, *A Proletarian Science*, Cambridge, 1980.
3. R.J.W. Selleck, *The New Education*, London, 1968.
4. Cyril Burt (ed.). *How the Mind Works* London, 1933, pp. 28–9.
5. Cyril Burt, *Listener*, 16 November 1950.
6. R.J.W. Selleck, *English Primary Education and the Progressives, 1914–1939* London, 1972, pp. 120, 156.
7. P. Bourdieu and J-C. Passeron, *Reproduction in Education, Society and Culture* London, 1977; S. Bowles and H. Gintis, *Schooling in Capitalist America*, London, 1976.

8. The first volume cited, New York, 1961, was edited by A.H. Halsey, Jean Floud and C.A. Anderson; the second, New York 1977, by J. Karabel and A.H. Halsey. This point is further developed on pp. 14-17.
9. P. Bourdieu, 'The School as a Conservative Force: Scholastic and Cultural Inequalities' in Roger Dale *et al.* (eds.), *Schooling and Capitalism*, London, 1976.

3

To Whom Do Schools Belong?

Perhaps I should start by confessing that my title, 'To whom do schools belong?' is filched from Lester Smith, a former distinguished Director of Education in this city. Lester Smith was, of course, also an historian, and it was under this title that he put together (from notes and drafts of lectures) the important book published in 1942 – a moment when widespread discussions relating to a new Education Act were under way. It may be asked how a busy Director, responsible for administering the education service of one of our greatest cities, at a time of stress, could find time not only to turn his mind to these issues but, much more arduous, produce a substantial volume in his own characteristically modest style drawing on a wide knowledge not only of educational but cultural and social developments more generally. His own answer – that during a wartime winter 'I experienced a good many unoccupied wakeful nights' – apparently covered the hours spent fire-watching in that well-known building in Deansgate, for nearly eighty years the focus, and administrative centre, of Manchester education. But it is only reasonable to suppose that other weekends, evenings and even the odd vacation saw Lester Smith working on his manuscript. However that may be, this pioneering book was the outcome, to be followed by others on the same subject – the

This is the fifth of a series of public lectures commemorating the work of Lady Simon of Wythenshawe for education in Manchester. It was given in the Great Hall of the Town Hall, Manchester, on 14 November 1978.
Lady Simon, Lady Mayoress of Manchester 1921–22, was a member of the Education Committee in 1924–33 and 1936–70, serving as Chair in 1932–33. She made a distinguished contribution to public life and especially to the development of the education service. The Freedom of the City of Manchester was conferred upon her in 1964.

government of education – when he eventually left
Manchester to become a Professor of Education in the
University of London.

It was Lester Smith's contention that 'the control of
education (should be) a subject of much wider discussion than
has hitherto been customary', that it is essential to tease out the
question as to 'where the seat of authority should be'. It could
be said, then, that he was very much on the ball in relation to
predicting current concerns. Evidently there were fears at that
time that a new educational dispensation might involve greater
centralised (and therefore bureaucratic) control at the expense
of the local authorities, for Lady Simon also took up the theme
in 1942 in a major address to a conference of the Institute of
Public Administration.[1] In any case the book by the director of
education for Manchester is a sustained celebration of what he
calls 'the English compromise' whereby the government of
education is shared between the state, local authorities and the
voluntary bodies.

The title of the book comes from Professor Rein, a leading
German (or Prussian) educationist at Jena, from a lecture
delivered at the University of Cambridge in 1900.[2] Lester Smith
relates ironically (some will remember with affection his dry
humour) that Rein told his audience how successfully Germany
had overcome what in England, from 1870, has been known as
'the religious question'. 'In Germany,' Rein affirmed, 'the
problem was solved by adjudging the school to the state. The
school is a "politicum"; it must educate citizens of the state.'
He then went on:

> The central point of dispute is: To whom does the school belong?
> To the family, to the community, to the Church, or to the state?
> All these are interested in the school. The problem is: can their
> various interests be united by a just consideration of their various
> rights and duties?

Then, 'proving how right Germany was in choosing the state as
the custodian for education' (as Lester Smith put it) Rein
proceeded:

> Compulsory education is closely connected with military service
> and manhood suffrage ... for this reason ... the state which
> embraces politically the social whole, is and must be the master of

the schools. Educational matters, just like all other public affairs, must have a central head, if they are to be carried on systematically, and if they are to flourish.

To Professor Rein, then, the solution seemed self-evident – so much so that it only required assertion, if spiced with an element of Hegelianism. But it was far from self-evident to Lester Smith that such a solution would (or could) be appropriate to this country. Nor was it only the example of what Hitler and the Nazis had done to the schools in Germany that was on his mind – though naturally this was very much to the forefront at the time. There were, also in England, some ominous signs of a resort to centralised state direction. In his preface Lester Smith specifically points to what he describes as the 'ill-starred' Physical Training and Recreation Act of 1937. This he characterises as 'undemocratic in its administrative clauses' – concentrating wide powers over an important area of education in the hands of non-elective Central and Regional Councils – as a piece of 'harmful legislation' which nonetheless had received 'a thoroughly undeserved welcome'. Here, clearly, is one of the factors that motivated him to produce the book he did at this particular time; to alert people to the specific traditions and historical experience of this country, and so to promote a deeper understanding of the real issues underlying the crucial question – who should control the schools. It was his own view that the 'Triple Alliance' in England had 'stood the test of time'; for 70 years – since 1870 – it had been 'as a bulwark against the winds and waves of controversy'.

2

Today few would deny that 'the English compromise' is under stress – and perhaps not only the compromise in a formal sense but the whole setting in which the business of education is carried on. This is certainly one of the main concerns of an analyst of contemporary modes of government, Professor Maurice Kogan. As social change has affected people's expectations of education, he says, 'so the institutional fabric

has found it difficult to contain the new forces pressing on it'.
In *The Politics of Educational Change*, Kogan discusses many of
the central issues emerging in the field of education in the late
1960s and 1970s – growing student and teacher militancy, the
drive for comprehensive education and the Black Paper
backlash, the Tyndale case and the Bennett Report on primary
teaching, Jim Callaghan's Ruskin speech and the so-called
'Great Debate'.[3] All these, and more, indicate that education
has become 'politicised' – a charged issue – and it is this that is
leading to institutional strain and changes in what Kogan calls
'the power structure'. Everything is now being called into
question, he suggests: the legitimacy of traditional procedures
and, more generally, the status of authority in education. From
other quarters there is a similar analysis. Indeed it is now
generally recognised that education has become a major issue
of social concern, its organisation and working subjects of
everyday controversy producing 'flashpoints of recurring
tension'.

In this situation there is a search for a nostrum, a
philosopher's stone, a panacea that will somehow put all
things right in a flash. If only someone would take control, in
Professor Rein's sense, as 'the central head' and ensure that
things are 'carried on systematically' as is necessary 'if they are
to flourish'. The plea for strong, centralised direction of
education has been heard with increasing insistence during the
last two years.

Two books – or, perhaps, polemical pamphlets – are in the
running, both published late in 1977. *Lessons from Europe* by
Max Wilkinson and *What Must We Teach* by Tim Devlin and
Mary Warnock begin by directing our attention to continental
systems of administration – the French, German, Swedish,
Dutch – in all of which the state has historically played a far
greater role in the control of education that it has ever aspired
to in Britain.[4] And not only in terms of the administrative
structure, but also the content of the curriculum. In some of
these countries both the objectives of schooling and precise
'guidelines' concerning the curriculum are laid down
statutorily – in Sweden they are embodied in detailed
curriculum programmes which are actually part of the law of
the country. In most cases the teacher is paid by the state and

is, in effect, a civil servant. Neither the teachers nor the local authorities can be said to have a recognised role in determining the curriculum – apart, in some cases, from participating in discussions as to its final form through representatives (and one wonders how these are chosen). Generally speaking none of these countries allows scope for responsible decision-making of the kind allowed under the English compromise, with certain qualifications – to local authorities (in terms of policy making) and to teachers (in terms of internal school organisation and the curriculum).

It is not actually proposed in the books referred to – one of them by a former educational correspondent of *The Times* and an Oxford philosopher of some standing – that we in this country should slavishly follow continental models. But the net outcome of what is proposed might be very similar – and this seems to be the underlying intention. Should these views be seen as idiosyncratic, or do they represent a trend of which we should be acutely aware – as Lester Smith warned in his day? Are they, to use a currently popular phrase in official educational discourse, a 'cause for concern'?

I suggest they are, and very definitely so. It is true that the tendency for tighter central control over educational administration and expenditure is not new, that it has been manifest over the last ten or twenty years – particularly in the area of finance, a vitally important matter. But what is new, and goes to the heart of the matter, is the tendency to claim more direct control over the *process of education* itself – the curriculum, examinations and the like.

Consider the establishment of an Assessment of Performance Unit. This was a response to various pressures and public criticisms, but what are the implications in this sense? It is significant that Lord Alexander resigned from an advisory committee to this new body precisely on this question. The curriculum circular issued by the Department of Education and Science in 1977 is apparently to be followed by the formulation of national guidelines, while options to take more drastic action are kept open in the Green Paper formulations. Then we should take note of the *de facto* abolition of the Central Advisory Councils on the grounds that DES officials (or *ad hoc* committees) can do the job better; also of the ruthless reorganisation of Colleges of Education carried through during the last few years. Another innovation, which has much disturbed some people, is the Manpower Services Commission – a highly centralised system of administrative control in a field bordering directly on education. All this indicates increased bureaucratic, or remote, control over matters closely affecting all educational institutions, the very nature and quality of the educational process itself, and goes beyond what has traditionally been accepted as the legitimate role of government in education, even as defined by the DES. It would be in the Manchester tradition, I suggest, to call a halt and take stock. Where, precisely, are we heading?

3

In her 1942 lecture Lady Simon – teasing out in her clear, analytical manner, the full implications of the provision of equal educational opportunity – touched on what she called delicate 'political' issues. Equality of opportunity might effectively be achieved, it had been suggested, if both the finance and control of education were fully centralised, but this, she insisted, would necessarily involve a revolution in our present system with detrimental effect. As things were, the maintenance of minimum standards was ensured by the threat of reducing grant to recalcitrant local authorities, but to vest total financial control in the central authority meant setting a national norm and forbidding authorities to go beyond it, by raising extra money from the rates. If this was the way taken to secure equal educational provision 'education would become a state function, like unemployment, health insurance, the Post Office and the main roads'.

The chief argument against such a course is then deployed, and it is on this that I want to focus attention. It is well known, Lady Simon went on, that 'all experiment in education so far has come from below', from 'enterprising local authorities'. When a new move is successfully established in this way it has been taken up centrally, first by recommending the practice to other authorities and in due course in terms of introducing a new statutory duty through Parliament. Here she glanced at the history of numerous important features of the educational system: the school medical service, nursery classes, child guidance clinics, school camps, and elementary school 'tops' which were the forerunners of senior schools. All these were originally the outcome of *local* initiatives by advanced authorities, going back to the School Boards which had that role up to 1902.

I do not believe that the central part played by local authorities in the progressive development and, when necessary, in the defence of the educational system, has ever received the proper and detailed analysis and recognition it deserves – either from historians or students of politics and government, with the possible exception of the Webbs, or from politicians operating on the national scene. It lacks the glamour of great national and Parliamentary conflicts, such as the massive battles over the 1902 Act and the way conflicts of interest were resolved in 1870, on which historians like to focus attention. In addition there has been the particular situation that the British 'genius' in education was for long held to find its expression in the creation of great 'public schools' – which are not, of course, public in the proper sense of the term. These were developed as a cohesive 'system' in the late nineteenth century just when, through the efforts of School Boards up and down the country, the proper publicly-provided system first came into being to cater for a different social class, predominantly the working class. There was little glamour in this, perhaps, by comparison. But it is in many ways a heroic story – an enormous amount of energy, much of it voluntary, was put into building up systems of education to serve localities, by what were *ad hoc* authorities elected by a form of proportional representation. And if we sometimes have cause to resent the lasting qualities of the actual buildings erected, these were a magnificent achievement at the time – rising above the small surrounding houses almost as cathedrals did in medieval towns.

If, then, the matter is assessed historically, it becomes evident that, within the confines of statutory legislation, it is the representative local authorities that have made the running; and, too, provided a strong bulwark in defence of the educational system when there was attack from the centre –

and this without reference to party allegiance. Here is one of the points that struck me most forcibly when studying the inter-war period. This was a black period for education if ever there was one; in fact, taking the century from 1870, the two decades 1920–40 were those during which the least progress was made. Despite the promise of the Fisher Act – the product of the First World War – the national system of education suffered a consistent series of hammer blows – going so far, in the case of the Geddes proposals of 1922, as to threaten its very viability. At this bleak and difficult time it was the local authorities, and their leading representatives, who most consistently fought to defend what they saw, and rightly, as their own school systems, serving the people of the locality, built up with much concern and effort. While the Association of Education Committees expressed total opposition to what were officially designated as 'economies', Spurley Hey, Manchester's Director from 1914, published the most acute analysis of the implications of the threatened financial cuts, set at around 30 per cent, which would certainly have turned the Fisher Act into a dead letter. 'Anyone who wishes to reduce expenditure by £10 million, £15 million or £20 million is not an economist,' he declared. 'He is a butcher who proceeds to kill by dismemberment.'[5]

Nor was it only against the Geddes proposals that the local authorities protested, with effect. They also took the lead in a national protest against another clumsy attempt to dismember the educational service only three years later – this time by Lord Eustace Percy, then President of the Board of Education, dragooned by the Cabinet – with the issue of the notorious Circular 1371. *The Times Educational Supplement* – a much smaller affair in those days – published page after page of resolutions of protest for several weeks, from local authorities all over the country. And the shire counties, some still virtually feudal, were quite as outspoken as the great urban authorities. These protests are evidence of a clear grasp of the implications, for Circular 1371 was directed to nullifying *the* crucial clause of the 1918 Education Act – one which introduced a percentage grant and guaranteed a mimimum Exchequer contribution of 50 per cent. It was this clause that Fisher regarded as the *central condition* for the progressive – and effective – development of education as a national system.

There can be no doubt that the defence of the school system, at this threatening time, was primarily conducted by local authorities, both singly and in their associations – notably the Association of Education Committees and, if to a lesser extent, the County Councils Association. Other were also involved, of course, not least the teachers associations. In the closest possible touch with the schools, teachers were, and are, in the best position to evaluate the effect of economy drives and the extent to which they prevent an effective education, particularly for those most in need of it – a matter to which I will return. But the point to stress now is that, in this country, the national system of publicly provided education is essentially made up of *local authority systems*. Those responsible for the effective functioning of schools and colleges are the elected local authorities. It is at this level that institutions have been provided and are run. And it is those who plan and provide the facilities, who engage within institutions in the tasks of education, who are best placed to assess needs – and likewise to understand the real meaning of financial parsimony and to rouse public opinion in defence of education.

By the same token the pressure for educational advance has also come from those working at the local level, both teachers and administrators. In 1929 a remarkable book was published – *The Rising Tide* subtitled 'An Epic in Education' – by J.G. Legge, Director of Education for Liverpool from 1906–21.[6] This helps us to understand the great and growing pride local authorities have taken, and still take, in their work for education.

Legge concentrates specifically on the systems of secondary education built up by the larger authorities after 1902 – under legislation which, carefully enough, had accorded them only permissive powers. When the most was made of these, authorities came up against essentially restrictive governmental policies which implied acute suspicion of the exercise of initiative at the local level. Ranging over this experience – indeed the whole period from 1902–21 – Legge pays tribute to the official staff of newly established local authorites, but most of all head-teachers, directors and secretaries of education,

themselves sprung from elementary schools, men of great ability,

tireless energy and burning sympathy, who know not only the
types and characters of the masses of children of this country, but
of their parents as well, and who are intimately versed in the
conditions of their lives.

Such men and women proved an 'invaluable counterpoise' to
what he describes as the 'predominantly academic influences'
at Whitehall, and to the body of headmasters of so-called
'public schools' whose pronouncements carried weight at the
time but who were prone to be less than generous in their
comments on local authority efforts to establish secondary
education and patronisingly contemptuous of their chief
officials. The comments are the more blistering in that Legge
was himself an Oxford man, with years of experience of
working in the civil service before moving into education and
local government. As for members of education committees –
the 'Great Unpaid' to whom he dedicates his book – many, he
says, 'have the rare quality of vision' and soon pick up the
threads of administration. 'Their charge is over 7 millions, as
against the 60,000 of the schools that claim to be public
schools.' The job of the large urban authority, Legge makes
clear, emphasising the central point, is to organise an entire
system of schools, both elementary and secondary ensuring that
'money and effort are not wasted in covering the same ground
twice, or pandering to one interest to the exclusion of another'
– a comment which goes to the very heart of the matter, not
only yesterday but today.

I have discussed the important part that local authorities
have played historically, within the 'English compromise', in
defence of education, of systems created locally. I have
referred, as one example, to the crucial influence of local
authority initiative in the evolution of secondary education;
recalling that central government, through Parliament, gave
only permissive powers in this respect; and that the leading
national politicians concerned with that statutory measure, the
1902 Act, were soon shaken by the energetic thrust forward in
this area, by local authorities responding to local demand and
expectations. Many other examples come to mind – for
instance, the provision of nursery schooling here in
Manchester in the inter-war period, when something like half

of all the available nursery provision in the country was in this one area. Lady Simon included child guidance, school camps, and other such developments, and, indeed, even within the severe restraints of the inter-war period, progressive authorities managed to make advances in favour of children least able to fend for themselves. The provision of school meals is one case when the Manchester Education Committee specifically refused to implement an edict of the central authority on behalf of the children.

Most important, however, is the way that local authorities have made the running in terms of persistent attempts to raise the level of education available to the mass of children, from the days of the School Boards down to the development of comprehensive secondary schools. Manchester had a notable Clerk to its Board, Charles Wyatt, acknowledged in his day to be a leading figure in the development of local educational administration and one of the founders of the School Board Association which was the forerunner of the Association of Education Committees. It was he who administered the work of the Manchester School Board and it was, of course, the School Boards which took the initiative in the establishment of higher grade schools in the 1880s and 90s. Manchester's Central School, with its famous head teacher Scotson, was among the pioneers of this movement – the fruits of which were deliberately destroyed by the central authority, by administrative means, as Professor Eaglesham has shown, beyond doubt, in his scholarly studies of the period.[7] When the higher grade schools were suppressed, local authorities sought new ways of meeting the needs of their populations for a fuller, more generous education than could possibly be provided within the normal elementary school under the elementary code of regulations. Hence the energetic actions to develop secondary schools as soon as this became possible, which Legge so vividly describes, and, when barriers were erected, the resort to establishing central schools, with which, in Manchester, the name of Spurley Hey is particularly associated. Subsequently, in 1928, when Hadow reorganis-ation became national policy, it was once again the advanced authorities, those which took their responsibilities seriously, that went ahead, so far as they were allowed, with the establishment of senior schools in new and specially designed buildings which, despite the limitations imposed, opened new perspectives. The move to comprehensive education after the Second World War was a further logical step in this direction. This was again very much a local authority issue as Manchester knows very well; one pressed doggedly, and persistently up to the mid-1960s, against the overwhelming tenor of 'advice' from the central authority coupled with adverse decisions, whatever the political colour of the government. If to promote this system is now national policy this is by no means thanks to a central initiative.

A point Legge emphasises in his book is that the very task set the local authority – that of meeting the actual needs of a specific area or community – creates an outlook quite different from that of officials of limited background and experience at the administrative and political centre – themselves, in his day, largely the products of 'public schools'. I have already referred to Spurley Hey as typical of the local authority administrator at his best, a man acutely aware that, if reforms are not implemented, if financial cuts cripple the education service only for a time, a whole generation of children suffers. But not only this, Hey was also an official expert in the logistics and administration of education with a fund of experience, including local knowledge, which could not be rivalled at the centre. Such a man was bound to carry considerable weight, nationally as well as locally. But there were also others of the kind. The three leading Directors in the 1920s – when education was so often at risk – were Spurley Hey of Manchester, Percival Sharp of Sheffield and James Graham of Leeds. Known as the Three Musketeers, these men were as ready as Athos, Porthos and Aramis to unsheathe their swords and wield them with great effect, in defence of education and of local government. There was also William Brockington of Leicestershire, who pioneered Hadow reorganisation before the Hadow Committee reported, and who, amazingly, held his post for forty-four years, finally retiring at the age of 75 in 1947. Another was Philip Morris of Cambridgeshire, who introduced the village – or community – college, now being transformed by Manchester in an urban setting, at the Abraham Moss Centre. Directors of Education are relatively unhonoured and unsung. I have no wish to make exaggerated claims, but, in my view, English education probably owes more to this single, relatively small, but certainly expert body of men than to any other. They are the products, and very characteristic ones at that, of the 'English compromise'.

Let us not forget either Legge's 'Great Unpaid' – those who up and down the country regularly took part in the work of Education Committees and their sub-committees and sub-sub-committees taking on particular responsibilities. And particularly the Chairmen (or in Manchester, especially, I should say Chairpersons) who have an exacting task. It happened that Lady Simon was the first woman to hold this post in Manchester, and perhaps also the first to acknowledge that she learned her job from the Director, or successive directors, namely Spurley Hey and Lester Smith. Many chairmen of education committees in the inter-war period, from which I have been taking examples, played an important part on the national scene representing the interests and traditions of very different localities – perhaps, particularly, when one comes to examine the matter, in the North of England. I have in mind such men as the redoubtable Sir Percy Jackson from the West Riding and Alderman Rowlinson of Sheffield, both also members with Lady Simon, of the Consultative Committee to the Board of Education which played so important a part at the time, but was to be eliminated by the 1944 Act. Indeed the crucial Chapter 9 of the Spens Report, where the Committee presented key proposals for a single code of regulations for post-primary education and the abolition of fees in secondary schools, was essentially the product of what might be called a tightly knit group of educationally motivated men (and women) – the local authority representatives on that Committee.[8] The proposals, it may be added, presented at the close of 1938, were rejected out of hand by the central authority, on the advice of civil servants, as Utopian or impossible – but as rapidly adopted only two or three years later as the essential basis of what became the second great education act to emerge from a world war. Had the war not broken out, recalling the atmosphere of the late 1930s as I can do quite vividly, one wonders how long it would have taken to get the necessary measures establishing secondary education for all on the Statute book; a perspective essentially opened up by the leading local authorities.

4

I have focused so far on one specific feature of the English tradition in education – the strength and vitality displayed historically through the forms of local control and initiative that have evolved over the last century. Whatever the stresses and strains this system is now subject to, we need to recall the underlying resilience and vitality of this tradition; one which, I suggest, in the interests of education, needs today to be strengthened against attempts to erode it. But to refer to local 'systems' of education is to deal in an abstraction. These systems are made up of people, combined in institutions – in schools and colleges. And it is here that the real business of education is carried on – by the teachers who, in this country, are appointed and employed by local authorities, not the central authority, a matter of very considerable significance. This fact alone allows to teachers a measure of autonomy not to be found in centralised systems on the Continent to which our attention has latterly been directed.

Just as the work of local authority officials has been largely ignored by historians, so also has the work of teachers. Or, if they are written about, then it is mainly in terms of the growth of the profession, or the history of teachers' associations.[9] Both these are important, of course, but where do we look to find any analysis – or even reconstruction – of the real life of the schools established by local authorities; the relations between school and community which have developed, in some cases over a century, and the part played by teachers in transforming the education and upbringing of generations of English children.

Earlier I mentioned Scotson, the expert and highly professional head of one of Manchester's first Higher Grade Schools, the Central School, visited and vividly described by the Royal Commission on Technical Education in 1884. Called 'The Prince of Schoolmasters' – in fact by A.J. Mundella – Scotson played an important part on the national scene at the turn of the century in his passionate defence of the concept and practice of the Higher Grade School movement. It was by this means that many of the large urban school boards, in the North of England in particular, sought to construct unified, organic local structures integrally relating each stage of education to the next, up to and including the university. This they could work towards up to the point when the central authority, by administrative measures followed by the 1902 Act, closed down the perspective, halting what we can now assess as a significant effort to build up a comprehensive system of education from below.

It is not, however, only a question of those who made a mark on the national scene. What about the day to day work of the heads and assistants in elementary schools? Here were teachers who worked under the most difficult – we would now say almost impossible – conditions whose contribution has yet to be fully recognised. A recent study of a heavily urbanised area in Yorkshire – based on oral discussion with groups of ex-pupils who attended a specific group of neighbourhood schools from the close of the nineteenth century – brings this to light in a dramatic way. May I name the main teachers concerned? Edgar Wolstenholme, head of a Church of England, or 'national' school (popularly known as 'the Natch'), Harry Duce his assistant for nearly forty years, and William Dawn head of the nearby Board school for roughly the same period. All three retired at the same time – in the early 1930s. The story of the contribution these teachers made to the life of the locality – having taught up to three generations of steelworkers' children – has been written by a local girl, herself now a teacher, Cheryl Parsons, under the title *Schools in an Urban Community*.[10] She describes the slow growth of confidence and local pride in the schools, the gradual building up of positive relationships, the occasional dramatic events; and the extent to which the schools, or their teachers, found ways to alleviate distress in time of extreme poverty and unemployment in the district. All this not only makes fascinating reading but brings to light, very concretely, the contribution teachers have been able to make when free to use their initiative. Before steps are taken to curb this, we need to think very hard indeed.

This is an important issue because it seems evident that the present trend towards seeking a centralised solution to current problems is, in part at least, based on a belief that teachers today have too much freedom. Hence the call for curriculum guidelines at a national level, to be enforced by a battery of devices – from the inspectorate to the imposition of mass testing and, perhaps, yet more periodical examinations. What seems to be suggested is a kind of straitjacket or corset (to use a monetary analogy) outside which none should stray. I have a vision of the ideal school according to these criteria; all the children of the nation sitting docilely in rows and the teacher at the blackboard daily dispensing chunks of the required curriculum – a veritable turning-back of the clock.

I am as aware as anyone of the force of the criticisms now being made, by industrialists and other. But I believe this idea is altogether out of touch with the realities. And this for more reasons than can be gone into here – the chief being that it takes no account of what is involved in teaching and learning, what education means. Despite the Tyndale affair, any conception that teachers generally are incapable of utilising current freedoms, both responsibly and creatively, is very wide of the mark. So far as research into primary schools goes – since these have been specifically singled out for criticism – the only hard evidence we have had, until very recently, comes from two surveys bearing on teacher control in the classroom. One, covering a city and county area in the Midlands, generally regarded as a home of 'progressive' education, concluded that so tight is this control, even in what is called an 'informal' situation, that it is even doubtful whether pupils have sufficient freedom and mobility to enable the development of initiative and a sense of responsibility for their own work generally held to be desirable.[11] The second, Bennett's survey of all the primary schools in Lancashire and Cumbria, categorised only 9 per cent of these as genuinely 'progressive'; and it is worth recalling the finding that the best results, in terms of learning on the criteria used, were achieved in one of these.[12] Preliminary results of a large research programme into primary education currently under way at the University of Leicester – which involves close and systematic observation of sixty primary classrooms over one, two, and in some cases, three years – point in the same direction. And there are also the general conclusions of a survey conducted by

Her Majesty's Inspectorate, set out in a substantial volume of 200 pages.[13] I quote from a summary of classroom organisation:

> The children behave responsibly and co-operate with their teacher and with other children. Discussion takes place between teachers and children and amongst children. A quiet working atmosphere is established when necessary.

This is a new dispensation which has brought new educational results. And in one of their final paragraphs the inspectors say, under the heading 'looking forward':

> During years when the public at large has seemed to be critical of schools the relations between teachers and individual parents have become closer and more friendly; and the curriculum has broadened to include much that is of value. Good relations within the schools, increasingly good relations with parents, and a thorough concern for teaching the basic skills are solid foundations on which to build further.

Recent research, therefore, indicates that criticisms highlighted in the press, or on television, may well not reflect accurately what 'the public at large' really thinks; that there is no good cause to jump to rash or 'instant' conclusions to the effect that greater centralisation is required as a means of curbing teachers. Here I would like to recall another lecture by Lady Simon, since a profound respect for teachers and their judgement was one of the things she acquired during forty years on an education committee.[14] The content of education, she argued on this occasion, in 1934, 'is just as technical a subject as methods of teaching and the proper balance of the curriculum'. These important issues 'should be thought out in teachers' conferences' or by expert committees appointed for the purpose. Freedom in this sense is 'just as essential for the teacher in the elementary school as for the professor in the university'. Nowadays many would add that due account should also be taken of the views of students. But essentially at issue here is scope for the teacher to function as a responsible individual with powers of decision – in co-operation with colleagues – on the central aspect of education, the teacher-pupil relationship which in turn relates directly to the content of education and methodology. Just as doctors exercise their professional expertise in determining treatment in matters of health, so teachers exercise theirs in questions of education. It is this principle – this degree of autonomy – that we need to preserve, if we are to reap the maximum advantage from the skill and expertise of teachers.

5

To each country its historical traditions. In Prussia the provision of education was seen as essentially a function of the state long before 1900 when Professor Rein lectured at Cambridge. In this connection it is worth recalling that the German Social Democratic party, in a programme of 1875, demanded that the state should provide elementary education, and that this elicited the strongest of protests, from Karl Marx who dismissed the concept as 'completely objectionable'. Certainly the state should provide the means to education, define and enforce certain regulations, but this is something quite other than appointing the state 'educator of the people'. Rather, Marx contended characteristically, it is 'the state that could do with a rude education by the people'. More specifically he pointed to the pattern in Switzerland and the United States where there were elected school boards.[15]

This has been the pattern in England, although the state has certain overriding powers and statutory legislation is imposed nationally by Parliament. Even so – according to Sir Fred Clarke in his seminal book *Education and Social Change*, published in 1940 – the nature of central control has been such as to prevent the development of

> a genuine *popular philosophy of education* such as exists in the United States and some commonwealth countries. The mass of the English people have never yet evolved genuine schools of their own. Schools have always been provided for them from above, in a form and with a content of studies that suited the ruling interests.[16]

And this despite the degree of local autonomy I have been at pains to underline.

It follows, surely, that even if recent developments in the nature of society – increased complexity, mobility and so on – seem to call for centralisation in the government of education, if we are to retain the characteristic resilience and vitality of our educational system, what is needed is a greater degree of local responsibility for the control of education – not curtailment of what we have. In this connection it should be recognised – and this is a vital point made by Bryan Keith-Lucas in his study of local government – that the demand for enhanced central control is often motivated not by considerations related to effective provision to meet social needs but by such criteria as managerial efficiency in the pursuit of economy.[17] There should, then, be due awareness of what may lie behind insistent demands for centralisation, and a readiness to resist moves in what can only be a retrograde direction.

This is not to contend that local government has no faults. There are shortcomings of various kinds to be studied and corrected, and, as we all know, there are good local authorities and bad, in different places from time to time. What is worth insisting on, at this point, however, is that if there is to be enhanced responsibility for the all important education service, new initiatives are called for which stimulate and ensure *community* involvement. There are already various moves in this direction and, interestingly enough, some realise points which Lester Smith – as Director of Education for this City forty odd years ago – clearly foresaw and sought to encourage. In the book taken as my text he specifically stressed the need to find new forms of community participation – of the kind now being implemented on new lines, in Manchester and elsewhere, with the establishment of schools as an integral part of community colleges. He pointed also to the need to develop the English tradition of collegiate responsibility within institutions, now being implemented in a new way in terms of greater participation in the government of community colleges and comprehensive secondary schools, as also in terms of staff involvement in the government of colleges of education and technology following on the recommendations of the Weaver Report. Again, Lester Smith insisted on the importance of 'personalising' local services and this, too, is now better understood and being translated into practice – if there is still a good way to go.

And this brings me back to my title, 'To Whom Do Schools Belong?' Perhaps, it may be suggested at this point, the question is wrongly posed; and, so put, positively precipitates us into a dispute about 'ownership' of property. In a sense it is essentially correct to say, as Maurice Kogan does in the book I referred to earlier, that schools are 'maintained, staffed and owned by local education authorities'. This is so, of course, in a formal sense – if with certain provisos – but statements of this kind always raise additional questions. What, after all, *is* a school, in the human and social sense? Surely a community of teachers and pupils (or, better, students) engaged in educational activities; and how can it be said that the local authority, however democratically elected, owns these? To claim as much is to evoke cries of protest – about the rights of parents, for instance. But parents do not 'own' children either, as I think we would all agree if pressed, apart from the fact that – once more in this case – we are well aware of the line of policy that lies behind such claims; and also cognisant that local authorities are bound to run certain services specifically designed to protect children from parents and, for that matter, the community from certain children. Maybe the school buildings legally belong to local authorities, maybe they plan the local system, pay the teachers (if largely with funds allotted by the central authority), provide resources, administer and govern in various ways with varying degrees of devolvement. But these, however important, are all enabling activities. Schools are communities organised for the purpose of teaching and learning; education results from the interaction and activities of teachers and children, and the facilities provided for the purpose will only be the best, and the best used, when this is understood – as against balancing competing claims to ownership of the component parts. But it is also necessary to remember that learning does not only go on in schools and that other relationships are important to all those involved – as has recently been emphasised in relation to village schools, and how much they mean to the local community and the community to them. It is in the same sense that, in many towns, the neighbourhood school is valued both in educational and community terms.

That said, there is no question of the key importance of the elected local authority and its education committee so long as this acts – in the words of Lady Simon in her Warburton lecture in 1934 – as 'the touchstone of public opinion'; as the representative of community interests as a whole. For the education committee, as she said speaking specifically of this city, not only plans and implements policy but 'stands in the eyes of the public, the teachers, the officials, for the whole complicated structure loosely known as Manchester education'. It follows that, after arriving at a policy which can best serve the interests of the locality and the communities composing it, it is important to find ways of explaining that policy, and the underlying issues. Lady Simon intended to write on this theme when she retired from the education committee. It was to fulfil the wish, as she was unable to do, that the set of lectures, of which this is the final one, was inaugurated five years ago.

Perhaps it is worth recalling, in conclusion, that it was here, in Manchester, in the 1850s that the whole story of local authority involvement in education began. For the Lancashire Public School Association based on this city – later to be called the National Public School Association – was the first body to launch an effective, nation-wide campaign for locally controlled and rate-supported, but universal, systems of schooling.[18] The citizens of Manchester are, therefore, heirs to a great tradition – one that we today can and should build upon and strengthen for the tasks that lie ahead.

Notes

1. 'Equal Educational Opportunity: What it Means', *Public Administration*, Vol. XX, No. 2 (1942).
2. W. Rein, 'Outlines of the Development of Educational Ideas during the Nineteenth Century' in R.D. Roberts (ed.), *Education in the Nineteenth Century*, 1901.
3. Maurice Kogan, *The Politics of Educational Change*, Manchester, 1978.
4. Max Wilkinson, *Lessons From Europe: A Comparison of British and West European Schooling*, London, 1977 and Tim Devlin and Mary Warnock, *What Must We Teach?* London 1977.
5. *Education*, 10 February 1922.

6. J.G. Legge, *The Rising Tide*, Oxford, 1929.
7. Eric Eaglesham, *From School Board to Local Authority*, London, 1956.
8. Joan Simon, 'The Shaping of the Spens Report on Secondary Education 1933–38: an inside view', Parts I and II, *British Journal of Educational Studies*, Vol. XXV, No. 1, February 1977 and Vol. XXV, No. 2, June 1977.
9. P.H.J.H. Gosden, *The Evolution of a Profession* (1972); Asher Tropp, *The School Teachers*, London, 1957.
10. Cheryl Parsons, *Schools in an Urban Community*, London, 1978.
11. 'The Organisation of Junior School Classrooms', by D. Bealing, *Educational Research*, June 1972.
12. Neville Bennett *et al., Teaching Styles and Pupil Progress*, London, 1976.
13. *Primary Education in England,* London, 1978.
14. *How the Manchester Education Committee Works* (The Warburton Lecture), 1934.
15. Karl Marx, 'Critique of the Gotha Programme' in David Fernbach (ed.), *The First International and After*, Harmondsworth, 1974, p. 357. For a more detailed analysis of Marx's view, see pp. 100 ff.
16. Fred Clarke, *Education and Social Change*, London, 1940, p. 30.
17. Bryan Keith-Lucas and Peter G. Richards, *A History of Local Government in the Twentieth Century*, London, 1978.
18. Donald Jones, *The Making of the Education System 1851–81,* London, 1977 pp. 13–28; see also Donald Jones, 'Lancashire, the American Common School, and the Religious Problem in British Education in the Nineteenth Century', *British Journal of Educational Studies*, Vol. XV, No. 3, October 1967; and 'The Educational Legacy of the Anti-Corn Law League', *History of Education*, Vol. 13, No. 1, January 1974.

4

Why No Pedagogy in England?

The term 'pedagogy' is used here in the sense of the 'science of teaching' (OED). The title of this paper is meant to imply that no such science exists in England; the fact that the term is generally shunned implies that such a science is either undesirable or impossible of achievement. And such, it is argued, is the situation.

The contrast here with other European countries, both west and east, is striking. In the educational tradition of the Continent, the term 'pedagogy' has an honoured place, stemming perhaps particularly from the work and thinking of Comenius in the seventeenth century, but developed and elaborated in the nineteenth century through the work of Pestalozzi, Herbart and others. The concept of teaching as a science has strong roots in this tradition.

Not so in England. It is now more than one hundred years since Alexander Bain published *Education as a Science*.[1] Since then, less and less has been heard of this claim. The most striking aspect of current thinking and discussion about education is its eclectic character, reflecting deep confusion of thought, and of aims and purposes, relating to learning and teaching – to pedagogy.

As an example we may look briefly at the work of the Schools Council, which, after its establishment in 1962, had had the task of stimulating change in the curriculum in an

This paper was originally published as a chapter in a symposium entitled *Education in the Eighties, the central issues*, edited by Brian Simon and William Taylor (Batsford 1981). The author wishes to thank Dr T.G. Whiston, of the Science Policy Research Unit, University of Sussex, for extremely helpful and stimulating discussions on this issue, as also for commenting on an early draft of this paper. Thanks are also due to Professors E. Stones and J.F. Eggleston for very useful comments on an early draft.

attempt to bring it up to date in the light of modern knowledge
and of social and economic change. But the key feature of this
effort has been the atheoretical, pragmatic approach adopted
(together with the implicit acceptance of the status quo in
organisational or administrative terms). The technique used
has been the funding of teams of teachers and others with the
brief of producing 'curriculum reform' plans, syllabuses and
packages. These have worked out their own ideas based on
'good practice' implying an emphasis on grass-roots
experiences, on curriculum reform from below as compared to
reform from above as in the United States and the USSR. Thus
some projects have focused on the teaching of individual
subjects at various levels, others on the integration of subject
matter, yet others on 'the whole curriculum'. Some have
focused (like the early Nuffield Science Projects) on 'top ability'
pupils; others specifically on curricula considered appropriate
for 'the young school leaver'. The overall approach can hardly
be called systematic, and certainly has not been informed by
any generally accepted (or publicly formulated) ideas or
theories about the nature of the child or the learning/teaching
process – by any 'science of teaching' or 'pedagogy'. In
particular there has been an almost total failure to provide
psychological underpinning for the new programmes proposed.[2] In general the Schools Council approach has reflected
a pluralism run wild – a mass of disparate projects. In these
circumstances, there is, perhaps, little wonder that the 'take up'
in the schools seems to have been vestigial.

This is not intended as a criticism of the Schools Council. No
other outcome could have been expected; not so much because
of the make-up and constitution of that body itself (revised in
1979) but more because the concept of 'pedagogy' – of a
science of teaching embodying both curriculum and
methodology – is alien to our experience and way of thinking.
There are, no doubt, many reasons why this is so; among them
wide acceptance of the unresolved dichotomies between
'progressive' and 'traditional', 'child-centred' and 'subject-
centred' approaches, or, more generally, between the
'informal' and 'formal'. Such crude, generalised categories are
basically meaningless but expressed in this form deflect
attention from the real problems of teaching and learning.

Indeed, so disparate are the views expressed that to resuscitate the concept of a science of teaching which underlies that of 'pedagogy' may seem to be crying for the moon. I hope to indicate that it is, in fact, a realistic proposition; that the knowledge base for a science of teaching does exist, and that circumstances urgently demand that the matter warrants serious and close attention.

But first, it may be useful to advance an interpretation as to why the concept of 'pedagogy' has been shunned in England, and why instead our approach to educational theory and practice has tended to be amateurish, and highly pragmatic in character.[3] Relevant here is the practice and approach of our most prestigious educational institutions (historically speaking), the ancient universities and leading public schools. Until recently, and even perhaps today, these have been dominant, both socially and in terms of the formation of the climate of opinion. It is symptomatic that the public schools, in general, have until recently contemptuously rejected the idea that a professional training is in any sense relevant to the job of a public school master. Although toying with the idea in the late nineteenth century, the Headmasters Conference has never adopted a positive attitude to such training, which traditionally has been seen as perhaps relevant and important for an elementary school teacher, but certainly not to someone taking up the gentlemanly profession of teaching in a public school. This was seen, perhaps, not so much as a job anyone from the middle or upper class could do, but as something those who wished to teach, having the appropriate social origins including a degree at Oxford or Cambridge, could learn, through experience, on the job. Certainly no special training was necessary.[4]

The reasons for this are not far to seek. The public schools developed as a cohesive system from the mid to late 1860s serving the new Victorian upper middle class; indeed they played a major role in the symbiosis of aristocracy and bourgeoisie which characterised the late nineteenth century. As Honey makes clear, these schools were centrally concerned with the socialisation of these classes which could not be effectively undertaken in the home. This, he argues, is why, in spite of the epidemics, outrageous bullying, sexual dangers and insanitary conditions to which their pupils were exposed (and all of which took their toll), the popularity of these schools mounted irresistibly at this time.[5]

Socialisation, as the major function of these schools at this time, involved little emphasis on intellectual (or cognitive) development. More important, especially in conditions of developing imperialism, was the formation of character, specifically of the qualities embodied in the concept of 'manliness' which, in its late nineteenth century form, involved the religion of games. This is not to argue that intellectual development was totally neglected. The tradition of classical teaching was, in fact, reinvigorated at this period, both at Oxford and Cambridge and in the schools. But the area of studies was limited and a major effort in this direction confined to a small number of schools which had a tradition of success in winning scholarships at Oxford and Cambridge (for instance, Shrewsbury, and later, Winchester). The burden of the interpretation by modern scholarship of the evolution of the public schools in the nineteenth century focuses on the transition from the Arnoldian ideal of 'Godliness and Good Learning' in the early part of the century to the cult of manliness and games towards the end, the transition having been effected with the aid of 'muscular Christianity' personified by Hughes (*Tom Brown's Schooldays*) and Charles Kingsley.[6]

This is a world far removed from pedagogy – the science of teaching – and from its concerns. Bourdieu's analysis may be relevant here.[7] Teachers and pupils at the public schools, and in general also at the university, came from similiar backgrounds and shared a common culture. They talked the same language and were interested in the same things. The schools, in an important sense, were extensions of the home, largely financed by the parents themselves (though the value of endowments should not be underestimated), the products of a close collaboration between parents and teachers. The teacher's pastoral responsibility – in terms of upbringing – was as important, or more so than his intellectual (teaching) responsibility. In this situation upper middle class culture and attitudes were 'naturally' assimilated and reinforced – the process did not require the application of specifically 'pedagogical' means. Approaches to teaching were traditional, handed down from generation to generation, though here there were exceptions, and certain schools (and teachers) did contribute to new thinking and practice relating, perhaps particularly, to science (Rugby). Again, as far as pedagogy is concerned, one public school head stands out in the late nineteenth, another in the early twentieth century: Thring of Uppingham, who was particularly concerned with the development, mental and moral, of the normal or 'average' boy; and Sanderson of Oundle whose innovations in the area of science, crafts and technology are of outstanding interest. Of course there were others, but these are exceptions; the general picture is as described.

The (historical) denigration of the value of professional training by the public schools, then, falls into place; it simply did not appear as relevant to the schoolmaster's profession, as defined in terms of public school objectives and practice. And this, of course, implies disdain for the concept of pedagogy – or of a science of teaching – since the function of professional training is, in theory, to lay the basis in science of the practice or art of teaching. At no time over the last hundred years (the period of existence of public schools in their modern form as a system) have the public schools, as such, expressed more than a remote, or distant, interest in or concern with this process. While the proportion of public schoolmasters who have been trained has risen over the last twenty to thirty years, the amateur still reigns supreme.[8]

The situation is precisely reflected in Oxford and Cambridge, which, of course, have had the closest links with the public school system over the last century. Neither of these universities has, until perhaps recently, contributed to any serious extent to the study of education or to the development of educational theory and practice. This may seem an extraordinary thing to say; nevertheless it is the case. Cambridge, admittedly, made a start in 1879–80 when a delegacy was formed concerning teacher training, and lectures given covering the history, psychology and the practice of teaching. But this initiative did not prosper, and Cambridge was, in fact, among the last of all British universities to appoint a Professor of Education (in 1948) though, even here, it is ahead of Oxford which still does not recognise the subject in terms of establishing a Chair. Although departments of education have existed at both Universities for several decades now, these have been undistinguished and little regarded, both inside and outside the respective Universities. The low prestige of education as a subject of study, the few resources devoted to it, and the lack of serious experimental or scholarly studies undertaken, all these (and other factors) reflect general attitudes.[9]

The result has been that education, as a subject of enquiry and study, still less as a 'science', has, historically, had little prestige in this country, having been to all intents and purposes ignored in the most prestigious educational institutions. As Matthew Arnold tirelessly pointed out over one hundred years ago, in France, Prussia and elsewhere the problems of education for the middle class were taken really seriously. In Britain, on the other hand, everything was neglected; a *laissez-faire* pragmatism predominated.[10] This situation has, to some extent, been perpetuated. The dominant educational institutions of this country have had no concern with theory, its relation to practice, with pedagogy. This is the first point to establish.

But this, of course, is only part of the picture, if an important one. For while the public schools expressed, at least in their practice, a total disregard for pedagogy, in fact a systematic, rational approach was being developed elsewhere – as an indigenous growth within the system of elementary education, and specifically in the last decade of the nineteenth century, just as this system 'became of age', as it were, after its establishment in 1870. This is an interesting and relevant phenomenon, and worth serious attention for its lessons today.

The context of what was, in fact, a serious attempt to integrate theoretical knowledge with the practice of education is to be found in the work of the advanced School Boards in the main industrial cities at this time. Described as 'citadels of radicalism' by Elie Halévy, the French historian, these, with their higher grade schools, pupil-teacher centres, and technical institutions of various kinds (some of which supported, or merged with local universities) were now, in co-operation with the Technical Education Boards established after 1888, deliberately developing cohesive systems of education with an organic relation between the various stages, having the perspective of covering the whole field from infant school to university. This potential development was sharply cut off and circumscribed by a series of administrative and legislative measures brought in by a deeply Conservative government in the period 1899–1904.[11] But through the 1890s, such a perspective appeared realisable. Now at last the mass of the children had been brought into the schools; buildings were erected (some of them massive); teaching was developing as a profession. The so-called 'extravagance' of the School Boards, as seen by such as Sir John Gorst (and the Tories generally), had some basis in fact. The outlook was optimistic. This was the context of the quite sudden, and apparently rapid, development of educational theory and practice – of positive, all-embracing, pedagogical means.

The social context of this development has been outlined; its theoretical context is equally important. This is personified – or crystallised – in Alexander Bain's *Education as a Science*, published in 1879, reprinted six times in the 1880s, and a further ten times before 1900.[12] Examination of a number of student-teacher manuals, which proliferated in the 1890s, indicates their indebtedness to Bain's approach – or the extent to which they shared common interpretations both of theoretical issues relating to education, and of the practice of teaching.

Bain, Professor of Logic at Aberdeen, author of two large treatises on psychology (*The Senses and the Intellect* and *The Emotions and the Will*) biographer (and to some extent disciple) of James Mill and friend of John Stuart Mill, is perhaps best known, at least to historians of psychology, as the last of the classic line of associationists (stretching from John Locke, through David Hartley, Joseph Priestley, James and John Stuart Mill, to Bain's near contemporary, Spencer).[13] It was among the early associationists, in particular Joseph Priestley and Richard Edgeworth, that the concept that education might be a science, or at least could adopt scientific procedures, originally developed.[14] It is worth noting that Bain's book was published in Kegan Paul's International Scientific Series (comprising 54 volumes) alongside books by Tyndall, T.H. Huxley, and others. In this book, Bain firmly adhered to the view that education should be considered as a science.

The crucial basis for this approach lay in the theory, announced by Bain as fact, that the formation of associations of ideas in the mind was accompanied by (or was the resultant of) new connections, linkages, or 'paths' formed in the substance of the brain. The process of education since it consisted in the planned ordering of the child's experiences, must therefore have a necessary effect (as Priestley had argued one hundred years earlier), and this, of course, had been the basis of the theory of human perfectibility characteristic of the Enlightenment. This approach not only posited the educability of the normal child, it stressed the 'plasticity', as Bain put it, of brain functioning and processes. Education, then, as again Bain defined it, was concerned with *acquired* capacities and functions. It was about human change and development.

Empirical support for the theory of the formation of new connections in the brain as underlying the acquisition of new associations was available to Bain particularly from the work of his contemporary, the neuro-physiologist Henry Maudsley. Every sense impression resulting in a 'current of molecular activity' from one part of the brain to another, Maudsley wrote, 'leaves behind it ... some after-effect' or 'modification of the nerve elements concerned in its function'. This physiological process, he claimed, 'is the physical basis of memory', the 'foundation of our mental functions'.[15]

It followed from this approach that, to order education aright in terms of the acquisition of knowledge, two things were necessary. First, to obtain a psychological (and physiological) understanding of the growth of human powers through infancy, childhood and youth; and second, to analyse the content of subject matter in terms of its own inner logic. Together these underlay the determination of the curriculum. But Bain was also closely concerned with motivation, discipline, teacher-pupil relationships, moral education, as well as with the mode of teaching the main curriculum areas. Seeing 'education' specifically as schooling, he covered in his book almost every relevant aspect of teaching, learning, and classroom organisation.

As suggested earlier, advances relating to pedagogy were an indigenous development from within the elementary school system. This is the case, in the sense that the many manuals for student-teachers published towards the end of the century were written by men working in the teacher-training institutions of the time, all of which prepared students specifically for the elementary schools.[16] The training colleges and pupil-teacher centres involved existed to serve the *elementary* system, or were outgrowths from it. To men working in this field, Bain clearly brought a wider view and deeper knowledge than they were likely to achieve themselves; and, without exception, these manuals reflected what might be called Bain's educational optimism. What is noticeable, particularly to the modern reader, is the stress laid on the extent to which failure to develop positive attitudes, skills, and abilities in the child may be a product of the teacher's own behaviour, or lack of skills, knowledge and method. Later interpretations of failure as the inevitable function of innate disabilities *in the child*, e.g. 'lack of intelligence', do not figure. It can be argued, with Joseph Priestley, that the theory which underlies these manuals – that educational actions have a necessary effect (even if this is not always identifiable) – also underlies the science of education; that is, pedagogy.

Of course the theories, and the practices, advocated by Bain and the authors of these manuals, had their limitations as well as theoretical weaknesses. That goes without saying. But, in the 1890s, the approach was serious, systematic, all-embracing. The pedagogy of this specific decade pointed the way to universal education, and was seen as such by its progenitors. What happened? Why was this embryo pedagogy not systematically developed? What went wrong?

First, the social and political context underwent an abrupt change, as indicated earlier. The development referred to took place within the *elementary* system, but one having for a short period a realistic perspective of organic growth. This was the backcloth, the crucial feature, of this movement as a whole. The administrative and legislative events of 1899 to 1904, almost traumatic in their effects, put a stopper on this, and apart from abolishing the School Boards, confined elementary education within precise limits, setting up a system of 'secondary' schooling parallel to, but quite separate from, the elementary system.

This created a new situation. A positive pedagogy based on scientific procedures and understanding and relevant for *all* was no longer seen as appropriate, or required. Intellectual development in the elementary schools was now at a discount (in parallel with the public schools, but for different reasons). The social-disciplinary ('containment') function of elementary education was now especially emphasised. The soil required to nurture a science of education no longer existed.

However, with the demise of the elementary school as the ground of pedagogy, there now emerged the new local authority-controlled systems of secondary education; it seems to have been into these new systems that the most advanced local authorities put their main efforts. These new systems, although strictly contained in their development by the central authority (the Board of Education), and designed specifically for what can best be described as the lower middle class (all such schools had to charge fees), were the only growth points permitted in the new dispensation. The more advanced local authorities, determined to extend educational provision, approached this new field with energy and developed a considerable pride in the school systems so created.[17]

It was the establishment, and rapid development of this new system of secondary schools which underlay new developments in the theory and practice of education. This system insistently required a pedagogy – the development of effective pedagogical means. Thus we find, in the period 1900–1914, a renewed concern to develop a relevant pedagogy and it is this that lies behind the great interest in, almost the discovery of, the work of Herbart, and of the Prussian educators who had developed Herbartianism into a system – itself a phenomenon of some interest.

Herbart himself, a philosopher with special interests in psychology and education, in fact published his works, including his *Science of Education*, early in the nineteenth century.[18] Once again basing himself on associationism in his theory of the 'apperception mass', Herbart set out to explain the process of human acquirements, seeing them as the resultant of education, of teaching and learning. His ideas were developed and their practical application modified and refined in the work of Rein at the University of Jena and of other educators, and found expression in the German schools and thinking from the 1860s.[19]

It was not until the turn of the century, however, that Herbart's ideas began to make a serious impact in Britain; selections from his writings were first made widely available with the translation and publication of *The Science of Education* in 1892. By the first decade of the twentieth century most existing universities were developing and expanding their departments of education and a number of chairs in the subject now existed. Several of the new professors of education, for instance, J.J. Findlay, John Adams, J.W. Adamson, pronounced themselves as Herbartians. These and others wrote a number of books for teachers either explaining and interpreting Herbart, or elaborating on his work.[20] Here, if perhaps rather narrowly circumscribed in its context, was a new attempt, at a new level, to establish a science of education – a pedagogy. There was, then, a brief new flowering of pedagogy – a serious concern with the theory and practice of education. But this new, and to some extent hopeful, development was in effect only partial (concerned with secondary schools, and related to their upthrust); and, in the circumstances that developed following the First World War, it did not, and could not, persist.

The reasons for this are complex, and relate both to the structure and nature of the system that developed in the inter-war years and after, and to the movement of ideas and their relation to that system. Briefly, selectivity became the central focus of the whole system, the classification of pupils and their categorisation became a main principle of school organisation. That system urgently required a rationale – legitimisation in the eyes of parents, teachers, pupils and the public generally. Such legitimisation was, by the mid-1920s, at hand in the theories (and the practice) of mental measurement, particularly, intelligence testing.

Until then, the rational foundation for pedagogical theories – for the concept of education as a science – had lain in associationist psychological theories concerning learning. These were espoused by Bain, as we have seen, and underlay his whole approach; as also by Herbart and his protagonists (or elaborators). So it was theory and practice based on these ideas which gave rise both to the positive, or optimistic, pedagogics of the 1890s relating to elementary education, and to those of the period 1900–1920 relating to the new system of secondary education. But it was just at this period that new approaches came to predominate in the field of psychology which either relegated associationism to the background, or denied its significance altogether.

The two major influences leading to the demise of associationism as a major determinant of pedagogy were, on the one hand, the rise of philosophic idealism which denied the material basis of mind and decisively rejected the model of human formation of the strict materialists of the late eighteenth century (with its emphasis on man as the passive product of external stimuli); and, on the other hand, the triumph of Darwinism with its emphasis on heredity.[21] With the latter is linked Galton's work (*Hereditary Genius* was published as early as 1869), the rise of the eugenics movement with its associated theories (the Eugenics Education Society was found in 1908), and the work of the Galton Laboratory at University College, London, associated with the names of Pearson, Spearman, and later Cyril Burt. 'No request is more frequently made to the psychologist' wrote Burt in 1921, when he was educational psychologist to the London County Council,'than the demand for a simple mental footrule.'[22] It was precisely this that the psychologists were now ready to supply.

The demands of the system and the movement of ideas now coincided. In the field of educational theory psychometry (or mental testing) now established its hegemony which lasted over forty years from the 1920s. The triumph of psychometry tied in with a new stress on individualism after the First World War and a kind of reductionist biologism, both of which are central to the thinking of Sir Percy Nunn whose *Education, its Data and First Principles* was the central student manual of the inter-war years.[23] For reasons which will be discussed later, this spelt the end of pedagogy – its actual death. If education cannot promote cognitive growth, as the psychometrists seemed to aver, its whole purpose or direction was lost. 'Othello's occupation gone', as Hayward, an LCC Inspector, once put it.

This, I suggest, is the background to our present discontents. For a combination of social, political and ideological reasons pedagogy – a scientific basis to the theory and practice of education – has never taken root and flourished in Britain. For a single decade in the late nineteenth century in the field of elementary education; for a similar short period early this century in secondary education, pedagogic approaches and analyses flowered – though never in the most socially prestigious system of the public schools and ancient universities. Each 'system', largely self-contained, developed its own specific educational approach, each within its narrowly defined field, and each 'appropriate' to its specific social function. In these circumstances the conditions did not, and could not, exist for the development of an all-embracing, universalised, scientific theory of education relating to the practice of teaching. Nor is it an accident that, in these circumstances, fatalistic ideas preaching the limitation of human powers were in the ascendant.

Education and the Technological Revolution

The main objective of this paper is to argue first, that we can no longer afford to go on in the old way, muddling through on a largely pragmatic, or historically institutionalised basis, tinkering with this and that, but that a really serious effort can and should now be made to clear up current confusions and dichotomies. Second, in spite of what must surely be temporary setbacks in the provision of educational facilities, the conditions now exist for a major breakthrough in terms of pedagogy. This statement is made on the basis of two contemporary developments, the one structural, the other theoretical. Of major importance here is the insistent tendency towards unification of the historically determined separate systems of schooling through the transition to comprehensive secondary education. This has been accompanied, in the realm of ideas or theory, by a shift in the concern of educators and psychologists from static concepts of the child (derived from intelligence testing) towards dynamic and complex theories of child development. Both open new perspectives relating to the grounding of educational theory and practice on science (or on scientific procedures).

It is a commonplace that Britain now faces a deep economic crisis the especial severity of which arises from the relative obsolescence of British industry, as also from long-standing production and managerial inefficiencies.[24] Of particular importance, then, to the survival of this country in an increasingly competitive, and capitalised world, is the micro-processor revolution. It is argued authoritatively, by those making a special study of the matter, that, due to the cheapness, reliability and safety of the new technology, it is quite certain to be applied whatever the situation and the consequences.[25] It is these that deserve consideration.

Experts are agreed that, although without further research and experience much remains unpredictable (especially in a society that rejects planning), the micro-processor revolution may itself have a twofold, dichotomous effect on human skills. First, the demand for people with high-level skills and knowledge will increase greatly as production and other processes become both more complex, and subject to highly skilled control. Second, as has been the case with much technological advance, the mass of 'ordinary' jobs in manufacturing and industry generally may be subject to a de-skilling effect depending upon the form and degree of mechanisation that is introduced. Finally, in addition to this contradictory effect on skills, the introduction of micro-processors may well lead to massive 'labour-shedding' in some industries and service sectors. The extent to which this introduces a new element of structural unemployment will depend, of course, upon the extent to which alternative industries and growth-demand can compensate.

There is, however, a further possibility to be taken into account – the implementation on a large scale of automation. The importance of this in terms of education lies in the possibility automation holds out of systematically eradicating jobs which are essentially routine – specifically involving relatively simple forms of visual-motor co-ordination. Automation has now reached a stage where such functions, by which the worker relates one particular movement to the visual inspection of the object in process of manufacture, can be performed more economically by machinery (through the development, in particular, of robotics). It is estimated that jobs on this level today constitute some 40 per cent of all; it is their essentially monotonous (and alienating) nature and comparative simplicity (many occupations can be learnt with very little training – in some cases in a few days or even hours) that accounts, in part at least, for the disparity between the knowledge/skills demands of industry, and human potential, released partially through improved education, a standpoint interestingly developed by T.G. Whiston in a series of publications. To bring the two into a closer relation Whiston regards as a major objective in terms of human values, arguing that the relevant techniques regarding automation are now – or are becoming – available, though their implementation requires the thrust of deliberate policy. In this connection it is important to recognise that there is already today a great national shortage of highly skilled labour in many industries.[26]

It seems, then, that at the extremes, two opposite policy options are available. One is to allow the application of micro-processors to be determined entirely through the operation of *laissez-faire* (apparently the dominant trend in contemporary Conservative politics), relying on market forces alone to determine outcomes. In this case possible developments include mass structural unemployment as a permanent feature; domination by an expanded technocratic élite, accompanied by massive de-skilling for the majority of those remaining in employment – that is, the actual enhancement of the present bi-modal distribution of the knowledge/skills component of work. The second option is deliberately devised to exclude or counter such effects, and requires foresight, judgement and planning, no doubt of a highly sophisticated character and covering both short and long term objectives. By this option, the potential de-skilling effect of micro-processor applications may be countered by an active policy of automation (in mechanised industry), with the specific aim of achieving an all-round raising of the skill levels of employment, so, apart from other effects, both rendering work intrinsically more satisfying and overcoming (in the long run) the bi-modal distribution of the knowledge/skills demands of work.

Such a policy itself counters the establishment of a technocratic élite, since it implies that all, or the great majority of, the work force is capable, given extended and relevant education, of work at the level now required, and that the nature of work itself in industry will generally, over time, approximate to that level. In addition, a deliberate policy of diffusing responsibility and control both through the extension of participation and decision-making at all levels in industry, and through regional and local organisations (as well as national) becomes a possible, and, indeed, a necessary means of democratic development, itself requiring the diffusion, or, better, formation of knowledge and skills covering a wide area among the population as a whole. Finally, this policy option requires the deliberate expansion of labour-intensive employment across a wide range of social and community services – that is, particularly, the areas of health, education, the 'caring' professions generally, the leisure industry, and so forth. Such measures, which enhance the quality of life, provide the means, and the only ones, where new employment, on a mass scale, can be provided, given the consistent, long-term reduction in the labour demands not only of the primary sectory (agriculture, mining, quarrying, etc.), but also of manufacture and indeed certain sections of the tertiary sector itself, for instance, clerical work where micro-processors have many applications. Such a policy involves a deliberate shift of employment through the rationalisation of production (and the office service sectors) towards expansion in human and socially satisfying areas.

This is not the place to argue the options. It will be assumed here, as axiomatic, that the second is the only one of the two which can be acceptable as a perspective for an advanced industrial society such as Britain. In what follows, the *intention* to implement policy on these lines is assumed.

Such a perspective has important educational implications. It posits the development of high-level human skills and knowledge across the entire population, and, it is important to recognise, not only technological and scientific skills, but also those required to support responsible democratic decision-making and those underlying a massive expansion of employment in tertiary industries and services, such as education. In this context, limited, pragmatic measures to cope with the micro-processor revolution simply by expanding, and making more specialised, higher education alone (and perhaps technical education) will be entirely inadequate – such measures relate directly to the first option, not the second. To develop a population with the qualities and knowledge base required involves raising educational sights at all levels, primary and secondary, as well as tertiary. And this involves rendering the process of education more effective, once again right across the board. Hence the urgent requirement now to begin, quite consciously and deliberately, to develop effective pedagogic means.

As already indicated, the establishment of comprehensive secondary education, while no panacea in itself, does provide the conditions in which the target of high level mass secondary education appropriate for all becomes a possibility. This was excluded under the divided system of the past, which now appears as a simple reflection of the bi-modal distribution of job requirements. The comprehensive school, on the other hand, can be seen as one condition for overcoming this bi-modality, and to reflect, in its organisational form, a situation where the skills and knowledge requirements not only of industry but also of social and political life generally may be greatly raised as compared with the past. In this sense a base is coming into being from which a major advance may be made. The virtual elimination of streaming in the primary schools – a product of the last ten to fifteen years – is another reflection of the same approach. In a sense, educational change has taken the lead, and created new conditions appropriate to current and future requirements. The agony of the transition, and the nature and significance of educational developments in the 1950s and 1960s, can now be more fairly assessed for what they are. It is true that the independent schools still remain as a separate system, with their own goals and objectives – and functions. Indeed recent legislation has strengthened their position. If these could be brought functionally within the publicly maintained system of education, this dichotomy would be overcome. However it can be argued that these schools no longer have the same overriding importance and position, relative to the public system, that they had in the past, and are no longer as influential in determining the climate of thought or practice in education as they were a century ago.

Finally, and most important, there is the shift towards dynamic concepts of child development and learning, referred to earlier. This represents a new situation in terms of educational studies – of, to use Bain's term, 'systematic (educational) knowledge'. As a result the prospect exists of reinstating pedagogy as the basis for educational practice in the period that lies ahead – one which provides a perspective of a more satisfying humanised life for all. Provided social changes, where necessary, can be made, education has the opportunity now to come into its own, as one – *the?* – essential component of the society of the future.

A Revitalised Pedagogy?

What, then, are the requirements for a renewal of scientific approaches to the practice of teaching – for a revitalised pedagogy?

First, we can identify two essential conditions without which there can be no pedagogy having a generalised significance or application. The first is recognition of the human capacity for learning. It may seem unnecessary, even ridiculous, to single this out in this connection, but in practice this is not the case. Fundamentally, psychometric theory, as elaborated in the 1930s to 1950s, denied the lability of learning capacity, seeing each individual as endowed, as it were, with an engine of a given horse-power which is fixed, unchangeable and measurable in each particular case, irrevocably setting precise and definable limits to achievement (or learning). It was not until this view had been discredited in the eyes of psychologists that serious attention could be given to the analysis and interpretation of the *process* of human learning.

The second condition has been effectively defined by Professor Stones in his helpful and relevant book *Psychopedagogy*.[27] It is the recognition that, in general terms, the process of learning among human beings is similar across the human species as a whole. The view on which Stones's book is based is that 'except in pathological cases, learning capability among individuals is similar', so that 'it is possible to envisage a body of general principles of teaching' that are relevant to 'most individual pupils'. The determination, or identification, of such general principles must comprise the objectives of pedagogical study and research.[28]

One further point may be made at the start. The term 'pedagogy' itself implies structure. It implies the elaboration or definition of specific means adapted to produce the desired effect – such-and-such learning on the part of the child. From the start of the use of the term, pedagogy has been concerned to relate the process of teaching to that of learning on the part of the child. It was this approach that characterised the work of Comenius, Pestalozzi and Herbart, and that, for instance, of Joseph Priestley and the associationist tradition generally.[29]

Both the conditions defined above are today very widely accepted among leading psychologists directly concerned with education and with research into human cognitive development. When Bruner claimed, in a striking and well-known statement, that 'any subject can be taught to anybody at any age in some form that is both interesting and honest', he was basing himself on a positive assessment of human capacity for learning, and deliberately pointing to the need to link psychology with pedagogy. In an essay aimed at persuading American psychologists of the need to concern themselves with education – to provide assistance in elucidating the learning process for practising educators – he stressed his central point, 'that developmental psychology without a theory of pedagogy was as empty an enterprise as a theory of pedagogy that ignored the nature of growth'. 'Man is not a naked ape,' writes Bruner, 'but a culture clothed human being, hopelessly ineffective without the prosthesis provided by culture.' Education itself can be a powerful cultural influence, and educational experiences are ordered and structured to enable people more fully to realise their humanity and powers, to bring about social change – and so create a world according to their felt and recognised objectives. The major problem humanity faces is not the general development of skill and intelligence, but 'devising a society that can use it wisely'.[30]

When writing this, Bruner was clearly concerned with social change, and with the contribution that pedagogical means might make to this, as we must be in Britain in face of the dramatic social challenge that technological change now presents. And in considering the power of education, rightly ordered, to play a central part in this, it may be as well to recall that, while the simplified and certainly over-mechanistic interpretations of the associationist psychologists of the nineteenth century are no longer acceptable in the form, for instance, expressed by Alexander Bain (and his predecessors), the concept of learning as a process involving the formation of new connections in the brain and higher nervous systems has in fact not only retained its force, but been highly developed by neuro-physiologists and psychologists specifically concerned to investigate learning. Among these, perhaps the greatest contribution has been made by A.R. Luria in a series of works relevant to teaching, education and human development generally; but perhaps particularly in his work on the role of language in mental development, and in his theory of the formation of what he calls 'complex functional systems' underlying learning.

> It is now generally accepted that in the process of mental development there takes place a profound qualitative reorganisation of human mental activity, and that the basic characteristic of this reorganisation is that elementary, direct activity is replaced by complex functional systems, formed on the basis of the child's communication with adults in the process of learning. These functional systems are of complex construction, and are developed with the close participation of language, which as the basic means of communication with people is simultaneously one of the basic tools in the formation of human mental activity and in the regulation of behaviour. It is through these complex forms of mental activity ... that new features are acquired and begin to develop according to new laws which displace many of the laws which govern the formation of elementary conditioned reflexes in animals.[31]

The work and thinking of both Luria and Bruner (as representative of their respective traditions) point in a similar direction – towards a renewed understanding both of the power of education to effect human change and especially cognitive development, and of the need for the systematisation and structuring of the child's experiences in the process of learning. And it is precisely from this standpoint that a critique is necessary of certain contemporary standpoints, dichotomies and ideologies, and, in particular, of the whole trend towards so-called 'child-centred' theories, which have dominated this area in Britain basically since the early 1920s, to reach its apotheosis in what is best called the 'pedagogic romanticism' of the Plowden Report, its most recent, and semi-official expression.

It may be unfashionable, among educationists, to direct attention specifically to this point, more particularly because a critique of 'progressivism' was central to the outlook expressed in the Black Papers in the late 1960s, and early 1970s; but to make such a critique does not imply identification with the essentially philistine and a-theoretical standpoint of the Black Paperites, as I hope to show. Indeed the dichotomies which these and other critics sought to establish, for instance between progressive and traditional approaches, between the 'formal' and 'informal', do not reflect the options now available, nor even contemporary practice as it really is.

The basic tenets of child-centred education derive in particular from the work of Froebel who held that children are endowed with certain characteristics or qualities which will mature or flower given the appropriate environment. The child develops best in a 'rich' environment. The teacher should not interfere with this process of maturation, but act as a 'guide'. The function of early education, according to Froebel, is 'to make the inner outer'.[32] Hence the emphasis on spontaneity, as also on stages of development, and the concomitant concept of 'readiness' – the child will learn specific skills and mental operations only when he or she is 'ready'.

That there is a fundamental convergence between this view and the theories (or assumptions) embodied in Intelligence Testing has been overlooked; nevertheless it is the close similarity between both sets of views as to the nature of the child which made it possible for both to flourish together in the period following the First World War and after. Intelligence Testing also embodied the view that the child is endowed with certain innate characteristics; in this case a brain and higher nervous system of a given power or force – Spearman's 'Mental Energy or Noegenetics' – and that the process of education is concerned to actualise the given potential, that is, to activate and realise the 'inner' (in Froebel's sense).[33] Both views in fact deny the creative function of education, the formative power of differential educational (or life) experiences.

The theoretical, or pedagogical stance of the Plowden Report represents an extension of these ideas. In their re-interpretation of the conclusions derived from psychometry they reject the concept of total hereditary, or genetic, determination. Development is seen as an interactional process, in which the child's encounters with the environment are crucial. Yet Plowden takes the child-centred approach to its logical limits, insisting on the principle of the complete individualisation of the teaching/learning process as the ideal (even though, from a pedagogic standpoint, this is not a practical possibility in any realistic sense). In their analysis the hereditary/environmental interactional process is interpreted as exacerbating initial differences so greatly that each child must be seen to be unique, and be treated as such. The matter is rendered even more complex by their insistence that each individual child develops at different rates across three parameters, intellectual, emotional and physical; and that in determining her approach to each individual child each of these must be taken into account by the teacher. The result is that the task set the teacher, with an average of 35 children per class when Plowden reported, is, in the words of the report itself, 'frighteningly high'.[34]

I want to suggest that, by focusing on the individual child ('at the heart of the educational process lies the child'), and in developing the analysis from this point, the Plowden Committee created a situation from which it was impossible to derive an effective pedagogy (or effective pedagogical means). If each child is unique, and each requires a specific pedagogical approach appropriate to him or her and to no other, the construction of an all-embracing pedagogy, or general principles of teaching, becomes an impossibility. And indeed research has shown that primary school teachers who have taken the priority of individualisation to heart find it difficult to do more than ensure that each child is in fact engaged on the series of tasks which the teacher sets up for the child; the complex management problem which then arises takes the teacher's full energies. Hence the approach of teachers who endeavour to implement these prescripts is necessarily primarily didactic ('telling') since it become literally impossible to stimulate enquiry, or to 'lead from behind', as Plowden held the teacher should operate in the classroom. Even with a lower average of 30 children per class, this is far too complex and time-consuming a role for the teacher to perform.[35]

The main thrust of the argument of this paper is this: that to start from the standpoint of individual differences is to start from the wrong position. To develop effective pedagogic means involves starting from the opposite standpoint, from what children have in common as members of the human species; to establish the general principles of teaching and, in the light of these, to determine what modifications of practice are necessary to meet specific individual needs. If all children are to be assisted to learn, to master increasingly complex cognitive tasks, to develop increasingly complex skills and abilities or mental operations, then this is an objective that schools must have in common; their task becomes the deliberate development of such skills and abilities in all their children. And this involves importing a definite structure into the teaching, and so into the learning experiences provided for the pupils. Individual differences only become important, in this context, if the pedagogical means elaborated are found not to be appropriate to particular children (or groups of children) because of one or other aspect of their individual development or character. In this situation the requirement becomes that of modifying the pedagogical means so that they become appropriate for all; that is, of applying general principles in specific instances.

What is suggested here is that the starting-point for constructing the curriculum, or children's activities in school, insofar as we are concerned with cognitive development (the schools may reasonably have other aims as well) lies in definition of the objectives of teaching, which forms the ground base from which pedagogical means are defined and established, means or principles which underlie specific methodological (or experiential) approaches. It may well be that these include the use of co-operative group work as well as individualised activities – but these are carefully designed and structured in relation to the achievement of overall objectives. This approach, I am arguing, is the opposite of basing the educational process on the child, on his or her immediate interests and spontaneous activity, and providing, in theory, for a total differentiation of the learning process in the case of each individual child. This latter approach is not only undesirable in principle, it is impossible of achievement in practice.[36]

In a striking phrase Lev Vygotski summed up his outlook on teaching and learning. Pedagogy, he wrote, 'must be oriented not towards the yesterday of development but towards its tomorrow'. Teaching, education, pedagogic means, must always take the child forward, be concerned with the formation of new concepts and hierarchies of concepts, with the next stage in the development of a particular ability, with ever more complex forms of mental operations. 'What the child can do today with adult help,' he said, 'he will be able to do independently tomorrow.' This concept, that of the 'zone of next (or "potential") development' implies in the educator a clear concept of the progression of learning, of a consistent challenge, of the mastery by the child of increasingly complex forms – of never standing still or going backwards. 'The only good teaching is that which outpaces development,' insisted Vygotski.[37] Whether the area is that of language development, or concepts of number and mathematics – symbolic systems that underlie all further learning – or whether it covers scientific and technological concepts and skills as well as those related to the social sciences and humanities, appropriate pedagogical means can and should be defined, perhaps particularly in areas having their own inner logical structures. In this sense, psychological knowledge combined with logical analysis forms the ground base from which pedagogical principles can be established, given, of course, effective research and experiment.

This chapter has been strictly concerned with cognitive development, since it is here that technological/scientific and social changes will make their greatest impact and demands. But for successful implementation of rational procedures and planning, in the face of the micro-processor revolution, more than this needs consideration. There is also the question, for instance, of the individual's enhanced responsibility for his own activities; the development of autonomy, of initiative, creativity, critical awareness; the needs on the part of the mass of the population for access to knowledge and culture, the arts and literature, to mention only some aspects of human development. The means of promoting such human qualities and characteristics cannot simply be left to individual teachers, on the grounds that each individual child is unique so that the development of a pedagogy is both impracticable and superfluous. The existing teaching force of half a million have, no doubt, many talents, but they need assistance in the pursuit of their common objective – the education of new generations of pupils. The new pedagogy requires carefully defined goals, structure, and adult guidance. Without this a high proportion of children, whose concepts are formed as a result of their everyday experiences, and, as a result, are often distorted and incorrectly reflect reality, will never even reach the stage where the development of higher cognitive forms of activity becomes a possibility. And this implies a massive cognitive failure in terms of involvement and control (responsible participation) in the new social forms and activities which the future may bring.

Notes

1. Alexander Bain, *Education as a Science*, London, 1879.
2. An attempt in 1962 by Nuffield Science project teams to gain assistance from psychologists was entirely negative. At a meeting convened to discuss possible research on the intellectual development of children in areas relevant to the projects, leading psychologists held that little advice was possible since 'so little research had, as yet, been undertaken with British children' on teaching and learning. See M. Waring, *Social Pressures and Curriculum Innovation*, London, 1979, p. 133.
3. The English failure to take pedagogy seriously is stressed in an article on the subject in an educational encylopedia of a century ago. Interest in pedagogy 'is not held in much honour among us English'. The lack of a professional approach to teaching means that 'pedagogy is with us at a discount'. This, it is held, 'is unquestionably a most grievous national loss ... Without something like scientific discussion on educational subjects, without pedagogy, we shall never obtain a body of organised opinion on education.' A.E. Fletcher (ed.), *Cyclopaedia of Education*, New York, 1889, pp. 257–8.

4. An exception here was R.H. Quick, author of *Essays on Educational Reformers*, 1869, a public school master himself who fought hard for professional training and who appears to have been largely instrumental in setting up the Cambridge Syndicate which organised (prematurely) the first systematic set of lectures on education in an English university; those delivered at Cambridge in 1879–1880 (see F. Storr, *The Life and Remains of the Revd R.H. Quick*, Cambridge, 1889, pp. 349–388). For a young teacher's experience of 'learning on the job' in the 1930s, see T.C. Worsley, *Flannelled Fool*, London, 1967, Chapter 1.

5. J.R. de S. Honey, *Tom Brown's Universe*, London, 1977.

6. See D. Newsome, *Godliness and Good Learning*, London, 1961, especially chapter 4; B. Simon and I. Bradley (eds.), *The Victorian Public School*, Dublin, 1975, especially chapter 7 by Norman Vance, 'The Ideal of Manliness', and chapter 9 by J.A. Mangan, 'Athleticism: A Case Study of the Evolution of an Educational Ideology'.

7. P. Bourdieu and J-C. Passeron, *Reproduction in Education, Society and Culture*, London, 1977.

8. G. Kalton, *The Public Schools: A Factual Survey*, London, 1966, pp. 50–3. An unusual, but very sharp, critique of public school attitudes to this question was made by A.A. David, headmaster of Rugby and Clifton and later Bishop of Liverpool, in the early 1930s; see A.A. David, *Life and the Public Schools*, Edinburgh, 1932.

9. It is symptomatic that the most recent (and internal) examination of studies at Oxford ignores the topic altogether, *Report of Commission of Inquiry* (the Franks report), 2 vols., 1966.

10. See, for instance, M. Arnold, *High Schools and Universities in Germany*, London, 1874, which devotes a lengthy chapter to the professional training of schoolmasters for the *gymnasia* and *realschule* in Prussia (chapter 5).

11. I have analysed developments in this period in detail in B. Simon, *Education and the Labour Movement, 1870–1920*, London, 1965.

12. A. Bain, *Education as a Science*, London, 1879.

13. Bain developed his associationist theory most notably in his *Mental and Moral Science*, London, 1868. See also, *The Senses and the Intellect*, London, 1855 and *The Emotions and the Will*, London, 1859.

14. Priestley held that 'Education is as much an art (founded, as all arts are, upon science) as husbandry, architecture, shipbuilding'. Just as there are laws covering mechanics, chemistry, physics, so there are laws governing the functioning of mind – whether physical or moral. It is, therefore, possible to establish the causes (which must exist) by which the mind 'is truly and properly influenced – producing certain definite effects in certain circumstances'. It follows that there are laws governing education, discoverable by observation and experiment.

15. Quoted in J. Fitch, *Lectures on Teaching*, Cambridge, 1898, p. 129. The full quotation from Maudsley given by Fitch, who is explaining association, reads as follows: 'That which has existed with any completeness in consciousness leaves behind it, after its disappearance therefrom, in the mind or brain, a functional disposition to its reproduction or

reappearance in consciousness at some future time. Of no mental act can we say that it is "writ in water". Something remains from it whereby its recurrence is facilitated. Every impression of sense upon the brain, every current of molecular activity from one to another part of the brain, every cerebral reaction which passes into movement, leaves behind it some modification of the nerve-elements concerned in its function, some after-effect, or, so to speak, memory of itself in them, which renders its reproduction an easier matter, the more easy the more often it has been repeated, and makes it impossible to say that, however trivial, it shall not in some circumstances recur. Let the excitation take place in one or two nerve-cells lying side by side, and between which there was not originally any specific difference, there will be ever afterwards a difference between them. This physiological process, whatever be its nature, is the physical basis of memory, and it is the foundation of our mental functions.'

16. For instance, A.H. Garlick, 'Headmaster' of the Woolwich Pupil-Teacher Centre, *A New Manual for Method*, London, 1896; David Salmon, Principal of Swansea Training College, *The Art of Teaching*, London, 1898; Joseph Landon, Vice-Principal and 'Later Master of Method' of Saltley Training College, *The Principles and Practice of Teaching and Class Management*, Oxford, 1894; and many others.

17. See especially J.G. Legge, *The Rising Tide*, Oxford, 1929 on Liverpool, and P.H.J.H. Gosden and P.R. Sharp, *The Development of an Educational Service, The West Riding 1889–1974*, Oxford, 1978, pp. 77ff.

18. J.F. Herbart (1776–1841) published a work on Pestalozzi in 1804 and his *Universal Pedagogy* (*Allgemeine Pädagogik*, later translated as *Science of Education*) in 1806. In 1841 he published *Plan of Lectures on Pedagogy*. His works in philosophy and education were collected and published in twelve volumes in 1850–1852 by Hartenstein.

19. Herbartian associations were formed in many parts of Germany in the late nineteenth century, first, in the Rhine and Westphalia with over 400 members; later in East Germany, Bavaria, Wurtemberg, Saxony and Thuringia. The first meeting of the latter, in 1892, attracted over 2,000 educationists, Professor Rein of the University of Jena being elected President. See H.M. and E. Felkin, *An Introduction to Herbart's Science and Practice of Education*, London, 1895.

20. For instance, the London County Council Inspectors, F.H. Hayward and P.B. Ballard, both of whom were prolific writers on education.

21. G. Murphy, *Historical Introduction to Modern Psychology*, New York, 1938, pp. 109–13.

22. C. Burt, *Mental and Scholastic Tests*, London, 1921, p.1.

23. Percy Nunn was Principal of the University of London Institute of Education from 1922 to 1936. His textbook went through over 20 reprintings between its publication in 1920 and 1940; it was required reading for many graduates training as teachers. For an acute critique of Nunn's biologism, see P. Gordon and J. White, *Philosophers as Educational Reformers*, London, 1979, pp. 207–13.

24. K. Pavitt (ed.), *Technical Innovation and British Economic Performance*, London, 1980.

25. C. Freeman, *Government Policies for Industrial Innovation*, London, 1978 and 'Government Policy' in K. Pavitt (ed.), op. cit.

26. This standpoint is argued in a series of papers by T.G. Whiston of the Science Policy Research Unit, University of Sussex. These include 'Technical Change, Occupational Skill and Retraining Issues' an unpublished paper given at a seminar on Employment and Technical Change, November 1978 and 'Technical Change, Employment and Education Policy', SPRU mimeo, July 1979; 'The Development of Education: Its Technological and Social Dimensions' in *The Future of Education and the Education of the Future*, [R.M. Avakov (ed.)], Paris, 1980 pp. 319–60; 'Education and Training for the Less Academic Young Person in Relation to Ongoing Social and Technological Change' in *Report of the Conference on Provisions to meet the Needs of less Academic Students between the ages 16–19*. Southern Regional Council for Further Education, Wokingham, Berks, June 1979; 'La prévision au niveau gouvernemental: orientation normative', *Conference of Institute International d'Administration Publique*, Paris, 1979, pp. 9–19. See also 'Population Forecasting: Social and Educational Policy', chapter 7 in T.G. Whiston (ed.), *The Uses and Abuses of Forecasting*, 1979, pp. 143–181.

27. E. Stones, *Psychopedagogy: Psychological Theory and the Practice of Teaching*, London, 1979.

28. Ibid., p. 453.

29. This point was clearly and emphatically made by James Ward in the first of his Cambridge lectures in 1879–80 (but only published in 1926). Entitled 'The Possibility and Value of a Theory of Education', this started by saying that a science of education 'is theoretically possible', and that such a science 'must be based on psychology and the cognate sciences'. He goes on, 'To show this we have, indeed, only to consider that the educator works, or rather ought to work, upon a growing mind, *with a definite purpose of attaining an end in view*. For unless it be maintained that systematic observation of the growth of (say) a hundred minds would disclose no uniformities; and unless, further, it can be maintained that for the attainment of a definite end there are no definite means, we must allow that *if the teacher knows what he wants to do there must be a scientific way of doing it*. Not only so. We must allow not merely the possibility of a scientific exposition of the means the educator should employ to attain his end, but we must allow also the possibility of a scientific exposition of the end at which he ought to aim, unless again it be contended that it is impossible by reasoning to make manifest that one form of life and character is preferable to another.' J. Ward, *Psychology Applied to Education*, Cambridge, 1926, p.1 (my italics, B.S.).

30. J.S. Bruner, *The Relevance of Education*, London, 1972, pp. 18, 131, 158.

31. A.R. Luria, *Voprosy Psikhologii*, 1962, 4.

32. F.W.A. Froebel, *The Education of Man*, New York, 1912, p. 32.

33. C. Spearman, *The Nature of 'Intelligence' and the Principles of Cognition*, London, 1927.

34. The Plowden Report, *Children and Their Primary Schools*, London, 1967, I, paras 75 and 875.

35. These points are argued in detail, supported by empirical evidence derived from systematic classroom observation, in M. Galton, B. Simon and P. Croll, *Inside the Primary School*, London, 1980.

36. For a critique of this approach by a psychologist who has worked closely with Piaget (regarded as the authority for individualisation, for instance, in the Plowden Report), see E. Duckworth, 'Either We're too Early and They Can't Learn it or We're too Late and They Know it Already: the Dilemma of "Applying Piaget"', *Harvard Educational Review*, Vol. 49, No.3.

37. See L.S. Vygotski 'Learning and Mental Development at School Age' in B. Simon and J. Simon (eds.), *Educational Psychology in the USSR*, London, 1963 and *Thought and Language*, London, 1962 and the Vygotskian Memorial Issue of *Soviet Psychology and Psychiatry*, 1967, 5, 3.

5

The IQ Controversy: the Case of Cyril Burt

There is no more important question – it could be argued – than the nature of human abilities, in particular of human beings' highest mental functions, intellectual powers – or, to adopt a static and individualist label – their 'intelligence'. Are people born all that they may become? Or, on the other hand, is our development primarily due to education, upbringing, life experiences?

The second interpretation points to a creative task for education, to a social obligation to provide as rich an educational experience as may be, particularly for the young, to develop their powers for the benefit both of society and individuals.

The former view – that propagated throughout his long life by Cyril Burt – insists that nothing can improve on the level of intelligence with which each individual is born. Accordingly the ideal social pattern he advocated was 'to discover what ration of intelligence nature has given to each individual child at birth, then to provide him with an appropriate education, and finally to guide him into the career for which he seems to have been marked out'.[1] In short, in Burt's ideal community people were ranged according to their 'intelligence quotients', or IQs. It was, then, pre-eminently the psychometrist or mental tester who could bring such a community into being – as inventor, operator, and as interpreter of tests designed to produce this all-important label which was held to stand as a measure of 'innate intellectual ability'.

This is a heady assumption, it cannot be denied, and such assumptions are dangerous to the scientific researcher whose

---

This paper is based on a popular lecture given to the Vancouver Institute, Vancouver, British Columbia, in October 1983.

most suitable attribute is humility before the immense complexity of the matters he is called upon to investigate and unravel. This is nowhere more the case than in the realm of psychology which has been late in moving towards scientific status. For it faces, more directly than most disciplines, the problems of what might be called participant observation, or close involvement with the very matters the researcher seeks to submit to objective investigation.

At the same time psychological findings can have a direct effect on the lives and fortunes of people. In the case of Cyril Burt this was certainly the case, for psychometry (or mental testing) played a key part in educational decisions and policy making in Britain over a long period. But the IQ controversy has not only been of moment in England, it has had a massive impact in the United States in both scholastic and racial matters. In other words, what might appear to be a purely scientific concern, is directly related to ordinary human aspirations, to deep-rooted preconceptions and to key issues of social policy and practice.

The case of Cyril Burt has to do with the highly sensitive issue of fraud in science, something which no one likes to envisage, scientists least of all. Nonetheless it is a matter now squarely in the public eye which demands attention. When a recently published study on the question of fraud in science was reviewed in *The Times Literary Supplement*, the reviewer, a distinguished mathematician, observed that, in all such cases, it is not 'the deceivers who deserve study, but their victims'. For the former presumably act out of 'rational self-interest' while revelation of the latter's 'gullibility and their reactions to its exposure' reveal significant factors about themselves as individuals and as 'social actors'. 'There is a treatise on the sociology of science to be read from the story of Cyril Burt,' the reviewer adds, 'who completely obfuscated the study of the inheritance of intelligence by his fabricated data on identical twins' and did so with the aid of an aggressive rhetoric against 'critics of his theories in order to divert attention from their transparently bogus statistical foundation'.[2]

Such is the now current view of the Burt case. But I do not see this as a matter of simple self-interest – although I was among those who dissented radically from all that he stood for and correspondingly was subject to aggressive rhetorical attack. As a researcher myself, into educational matters, I am acutely aware of the technical and theoretical pitfalls that may be met with. Inevitably there are moments when acceptance of one or another of alternative possibilities may bring some personal predilection into play, to say the least. But researchers – above all scientists involved in key fields – should, I believe, freely admit to such problems and be prepared to share the difficulties and responsibilities with those who will benefit, or suffer, from the results of their work. On the other hand the reviewer just quoted is surely right when he suggests that one of the most interesting aspects of the Burt case is the degree to which colleagues were taken in, to the extent of failure to question what seem – with hindsight – the most blatant of errors, or defections from normal and scientific academic practice. This, again, is a matter of social concern and worthy of investigation as, too, is the way in which a succession of leading psychologists followed up and brought to the surface Burt's misdemeanours, at the cost of many hours of work unravelling fabricated statistics.

There is, then, no question of pursuing an unfortunate deviant. What is in question is arriving at an understanding of what went wrong in this case. For it is by no means a case merely involving backroom research, and related reputations. The investigations pursued by Cyril Burt, the data he presented, and the conclusions he drew and propagated were such as directly to affect the prospects of tens or even hundreds of thousands of English children over half a century or more – quite apart from the damage that mistaken conclusions may have caused in strictly psychological terms. In such a case sympathies cannot be solely with the sinner, other considerations must weigh more heavily and argue strongly for publicity, discussion and an attempt to reach conclusions guarding against any repetition.

1

The case to be considered may be briefly introduced. A key date is 22 December 1978, the date affixed to an 'Important

Note to the Reader' as he puts it, a late inclusion at the start of
a book by one of Britain's leading educational psychologists,
Philip Vernon, entitled *Intelligence: Heredity and Environment*.[3]
This note explains that the book includes several criticisms of
the methods of work of Cyril Burt but denies that 'he
perpetrated systematic fraud' – a view the author claims was
justified by the evidence to hand when it went to press. 'Now,
however, a biography of Burt is to be published by an author
with impeccable credentials who had access to Burt's own
diaries. He finds that Burt did perpetrate systematic fraud from
about 1950 onwards,' so that the findings produced in papers
cited in Vernon's own book dated 1956 and 1966 'are
worthless apart from their contributions to genetical statistical
methodology'.

The biographer referred to was another leading psychologist, Leslie Hearnshaw and his book, which duly appeared in
1979, was simply entitled, *Cyril Burt, Psychologist*.[4]

Doubts about the validity of early reports of misdemeanour
by Cyril Burt arose in part from the fact that these had
appeared in the press, albeit in a quality newspaper, *The Sunday
Times*, over the name of the medical correspondent, Oliver
Gillie. It was on 24 October 1976, that is, two years earlier than
Vernon dated his note, that this paper carried a front page
story under the headline 'Crucial Data was Faked by Eminent
Psychologist'. There followed a long 'investigative' article by
Gillie which included the statement that 'leading scientists are
convinced that Burt published false data and invented crucial
facts to support his controversial theory that intelligence is
largely inherited'. Among those cited were Professor Alan and
Dr Ann Clarke, of the University of Hull, both of whom had
been graduate students of Burt's studying for doctorates on the
way to qualification as educational psychologists and who had
submitted Burt's published studies in their field of early child
development to careful examination. This had brought to light
'gross inconsistencies and internal contradictions' and, they
added, 'since no one who knew Burt could possibly accuse him
of incompetence, there remains only the probability of
dishonesty'.

Another to comment was the then Chairman of the
Education Research Board of the Social Science Research

Council, the late Jack Tizard, Professor of Child Development at London University and a distinguished scientist and researcher. He saw the discrediting of Burt's work as casting doubt on his whole line of enquiry, and as likely to have the same effect on that branch of science 'as the finding that the Piltdown skull was a forgery had on palaeontology'. It had been immensely damaging.[5]

Meanwhile before these charges surfaced, Hearnshaw, the leading historian of psychology in Britain, had undertaken to write an 'official' biography of Burt who had died in 1971 at the age of 88. A great admirer of his subject's early work, he had delivered the main appreciation of his achievements and standing at the memorial meeting in that year. 'It never occurred to me to suspect his integrity', Hearnshaw was to write in his biography which was not published until 1979. Although his work was nearly completed, investigation of the charges made in 1976 necessarily involved much additional research and 'further detailed analysis of Burt's ... diaries and papers'. But, at last, the conclusion was inescapable. 'Gradually, as evidence accumulated from a variety of sources,' Hearnshaw writes, 'I became convinced that the charges against Burt were, in their essentials, valid.'[6]

In examining the case further I propose first to discuss aspects of Burt's work and ideas, particularly relating to intelligence and education; then to say a little about my own involvement insofar as it activated both controversy and cover-up, before considering the reports of those who examined Burt's publications in detail. Finally I will briefly consider some of the issues arising from this case.

2

Burt remained active in his own field until the end of his life, into his late eighties. His last lecture, arguing the case for heredity as the major determinant of intelligence, was delivered (by a reader) as the Thorndike Memorial Lecture, to the American Psychological Association in the year of his death, 1971. Ironically, it was this that was the catalyst precipitating close examination of his work by Leon Kamin, Professor of

Psychology at Princeton, which brought to light unexpected features.

From his earliest work – not long after the turn of the century – Burt was concerned to uphold three interrelated concepts. First, that intelligence is the most important factor of the mind; second, that it is largely innate or inherited. Third, that its distribution among the population conforms to the 'normal' (or bell-shaped) curve. In ordinary parlance, in any population, there are always a few highly intelligent people, a few very unintelligent, while the mass cluster around the mean, or average.

Over and above this Burt held that intelligence relates closely to social class. Tables of data figure in several of his works indicating that the higher the social (or occupational) grouping tested, the higher their average intelligence scores (or IQs) and vice versa. Here was the source of a theoretical model which, taking social mobility into account, appeared to justify the prevailing structure of society with wide social class differences on biological grounds.

In 1912 the first educational psychologist to a local authority in England was appointed, by the important London County Council. It was Cyril Burt. His early work on intelligence testing and its educational implications had brought him this position through which he became established as a leading technician, theorist and practitioner in this field. He continued subsequently to work in it throughout the inter-war period, first at the London Day Training College (now the London University Institute of Education) and then (from 1932) as holder of the Chair of Psychology at University College, London.

The most important policy-making reports on education of the late 1920s and 1930s in England were those of the Consultative Committee of the Board of Education (as it then was) relating to the organisation of both primary and secondary schooling. Wherever these reports make reference to expert psychological advice, this came from Cyril Burt. During these decades the English school system developed on a hierarchical pattern, only somewhat softened by a 'scholarship' system allowing a small degree of mobility – later known as '11+' selection or 'The 11 plus'. Not only were schools themselves arranged in a pyramid with grammar schools at the apex and non-selective schools at the base, but, as the system was streamlined at these levels each school was officially advised to group pupils in separate streams, or tracks, from the age of 7, or before – group them, that is according to intellectual ability. The theoretical justification for this pattern of education derived primarily from Cyril Burt.

He himself propagated his ideas in popular form, as well as in terms of professional advice to leading committees. An example is a passage in *How the Mind Works*, published in 1933 which is remarkable for its certainty that intelligence is 100 per cent innate.

> By intelligence the psychologist understands inborn, all-round intellectual ability. It is inherited, or at least innate, not due to teaching or training; it is intellectual, not emotional or moral, and remains uninfluenced by industry or zeal; it is general, not specific, i.e. it is not limited to any particular kind of work, but enters into all we do or say or think. Of all our mental qualities, it is the most far-reaching.

And there followed a most misleading statement – although evidently made in the light of a strong belief:

> fortunately it can be measured with accuracy and ease.[7]

Here, now, is a paragraph from the report of the Consultative Committee (the Spens Report), which advanced important recommendations about the extension of secondary education to all in 1938. It will be clear how far it derives from the advice offered by Burt, and it was in fact taken from his written evidence to the committee:

> Intellectual development during childhood appears to progress as if it were governed by a single central factor, usually known as 'general intelligence' which may be broadly described as innate, all-round intellectual ability. It appears to enter into everything which the child attempts to think, to say, or do, and seems on the whole to be the most important factor in determining his work in the classroom.

And there follows what turned out to be misleading guidance attributed directly to 'our psychological witnesses', namely that this key factor 'can be measured approximately by means of intelligence tests' and that 'with few exceptions, it is possible at a very early age to predict with some degree of accuracy the ultimate level of a child's intellectual powers'.[8]

It was only natural for the committee to conclude that, after the initial grading of children in parallel A, B and C streams in junior schools, from the age of 11 the type of education should vary 'in certain important respects', a view which in turn led to a recommendation that there should be three different types of post-primary or secondary schools.

No wonder that Cyril Burt claimed, in later life in a retrospective article, to have exercised a material influence on the development of the English system of schooling.[9]

3

My own involvement in this matter dates from the immediate post-war period. On release from the army in 1945 I taught in Manchester and Salford, in primary, secondary modern and selective grammar schools which accepted only some 25 per cent of children of secondary school age. The rigidity of the hierarchical structure shocked me – especially since the Education Act of 1944 had seemed to promise to reorientate and humanise the school system. Yet streaming of little children in junior school, exposure in and, for the majority, failure in the 11+ selection examination, which determined entrance to the grammar school, followed by yet more segregation at the secondary level made up an educational pattern which determined the prospects of children rather than opening up opportunities and minds. The whole set-up took on the aspect of a vast machinery of selection. What counted was initial placement at the age of 7 – for transfer between one stream and another was minimal. Only an A placement, then, gave the opportunity of success at 11 and so a selective place in one of the grammar schools which monopolised the road to higher education. The independent, so-called 'public' schools provided, of course, for those with the means (a small proportion of the population) an additional highway outside all this.

There was only one way of modifying this system and that

was to supersede it as a whole by establishing a single, common secondary school – the comprehensive school, as it is now called. But the system then seemed unbreakable – practice seemed to bear out the dominant theories on which the selective system depended. It was, then, the theories that required investigation. How far were they justified? It was by this route that I, and others, began to turn attention to the theory and practice of 'intelligence' testing, or what appeared to be the iron laws of psychometry, although these passed as unassailable scientific findings which no one at that time called in question.

Accordingly I found myself as a practising teacher seeking knowledge in a class studying aspects of psychometry at the University of Manchester, and soon entangled with the whole issue. The outcome was a short study published in 1953, *Intelligence Testing and the Comprehensive School*, which was sharply critical of the theory and practice of intelligence testing and of what I saw as its malign influence on the education of countless children.[10] It seems that this book was read by Burt, then in his seventieth year but by no means retired from the scene. So, too, was a book by a qualified psychologist, Alice Heim, published a year later, taking up points critically from this angle. According to Hearnshaw's biography there is little doubt that it was these criticisms – new and surprising as a phenomenon to one who, for half a century and more, had ruled the roost – that first stirred Burt to seek fresh argument, and data, to support his strictly hereditarian concept of intelligence. In short, as Hearnshaw puts it, they led him 'to take up the cudgels, and turn again to the exposition of his views, and' – here is the ominous addition – 'search for evidence to support them'.[11]

The articles that resulted are described by Hearnshaw as 'mainly of a defensive kind', directed 'against environmentalist and other attacks'. A pair of crucial articles of 1955 and 1966 were plainly rejoinders, as Burt himself makes clear, motivated (as Hearnshaw puts it), by 'a determination to get the better of his critics'; they were 'written in haste and anger'.[12] The arguments advanced were supported by fabricated data – nor, as will later appear, was this the first instance of the kind.

My book sought to demystify intelligence testing – it was written for teachers and educationists, indeed also parents who had to cope with the disappointments and miseries inflicted on children by the selective system. To this end it examined the assumptions underlying the practice, the statistical scaffolding and procedures utilised, and the nature of the actual tests themselves including the precise questions children had to answer. It was not necessary to enter very deeply into things to discover that the idea of intelligence as a discrete, primary mental function is itself highly controversial; that then current tests embodied, and so measure, what can best be described as a professional middle class concept of intelligence, so favouring children from this background; and that the evidence adduced in the claim that intelligence is largely inherited was unconvincing to say the least. Finally, that the assertion that intelligence is distributed according to the normal or bell-shaped curve in any society was no more than an initial assumption which is built into the technology of testing.

Just how naïve was the approach at this period may be illustrated by the content of a test, constructed by Burt in the 1920s and still used for selection purposes in the 1930s and later – one which I selected at random for close examination. This was designed for *all* children, whatever their background, social class, or life experiences and was supposed not to involve any acquired knowledge and so to test 'pure intelligence', whatever that may be. But even to begin to answer some of the questions there were things a child had to know. The meaning of such words as 'spurious', 'antique', 'external', 'irregular', 'inexpensive', 'affectionate', 'moist' – how many 10 or 11 year-olds, particularly those with a working-class background – exchange such verbiage.

They also needed to know that a sovereign was made of gold while a florin is of silver, that pearls, emeralds, sapphires, diamonds and rubies are precious stones, while gold is not; the relative functions of telephone and telegraph; the use of thermometers; the reasons for saving money; the purpose of charitable societies; what a cubic block is; what a clerk's job is; that ledger-clerks work in banks; what is meant by an individual's 'mechanical bent' or his 'inclinations'; that a shorthand typist is expected to be able to spell well; what 'the adjustment of an individual to his vocation' means; and finally – the gem of the collection – that a parlour maid is not expected to do the sewing in a house. On this test the 'inborn ability' or 'intelligence' of children was, supposedly, measured with accuracy and ease. There is a degree of blindness here – not only in the test constructor but those who used it – that today seems almost inconceivable.

Once having broken the shell of the system, as it were, the rest followed – in terms, virtually, of reversing the views imposed by Burt. Clearly 'intelligence' tests were not scientifically viable, nor could it be maintained that only innate ability, not acquired knowledge, was tested, nor that these tests did not discriminate against working-class children – they clearly did. At a moment when, in the wake of a devastating war, there were moves to realise the promise of new educational legislation, hopes, efforts, aspirations were fatally damped down at every turn by the denial that industry and zeal can have any effect in promoting intelligent behaviour, or improving mental powers. The crying need was to press the claims of education to enrich the lives of children as against a selective machinery and hierarchical educational structure which narrowed their experiences and seemed intent on nothing more than cutting them down to a predestined size.

If my concern was the educational aspect, Alice Heim's book *The Appraisal of Intelligence* published in 1954, took up points about the technology of testing and underlying assumptions with expertise.[13] Then the sociologists also entered on the scene, notably Jean Floud and A.H. Halsey who insisted that tests reflect social class, rather than any other factor. According to Hearnshaw all these contributions got under Burt's skin. This was the first critical wave, from 1953 to 1956, but then came a second, in 1963–4. At this point an important government committee, the Robbins Committee – whose report underlay the whole expansion of higher education in Britain from that date – overtly set aside the Burtian model which allowed only a small proportion of the population the inborn intellectual capacity to profit from higher education. At the same time an official report on schooling appeared entitled *Half our Future*, the Newsom Report. Here a new appreciation of intelligence, characteristic of that period, now surfaced. 'Intellectual talent', it reported, 'is not a fixed quality with which we have to work but a variable that can be modified by social policy and educational approaches ... The kind of intelligence which is measured by tests so far applied is largely an acquired characteristic.'

It was a notable turn around, making clear that Burt's ideas could no longer command the unquestioning assent they had enjoyed for so many years, or, to put it crudely, the 'intelligence' test had been rumbled.

4

It was one thing for a breakthrough to be made in the educational field at large. It was quite another to alter the minds of those who, with Burt, had been engaged in the essentially small and specialised area of psychometry. And there were others who continued to show extreme gullibility in terms of accepting, without question, articles produced by Burt at this point including data and tables incorporating manifestly suspicious items. Such materials figured as central items in the famous paper by Arthur Jensen, published in 1969 in the *Harvard Educational Review*, titled 'How Far Can We Boost the IQ?' This sparked off a massive and bitter controversy in the United States as to the relative intelligence of blacks and whites, a controversy as old as Galton but which still rumbles on. In England Hans Eysenck, a one-time student of Burt, and, like him, an inveterate controversialist, also used data since classified as fabricated as the main support for his arguments in a popular book entitled *The Inequality of Man*, published in 1973. Others did likewise.

Describing these materials Hearnshaw uncompromisingly characterises them as

'dirty data', collected for a variety of *ad hoc* purposes, by a variety of unco-ordinated techniques, administered by semi-trained assistants, and often 'adjusted' in the interests of immediate practical requirements.[14]

Still worse, as emerges from the investigations of another psychologist, Professor Dorfman of the University of Iowa, the great bulk of the evidence adduced in one of Burt's most telling articles, 'Intelligence and Social Mobility', derived from his inner consciousness; that is, represented what he *thought* the data should be according to the theory he sought to prove.[15]

To turn now to the work of those who brought errors to the surface, the first to locate definite fraud in important papers by Burt was Leon Kamin of Princeton.[16] And this brings us to identical twins, invariably met with when an attempt to prove hereditarian arguments are in train. The search for genetically identical twins has been long and persistent – the aim being to find both twins reared together, in a normal family situation, and, more important but far more difficult, twins separated at an early age to be reared apart in different circumstances. Measurement of the relationship between the IQs of such pairs of subjects leads directly to an assessment of the relative influence of heredity or environment – always supposing the premises are accepted. Now identical-twin data were presented in the paper Burt wrote for the American Psychological Association which was brought to Kamin's attention by a student. He soon perceived what were clearly highly suspicious items and followed the matter up. I will focus only on the main point at issue.

In a series of four papers, published between 1955 and 1966, Burt (and a collaborator Conway, of whom more later) claimed a steady increase in the size of the samples of identical twins he tested, and also that the test correlations – that is, the degree of similarity between their intelligence test scores – worked out precisely the same, to three decimal places in three out of four instances. Thus in 1955 there were 21 sets of identical twins, reared apart, under investigation. By 1958 the sample had risen to 'over 30' (as Burt vaguely claimed) but his collaborator Conway writing in another paper the same year gives it as 42. In 1966 the sample had increased to 53. In three of these instances, in spite of the differences in the size of the samples, the test correlation given is precisely 0.771, only in Conway's 1958 paper is there a slight difference at 0.778. Correlations for twins reared together, again with different numbers in the sample, also figure as identical in three cases out of four.

It is nothing short of astonishing that no one in the field noticed that Burt claimed to have discovered and tested no less than 53 pairs of identical, but separated, twins – the rarest of research material. There was, as Hearnshaw observed with hindsight, 'an incredible doubling of the number of this rather rare group in the space of three years', adding that continued exactitude to three decimal places is 'wholly incredible' but 'nobody at the time seemed to have noticed this'.[17]

By 1974, however, Kamin had carefully analysed the papers on twins and related work and pointed to the extent of the blindness. 'The absence of procedural description in Burt's reports,' he wrote, 'vitiates their scientific utility. The frequent arithmetical inconsistencies and mutually contradictory descriptions cast doubt upon the entire body of his later work. The marvellous consistency of his data supporting the hereditarian position often taxes credibility; and on analysis the data are found to contain implausible effects consistent with an effort to prove the hereditarian case.' It is his inescapable conclusion that the figures 'left behind by Professor Burt are simply not worthy of our current scientific attention'.[18]

Yet, so long as Burt lived, these same twin articles were the principle 'buttress of the hereditarian case' in Hearnshaw's estimation – and this is certainly right.[19]

The other relevant example is the crucial paper of 1961, 'Intelligence and Social Mobility', in which Burt replied to the sociologists.[20] This was analysed in detail by Professor Dorfman in 1978, too late for discussion in the Hearnshaw biography. But Hearnshaw does consider this paper and concludes that the material Burt 'dredged up from the past to serve as the basis for his calculations was, from a scientific point of view, mostly rubbish'; a 'dubious exercise', he adds, 'though perhaps "fraud" is too strong a word to use'.[21] Dorfman's analysis may seem to suggest the alternative.

In this case the model involved is one I have already mentioned which envisages a certain degree of social mobility within society on the assumption that the intelligence of children of parents in any social class will tend to regress towards the mean. Thus some children of higher professional parents will tend to have low IQs and, it is assumed, take up lower status occupations, and vice versa; the model even allows a tiny proportion of children of unskilled workers to attain a high IQ and so high status employment.

With this proviso intelligence is otherwise distributed according to occupational (or class) situation, with higher professional workers at the top and unskilled workers at the bottom. This model is actually Galton's dating from the 1880s, refurbished and re-presented by Burt eighty years on, accompanied by all the apparently scientific trappings and statistical exactitude latterly associated with testing.

What Dorfman shows, after detailed technical examination, is that Burt failed to reclassify actual data – as he said he had done – he merely 'constructed the distributions' of intelligence and social class in relation to the adult and child data. In other words in the crucial tables the data are simply invented, and the distribution pattern adopted relates systematically to that required by the theory Burt was intent on proving. This systematic, i.e. fabricated, data was then used both to test deductions from his genetic theory of social class and to answer criticisms of related work. 'Since constructions are not data,' Dorfman underlines, 'it is extraordinary for Burt to have discussed his tables as if they were actual data' – and he points to fifteen occasions when precisely this was done, appending illustrations, e.g. 'I propose to offer more detailed evidence to support the interpretations I put forward'. Again, 'When we turn to the data for children (Table 2)' and so on.[22]

Others have also examined these papers and commented on what they found. Professor and Dr Clarke found the paper full of errors and refer to his defenders' excuse that Burt was merely careless – if so, they say, his 'carelessness' was 'strangely systematic' with respect to his hypothesis since the evidence always 'fits the theory'.[23] For Professor Jones, of the Australian National University at Canberra, a perceptive analyst of Burt's work, the paper, 'as an example of systematic deception ... is a classic'.[24]

This brings us back to Dr Oliver Gillie who brought the whole business into the open in 1976, for he raised some of these points then and was strongly attacked for suggesting that Burt 'worked backwards' 'to fit data to his genetic theories. There is no question now but this is precisely what he did – as the most careful investigations by psychologists on three continents have shown.

Among the oddest of Gillie's propositions, shown to have

been justified, is the non-existence of the two named collaborators of Burt. One of these, Miss Conway, has figured in this last discussion but may never have existed, since it seems Burt himself wrote the papers making use of this name. Elsewhere he conjured up a Miss Howard and these instances bring to light another extraordinary realisation. For many years Burt was editor of the *British Journal of Statistical Psychology* with which he did as he liked, including writing half the articles under other names. Not only were the Misses Conway and Howard – or their names – so used but Alan and Ann Clarke found theirs had been. An 'unscrupulous' controversialist, according to his biographer, Burt also invented controversies, entered on them himself under pseudonyms on one or both sides, and generally made hay. Naturally antagonistic to Dr Halsey, a sociologist critic, Burt first published a critique of a study of which he was part-author over the name of Miss Conway, then invited a reply from Halsey, then weighed in with a crushing response over his own name and denied his victim any rejoinder. Of forty contributions to this journal, an official organ of the British Psychological Society, more than half carry the editor's pseudonyms. That he was accorded such control over a supposedly learned publication is an important aspect of a case which introduces one surprise after another.

Perhaps the most unforgiveable gambit, in his last years, was an article claiming that there was a remarkable decline in standards in English schools by comparison with 55 years earlier, i.e. prior to the First World War.[25] This was precisely the kind of information to be welcomed in the Black Paper of 1969, the first of a series of derogatory attacks on new developments in the public system of education. But this proved to be, like so much else, disinformation calculated to destabilise the comprehensive schools then, with difficulty but with a new hope, coming to birth. Burt's prestige and standing ensured enormous media coverage for charges at a moment when the schools, teachers and pupils, were working their way through all sorts of difficulties. Experts did, on this occasion, ask to examine the data but, as usual, Burt contrived to prevaricate. When, however, the crucial points were published the data turned out, in Hearnshaw's view to be 'at least in part, fabricated'. It is hardly surprising that Burt's biographer should be exasperated at one point into stating that his subject 'was quite capable of making statements which were demonstrably untrue in every particular'.[26]

5

No one now denies that Burt practised deliberate deception in later life. But when did this begin? Opinions vary. Hearnshaw thinks around 1940, when Burt was 57, a time, incidentally, when he was at the height of his powers and influence. Kamin is of the opinion that all the early work may be contaminated. The late Jack Tizard challenged the findings of two important books, *The Young Delinquent* of 1924, *The Backward Child* of 1937, on the grounds that it is difficult to pin down any of the research and there is no indication when the field work was undertaken.[27] So far as I know there has been no close analysis of all the early work. But we do know that, right from the start, Burt was inclined to table enormous claims on the basis of minimal data – a characteristic to which I referred (if obliquely) in my 1953 book.

One piece of so-called research of this order has fascinated me since I first started enquiries. It dates back to 1909, when Burt was 26, and has been described as a 'career establishing paper'.[28] It reported tests applied to two groups – one of 13 boys at the Dragon School at Oxford, mostly sons of dons, Fellows of the Royal Society, and bishops, the other 30 children from a local elementary school, sons of tradesmen and workers. In those days intelligence tests were yet to come but Burt devised some sensory-motor ones (tapping and the like) which, he reported, ranked the boys in roughly the same order as the headmaster ranked them in intelligence.

After tapping both lots of boys it emerged that the upper-class ones scored higher, indeed on certain tests their scores outdid even 'the cleverest sections of the elementary boys'. What did Burt then conclude, from this elementary exercise? That 'the superior proficiency at intelligence tests on the part of boys of superior parentage was inborn', adding, 'Thus we seem to have proved marked inheritability in the case of a mental character of the highest "civic worth".' For – you will remember – boys were sensitive to the taps in the same measure as they were to the headmaster's judgment of their intellectual powers. It was by this means that Burt reached the first of many similar conclusions tabled during a long life, that 'intelligence' had been shown to be 'inherited to a degree which few psychologists had hitherto legitimately ventured to maintain'.

It could be supposed that, having taken the first step in his career by this means, the young Burt saw no reason to alter so successful a pattern. Certainly to claim he had *proved* 'marked inheritability' of intelligence on the basis of data so flimsy points to an early tendency towards exaggeration, or triumphalism. Or, again, Burt is on record as saying that data do not really matter, what does is the theory. 'From his earliest writings,' Professor Jones of the Department of Sociology, Canberra, has said 'he advanced the view that statistical findings were nothing more than corroborative evidence to be weighed against deductive expectations from wider theory and the insights of introspection and clinical observation.'[29] No doubt future researchers will closely investigate all the early work – given how closely the whole evolution of psychometry is bound up with Burt's work and how many doubts have been raised. Meanwhile it would be premature to give the early work – influential as it was – a clean bill of health.

What led to all this? As befits a psychologist, Hearnshaw advances a psychological explanation, relating to his subject's early life, subsequent illnesses (he suffered from Ménière's disease) and the consequent distortion of his personality in later middle age and after retirement. There may well be some truth in this and similar analyses. Gillie had advanced an alternative psychological diagnosis. The Clarkes who knew Burt well from student days, testify that he was 'obsessed with the importance of heredity as a major determinant of human differences'.[30] Throughout a long life he is found reiterating the same idea in almost the same words, says Professor Jones. Surely, then, it must be counted a potent influence in the Burt tragedy that the social, political and educational situation was such as to permit this? Nor is it without significance that it was in the educational sphere that the breakthrough was made, heralded by a firm declaration from a committee of educational enquiry that 'the belief that there exists some easy method of ascertaining an intelligence factor unaffected by education and background' is outmoded.

This belief perpetuated the use of tests which tell us *nothing* about the acquisition of new abilities and skills, about the development of higher mental processes, but yet purport to grade children according to intelligence. In fact, psychometry, or mental measurement, merely classified people according to arbitrary criteria – that is all it can do. No account is taken of advances in other areas of psychology bearing on the working of the human brain and the processes of cognition. By contrast the work of such psychologists as Professor Jerome Bruner in the United States, the late Professor Alexander Luria in the Soviet Union and many others is based on the findings of neurology, concerned with cognitive processes, and so has much to tell us about teaching and learning whereby intellectual activity can be fostered and intellectual attainment increased. It is with such matters that educational psychology is, or should be, concerned and to such ends that the practice of education is rightly directed.

For many years the two-factor theory has been an obstacle, denying that children can make their own future, that it is worthwhile to exercise industry and zeal, preaching that the interaction of heredity and environment, and primarily heredity, inevitably shapes development. Since this idea was imported from biology, to become embedded at the base of psychometry, it is appropriate to give a distinguished biologist the last word. Shocked by the Burt case, Sir Peter Medawar deplored 'the extreme hereditarian view' (as he called it) that 'the whole course of development of a child's intellectual capabilities is largely laid down genetically', and recommended elimination of the very expression 'innate intelligence'.[31] Regrettably this hope has yet to be realised which is why it is so important for people to understand what the IQ controversy has been about and the nature of the case against Cyril Burt.

Notes

1. Cyril Burt, *Listener*, 16 November 1950.
2. 'Fudging the Facts', review of William Broad and Nicholas Wade, *Betrayers of the Truth: Freud and Deceit in the Halls of Science* (1983), by John Ziman, *The Times Literary Supplement*, 9 September 1983.
3. Philip Vernon, *Intelligence: Heredity and Environment*, San Francisco, 1979.
4. Leslie Hearnshaw, *Cyril Burt, Psychologist*, London, 1979.
5. *The Times*, 25 October 1976.
6. Hearnshaw, op. cit., p. viii.
7. Cyril Burt (ed.), *How the Mind Works*, London, 1933, p. 28–9.
8. *Secondary Education*, Report of the Consultative Committee to the Board of Education (the Spens Report), 1938, pp. 123–5.
9. Cyril Burt, 'The Examination at Eleven Plus', *British Journal of Educational Studies*, Vol. III, No. 2, May 1959.
10. Reprinted in *Intelligence, Psychology and Education*, London, 1978.
11. Hearnshaw, op. cit., pp. 227–8.
12. Ibid., p. 241; see also p. 228.
13. A.W. Heim, *The Appraisal of Intelligence*, London, 1954.
14. Hearnshaw, op. cit., p. 314.
15. D.D. Dorfman, 'The Cyril Burt Question: New Findings', *Science*, 28 September 1978, Vol. 201, No. 4362.
16. In Leon J. Kamin, *The Science and Politics of IQ*, Harmondsworth, 1977, chapter 3.
17. Hearnshaw, op. cit., p. 231.
18. Kamin, op. cit., p. 71.
19. Hearnshaw, *op. cit.*, p. 232.
20. *British Journal of Statistical Psychology*, Vol. XLV, pp. 10–21.
21. Hearnshaw, *op. cit.*, pp. 255-6.
22. Dorfman, op. cit.
23. *The Times*, 13 November 1976.
24. F.L. Jones, 'Obsession plus pseudo-science equals fraud: Sir Cyril Burt, Intelligence and Social Mobility', Mimeograph, Research School of Social Sciences, Australian National University, Canberra (nd, 1980?), p. 13.
25. Cyril Burt, 'The Mental Differences between Children', C.B. Cox and A.E. Dyson (eds.) *Black Paper Two*, London, (nd, 1969), see pp. 23–4.
26. Hearnshaw, op. cit, p. 290.
27. *The Times*, 25 October 1976.
28. Bernard Norton, 'Psychologists and Class', in C. Webster (ed.), *Biology, Medicine and Society, 1840–1920*, 1981, p. 306. The paper referred to is C. Burt, 'Experimental tests of general intelligence', *British Journal of Psychology*, Vol. iii (1909), pp. 94–177.
29. F.L. Jones, op. cit., p.9.
30. *The Sunday Times*, 24 October 1976.
31. *The Times*, 3 November 1976.

6

Samuel Taylor Coleridge: the Education of the Intellect

In February 1792, a group of fellow students were pursuing their riotous and uneven way back to their college (Jesus) at Cambridge. Stumbling over the loose stones, two of them lurched heavily and fell in the gutter. The third, the author of a letter describing the scene, went to help the nearest, only to be greeted with a Philip Sidney response: 'No, no! Save my friend there. Never mind me. *I* can swim.'[1]

This is as good a way as any to introduce Samuel Taylor Coleridge, the writer of this letter, in his youthful Cambridge days, when it seemed that poverty, slavery, and all the evils of a corrupt society were soon to be swept away not only through the cleansing power of the French Revolution, but also through the new vision of the perfectibility of man held out both by the French *philosophes* and their English counterparts, Joseph Priestley and the advanced democratic grouping of which he formed a part. Among these, of course, was William Frend, Fellow of Jesus, shortly to be put on trial by the University for subversion. The almost farcical semi-legal procedures by which Frend's trial was carried through in the Senate House, and Coleridge's vociferous part in this, have been well documented by Frida Knight in her biography of Frend,[2] as indeed has the widespread radical student movement in support of Frend and social change generally in B.R Schneider's *Wordsworth's Cambridge Education*.[3] It seems that even contemporary student movements could learn something from the techniques of agitation thought up by Coleridge and his friends, one of whose major coups was the burning by the use of gunpowder trails of the slogan 'Liberty and Equality' on the sacred lawns of Trinity.[4]

126

One point that Schneider makes, in his reconstruction of this movement and its significance, is that the strength of conviction and radical actions then shown were hidden and forgotten as its participants and chief actors – the *jeunesse dorée* of the time – moved into positions or power and responsibility in Church and state through the turbulent years of the early nineteenth century. Their own memoirs and those of their biographers, written in the 1830s, 40s and 50s, either ignored or glossed over their subjects' participation in what had been a widespread and advanced democratic movement.[5] It was partly through the (comparatively recent) discovery of Godwin's manuscript diary relating to this period and to Cambridge in particular, that Schneider was able to reconstruct the situation as it really was. Indeed, Coleridge himself, as of course is well known, through his 'abstruse metaphysical researches' as he put it, finally threw off the philosophic rationale of that movement – and also moved politically far away from the radical, democratic stance of his early days.

Yet his case was unique. Perhaps no one more than he embraced so wholeheartedly what he later called the 'mechanical philosophy' of the eighteenth century; certainly no one found it necessary to penetrate so deeply into its rational and scientific foundation before finally rejecting it in his move to philosophic idealism. In 1795, when aged 23, Coleridge named his first child Hartley, in deliberate celebration of his high regard for the teaching of the associationist psychologist (or philosopher) David Hartley, whose thinking underlay the concept of human perfectibility and, by the same token, provided the lynch-pin or cornerstone of Necessarianism, the strictly materialist world outlook developed and propagated with great force and power by Joseph Priestley, William Frend and many others.[6] Apostrophised in an early poem ('Religious Musings') as 'of mortal kind/wisest', Hartley is there described as the 'first who marked the ideal tribes/Up the fine fibres of the sentient brain', a poetic rendering of Hartley's theory of vibrations, of which more later. Although contradictory tendencies were certainly present in Coleridge's thinking from his youth (a sense of wonder, of religous awe), it was not until he reached the age of 30 that he began finally to break with his early outlook – and all his life he was to look back on this period with longing, as *the* period when all his forces, physical and mental, were harmonised in free activity.[7]

There is no doubt that David Hartley's systematic formulation of the theory of associationism, derived from Locke's *Essay on Human Understanding*, Newton's experiments in optics, and above all from contemporary medical knowledge relating to the functioning of the brain and nervous system, played an extraordinarily liberating role in the late eighteenth century (and later). As a theory of learning or human formation it provided, as suggested earlier, a rational basis for the theory of human perfectibility, underlying the enlightened outlook of the *philosophes*, as well as that of the utilitarian movement led by Jeremy Bentham and James Mill (for whom the theory of the human mind was, following Hartley, as clear and straightforward as the 'road from Charing Cross to St Paul's'). Associationist theory was also embraced by the early Utopian socialists; by Robert Owen (as encapsulated in his slogan 'Circumstances Make Man'), and by the French socialists Saint-Simon and Fourier. Above all its educational implications were clear and direct. Human beings were the product of their circumstances; to change people, surround them with positive circumstances, where all the external influences promote and fix desirable associations, and so, trains of ideas, attitudes and behaviour. This is precisely what Robert Owen set out to do at New Lanark – with evident success. In all these schemes, whether of the *philosophes*, the utilitarians or the socialists, education, conceived of in its widest sense, was central. A sympathetic summary, written in 1844, identifies the significance of this whole movement of thought:

> If man draws all his knowledge, sensations, etc., from the world of the senses and the experience gained in it, the empirical world must be arranged so that in it man experiences and gets used to what is really human and that he becomes aware of himself as man ... If man is unfree in the materialist sense, i.e. is free not through the negative power to avoid this or that, but through the positive power to assert his true individuality, crime must not be punished in the individual, but the anti-social source of crime must be destroyed, and each man must be given social scope for the vital manifestation of his being. If man is shaped by his surroundings,

his surroundings must be made human. If man is social by nature, he will develop his true nature only in society, and the power of his nature must be measured not by the power of separate individuals but by the power of society.

This was Karl Marx's response to the implications of the materialist outlook, as embraced by Coleridge and others in the late eighteenth century.[8] Here Marx does not set out his own critique of the deterministic nature of the mechanical materialism of the eighteenth century, but this was to prove the main focus of his rejection of this outlook as a sufficient explanation, in itself, of the complex relations between human beings and their external circumstances.

For Coleridge, it was also the highly determinist, or mechanistic, nature of contemporary materialism which became, for him, antipathetic. Although a liberating force in its day since it held out a rational prospect of human change, this determinism – the conviction that people we formed by their circumstances – allowed no scope for what may be called human 'self-activity'. The particular interest which attaches to Coleridge's painful, and lengthy, struggle to free himself from his early beliefs or world outlook, for educationists today, derives directly from evident similarities in the contemporary scene. For those who wish to underline similar values to those Coleridge came to hold dear; those related to autonomy, creativity, the development of initiative, intellectual courage and independence of thought, are today beset by a variety of equally determinist theories as those that faced Coleridge, and by even more threatening tendencies in practice. These include psychological theories, particularly in the area of psychometrics (or mental testing), theories relating to the primacy of biological determination, as well as sociological, stressing the helplessness of the individual in the face of formative social circumstances, each of which has its counterpart in specific educational policies and tendencies. Given this situation it is, perhaps, not surprising that Coleridge's encomium on Plato as educator, written after he had broken with what he called the 'mechanical philosophy', has a clear resonance. 'We see', he writes,

that to open anew a well of springing water, not to cleanse the stagnant tank, or fill, bucket by bucket, the leaden cistern; that the *Education* of the Intellect, by awakening the principle and *method* of self-development, was his proposed object, not any specific information that can be *conveyed into it* from without: not to assist in storing the passive mind with the various sorts of knowledge most in request, as if the human soul were a mere repository or banqueting-room, but to place it in such relations of circumstances as should gradually excite the germinal power that craves no knowledge but what it can take up into itself, what it can appropriate, and re-produce in fruits of its own. To shape, to dye, to paint over, and to mechanise the mind, he resigned, as their proper task, to the sophists, against whom he waged open and unremitting war.[9]

There are good reasons why this particular sentiment – or expression of an educational philosophy – strikes home closely today. For it is not difficult to recognise (or identify) our modern Sophists who seem concerned to mechanise the mind in the Coleridgean sense, furnishing it as a mere repository or banqueting-room, or filling it, bucket by bucket, as a leaden cistern. Even not very sensitive antennae cannot fail to pick up the major tendencies and direction in current pressures on education. These include the clear determination, by the central authority, to establish new forms of control over the curriculum, referred to in several papers in this volume, and indeed the whole (official) conception of the curriculum as something to be 'delivered' by teachers – as if it were an object having a material existence to be in some way directly transferred from the teacher to the child.[10] These tendencies have one thing in common; the reduction of the teacher's role to that of an agent in the promotion not of the *appropriation* and *transformation* of knowledge, as Coleridge puts it, but of its simple *assimilation*.

Such ideas and practices are put forward today in the name of the education of the *Intellect*; as a means of raising 'standards', or, as more usually presented, preventing a further decline. There are many, however, who assess these measures as profoundly philistine in conception; as anti-educational in the deepest sense. This is why the work and thought of Coleridge, specifically in its evolution, is closely relevant to contemporary issues in education.

2

Among English philosophers and educationists, it was Coleridge who first stressed the central importance of *self-activity* in education and in human development generally, as against the mechanistic world view which sees the human being as the passive product of external circumstances. What is particularly interesting is the process by which Coleridge climbed out of the mechanistic outlook, of which he was originally an ardent proponent, to perceiving the importance of self-activity for which the earlier views he espoused, as he came to realise, could make no allowance whatsoever. In this process, Coleridge formulated what he called 'the two grand problems' – central questions concerning people's relations with the external world. These he defines as 'How, being acted upon, we shall act,' and secondly, 'How acting, we shall be acted upon?' Already these formulations, which occur in a letter written in 1802, give the clue to Coleridge's own, idiosyncratic solution to these issues.[11]

What, then, was Coleridge up against? Hartley's associationism led to the conclusion that people's ideas (or sensations) are the direct resultant (or reflection) of external objects which impact on the brain through the senses; conveyed there by the movement of particles which transmit vibrations, emanating from the object perceived to the nerves, and so to the brain. All 'simple' ideas, for instance, of specific objects in the external world, are explained in this way, while what Locke called 'complex' ideas (for instance, love, honour, patriotism) were explicable as an amalgam of several simple ideas. Further, Hartley held that ideas were associated together in the mind through simultaneous, or successive, occurrence in the external world (and in the subject's perception), a phenomenon for which he provided a materialist explanation in terms of the connections, or relationships, formed in the brain as a result of excitation of the brain substance due to the impact of closely related events in the external world. On this basis, Hartley formulated the laws of association, and of trains of association linked together, which must determine, in his analysis, the direction of thought, and so, indeed, character, disposition, and so on. Human beings were thus interpreted as the *product* of this relationship with the external world (or surrounding circumstances) by which they were, quite specifically, *formed*.

Now it is worth noting that this theory is, in fact, a theory of learning; and that it was specifically developed as such by Joseph Priestley, who, in his own edition of Hartley's *Observations on Man*, though jettisoning the theory of vibrations (which Hartley himself regarded as speculative and no essential component of his theory), contributed an introduction of his own. 'I think myself more indebted to this one thesis', he wrote, 'than to all the books I ever read beside, the scriptures excepted';[12] elsewhere he claimed that Hartley had 'thrown more useful light upon the theory of the human mind than Newton did upon the theory of the natural world'.[13] It was partly because Hartleian associationist theory led to the conclusion that every educative action must have a necessary effect that Priestley, and others, now began to claim that education could be developed as a science – that is, studied according to the procedures of natural science (observation and collection of data, testing of hypotheses, the formulation of laws, etc.). For the same reason associationism laid the basis for the pedagogic optimism so characteristic of the Enlightenment, the utilitarians and the early socialists, already referred to. It provided, as it were, the psychological rationale for educative action – action which, if effectively planned and ordered, must inevitably lead to the desired result – that is, to achieving the educator's aim. Associationism, therefore, established a close link between theory and practice in education, and indicated how, through a restructured education, a fundamental change could be brought about in the nature of humanity – and this was the central concern both of the utilitarians and of the early socialists, though these movements had, of course, rather different objectives.[14]

It is worth noting here that, though Hartleian associationism was, fundamentally, a theory of learning (and this is its main significance), it contrasts sharply with modern deterministic theories of human formation, whether psychometric or sociological. These, in essence, evade the whole question of the nature of human learning in generalised assertions about innate limitations, or about the social determinants of educability. Nevertheless it is true that associationism, in its Hartleian form, certainly does assign an essentially passive role to man, who is seen as the subject of external stimuli – a 'lazy looker on', as Coleridge defined the role assigned to man in the Newtonian system when he himself was in the process of breaking out of it.

As is well known, Coleridge submitted Hartleian associationism to an extremely close analysis extending over four chapters of *Biographia Literaria*, published in 1817, when he was aged 44 – by which time he had made his transition to philosophic idealism. A quotation from Chapter 7 gives a taste of his new standpoint, as developed there. The chapter starts with a polemic against a system which assumes

> that the will and ... all acts of thought and attention, are parts and products of this blind mechanism, instead of being distinct powers, whose function it is to control, determine and modify the phantasmal chaos of association.[15]

By assigning primacy to the Will, Coleridge signifies his rejection of deterministic models, and in essence returns to the human mind a conscious, voluntary and directing capacity by which man is freed from external control and is endowed with the power to determine his own thought and action. 'Yet', Coleridge adds, referring to 'this blind mechanism',

> According to this hypothesis the disquisition, to which I am at present soliciting the reader's attention, may be as truly said to be written by Saint Paul's Church, as by *me*: for it is the mere motion of my muscles and nerves; and these again are set in motion for external causes equally passive, which external causes stand themselves in interdependent connection with every thing that exists or has existed. Thus the whole universe co-operates to produce the minutest strokes of every letter, save only that I myself, and I alone, have nothing to do with it, but merely the causeless and *effectless* beholding of it when it is done ... The sum total of my moral and intellectual intercourse dissolved into its elements is reduced to *extension, motion, degrees of velocity,* and those diminished *copies* of configurative motion, which form what we call notions, and notions of notions.[16]

Here, of course, Coleridge is satirising the whole mechanical materialist world view which came to be known as necessarianism, and which included associationism as an essential component. He does not, however, deny that associationism plays a part in influencing the direction of thought; indeed he gives a number of examples as to how it operates. What he does deny, and very vehemently, is that it causes, controls, or determines thought. The great error, he claims, is 'mistaking the *conditions* of a thing for its *causes* and *essence*'. Just as air is a conditions of my life, it is not its cause.[17] The relation between trains of thought, Coleridge asserts, can be determined by an 'act of consciousness', and he concludes:

> The true practical general law of association is this; that whatever makes certain parts of a total impression more vivid or distinct than the rest, will determine the mind to recall these in preference to others equally linked together by the common condition of contemporaneity or ... of continuity. But the will itself by confining and intensifying the attention may *arbitrarily* give vividness or distinctness to any object whatsoever ...[18] (my italics, B.S.).

So Coleridge has made his transition. He gives primacy to the will; finds a key place for imagination, and puts the Self, the I, in the central role with independent and autonomous power of *control* over thought and therefore, presumably, action. By this time, then, he has answered the questions he posed himself some fifteen years earlier very clearly and specifically. To the first he answers that we may act independently of the forces impinging on us from outside, while the answer to the second follows logically in the assertion that actions from without are of only minor conditioning significance. In essence, Coleridge is re-asserting the freedom of the Self – or, to put it in another way, the responsibility of the individual for his or her actions.

3

Let us now follow Coleridge as he goes, as he puts it, 'sounding on my dim and perilous way'[19] – just staying to acknowledge that his darts of thought, his digressions, his deep penetration and occasional fun and nonsense are always something of an intellectual adventure; somewhat like a walk over the Lakeland fells on a blustering windy day of the kind described by Coleridge himself in Eskdale,[20] with views of chasms, mountain tops, swirling spray, and the occasional distant glimpse of green, peaceful, fertile valleys far below – 'a green glade; fountainous and cool'. His life's intention, as is well known, was to produce the final (and total) philosophic system by which everything would be made clear and all the ends tied up in an intellectually satisfying manner. To this all his writings he regarded as Prolegomena. But this he never achieved; nor, as we can see now, was it ever possible that he should – given the direction of his thought.[21] What is important here, however, is what can be teased out from his thinking of particular relevance to our theme of 'the education of the intellect'.

As suggested earlier, the important feature here is Coleridge's stress on man's *activity*, in, as some might put it, the *creation* of his world. This seems to be the chief significance of his rejection of the mechanistic system of the eighteenth century (which Coleridge likened to death), and indeed a necessary condition for it. The fact that, with Coleridge, philosophic idealism took a fundamentally religious form is not particularly significant from out point of view, and I don't intend to follow him at all deeply in the famous distinction he made (derived from Kant) between Reason and Understanding (though something must be said of this), nor in the parallel distinction between the Imagination and the Fancy, interesting and highly controversial though they are. It seems now generally acknowledged that Kantian critical philosophy was the lever which enabled him to make the break,[22] and it is worth acknowledging here his almost unique knowledge (for his time) of the German language and of contemporary philosophical writings, including those of Fichte and Schelling, both of whom broadly developed the idealistic side of Kant's thought. [23] If Coleridge learned German to read abstruse philosophical treatises in 1799–1800 (at the age of 27 and 28), it is worth recalling that, even 20 years later, only two dons in the whole of Oxford had acquired the same capacity, in their case to study the new theology.[24] It was here, in German philosophic literature, that Coleridge found a distinct

rationale for his turn to idealism, and so to the restoration to
man of the power, or capacity, of *conscious self-activity* (a term
that seems best to express Coleridge's standpoint).

There has been much discussion as to how far Coleridge
arrived independently at an idealist world outlook (as he
himself tended to claim) in contrast to the materialist theories
he espoused in his youth.[25] This is essentially a matter for
specialist scholarship, but it seems certainly the case that at and
around the turn of the century (that is, by 1799 to 1800),
elements of idealism had entered Coleridge's thought, even
though its full and deliberate expression came later. His really
serious study of Kant, for instance, was undertaken only after
his return to England from his extended visit with Wordsworth
to Germany in 1798–99. But this tendency of Coleridge's early
thinking, which originally took a pantheistic form, was shared
and perhaps best expressed originally by Wordsworth. There is
little doubt that the two poets had begun to formulate their
shared philosophical outlook during the endless discussions
they had together when living close to each other at Alfoxden
and Stowey in the Quantock hills in 1797 and 1798; nor is
there any doubt that Coleridge's more metaphysical, analytic –
in short philosophic – approach profoundly influenced
Wordsworth at that time. 'Every poet must be a philosopher',
noted Coleridge, and certainly he held that Wordsworth's
greatness as a poet was due to the fusion of poetry with a
distinct philosophical outlook, one close to the direction of
Coleridge's mind at that time.

In the two early parts of *The Prelude*, originally intended for
The Recluse, but thought of by Wordsworth always as 'the poem
to Coleridge', Wordsworth expresses what may be called the
Coleridgean philosophic stance of that period – in a poem
which Coleridge felt at the time expressed the height of
Wordsworth's powers as poet.[26] Wordsworth is concerned to
explain how a heightened perception of nature (or the external
world) brings a new glory to everyday affairs and perceptions –
to the 'simple produce of the common day'; and how he hopes
that his poetry – his life's work – will help people to
understand and so achieve a higher state of being and
consciousness:

                                    ... by words
Which speak of nothing more than what we are,
Would I arouse the sensual from their sleep
Of Death, and win the vacant and the vain
To noble raptures; while my voice proclaims
How exquisitely the individual Mind
(And the progressive powers perhaps no less
Of the whole species) to the external world
Is fitted: – and how exquisitely, too –
Theme this but little heard of among men –
The external World is fitted to the Mind:
And the creation (by no lower name
Can it be called) which they with blended might
Accomplish: – this is our high argument.

There is no rejection here of the reality – or objective existence – of the external world (in the Berkleian sense), nor was there with Coleridge, even after the break with the 'mechanical philosophy'. There is the same equation of this philosophy (the sensual) with Death; above all there is the celebration (if I may make the leap) of what might be called the dialectical unity of mind and matter, being and consciousness (later so formulated by Marx) in the reference to the *creation* which their 'blended might' may accomplish – this, said Wordsworth, 'is our high argument'.[27]

It is the worth recalling at this stage that the two parts originally intended for *The Recluse* (never completed) were in fact dedicated to Coleridge. The first was written in Germany in 1799, that is, before any full immersion in German philosophical writing was experienced by Coleridge. Several references, both in his early notebooks and in his letters over the next three or four years, indicate that Coleridge was now already seeking a way out of the impasse, as he increasingly saw it, of mechanical materialism. Several writers have drawn especial attention to the 'excited' letter to Poole of March 1801, which claimed not only to have 'completely extricated the notions of Time and Space' but also to have 'overthrown the doctrine of Association, as taught by Hartley, and with it all the irreligious metaphysics of modern Infidels – especially, the doctrine of Necessity'. This, it appears, was an immediate reaction to the study of Kant, begun a month or so earlier, but was, perhaps, premature, in terms of his actual intellectual development.[28]

To pursue this further – the starting point of the 'dynamic philosophy' (as Coleridge later called it), and that which differentiates it from the 'merely mechanic' is, as Basil Willey writes in his interpenetration, the affirmation of self-consciousness – the 'I am', rather than the 'it is' of materialism. What takes place in perception (or in 'the act of knowledge') is an interpenetration of subject and object – that fusion or 'blending' of the external world as given through our senses with the mind (as Wordsworth puts it) or the Intellect (as Coleridge preferred). So, argues Willey, the external world is neither 'subjective' nor 'unreal', 'even though we "half-perceive and half-create" it'.[29]

So we reach the central point, the affirmation 'certainly not "demonstrable",' says Basil Willey, 'any more than religious faith is – that a bond exists, an affinity, between Nature and Man' (William Wordsworth's 'exquisitely fitted') 'whereby these interchanges and fusions … are not only possible … but truth-bearing' (as, for example in Wordsworth's 'Ennobling Interchange/of Action from without and from within,' in *The Prelude*). And so, now, to the *human power* that makes this possible – the 'Imagination'.[30]

'The Imagination then I consider either as primary or secondary, wrote Coleridge later. 'The primary imagination I hold to be the living Power and prime Agent of all human Perception, and as a repetition in the finite mind of the eternal act of creation in the infinite I AM.'[31]

Imagination, then, is a power given to people which underlies, forms the basis of, or is realised in, the act of perception. Coleridge, it has been suggested, assigns perception to 'Imagination' rather than to some purely intellectual faculty because he wishes to stress its *creative* nature – our mere perceptions contain something beyond purely intellectual analysis. But this goes much further in Coleridge's mature thinking. Human perception is a reflection, or repetition in miniature, of the act of creation itself. Human beings, made in the image of God who created Nature, participate in the creation or re-creation of nature 'every minute of our waking lives'. Basil Willey, a very sympathetic critic, comments here 'the mixture of sheer dogma and "revelation" with psychological experience in all this is very remarkable'.[32] Professor MacKinnon makes a rather similar point in an analysis of Coleridge's philosophical speculations. 'We cannot escape the sense,' he writes, 'that Coleridge approaches the sorts of issue that the empiricists seemed to him to have raised often as a seer or prophet rather than as a philosopher.'[33]

This seems an appropriate place to interpolate that there had, of course, always been a soul in man; a spirit, seen as having creative power linked to the divine. This had been central to medieval Christian thought and this concept was retained, and even embellished, by the Protestant Reformation. Locke first systematically removed it, in developing the materialist world outlook. Joseph Priestley, though a dissenting minister, denied the doctrine altogether, claiming (*inter alia*) that there was no authority for it in the Bible. He believed, and quite consistently in terms of logic, in the resurrection of the body. The significance of Coleridge's turn to idealism is that it allowed the reimplantation of the soul in Man, in the form of his concept of the 'creative imagination'.

So Coleridge restored to the human mind its creative function, and, as a result, was able to conceive of education also as having a creative function, as exemplified in the quotation given earlier on Plato as educator. But he was unable to base this restoration on a satisfactory philosophical or epistemological foundation. Its arbitrary nature is clearly exemplified in his distinction between Reason and Understanding, by which Reason represents the apprehension of the Divine – an act of faith, surely, which departs radically from Kant's own position – while the Understanding represents the grasp of empirical truths or objective knowledge (and was, therefore, banausic in character).[34] Once this central division is made, as Coleridge's one-time mentor, Joseph Priestley, pointed out in another context, there is no end to the blind alleys up which one may be led.[35]

Nevertheless there is a related aspect of Coleridge's thinking – not usually emphasised – which deserves attention. This is its dialectical character, a direction only now a possibility with the rejection of the mechanistic philosophy. The concepts of interpenetration, fusion (or interfusion in the *Ode to Immortality*), blending, flux, interdependence, interconnection, polarity – all concepts used by Coleridge – relate to the idea of movement, change, development, and it is this aspect of Coleridge's 'dynamic' philosophy that is certainly worth attention, in the sense that it is here in particular that Coleridge's outlook 'goes beyond' and transcends the billiard-ball philosophy of mechanical materialism. Coleridge's writing often reflects, or draws attention to, this sense of movement, of change, of impermanence co-existing with permanence; an outlook that was, of course, specifically developed by Hegel with whose work, however, Coleridge was not deeply familiar.[36] It was this aspect of Hegel's philosophy which so strongly appealed to the young Marx. 'All objects of sense,' writes Coleridge, 'are in a continual flux', so that 'the notices of them by the senses must, so far as they are true notices, change with them.'[37] It is relevant here to draw attention to Coleridge's very close relations with, and high admiration for, Humphrey Davy while living in the West Country at a formative phase in the life of both of them. The newly developing sciences of chemistry and electricity, with the discovery of the role of polarity, mutual attraction and repulsion, tension between opposites in particular brought new conceptions, new ways of thought, new models to explain the universe.[38]

'The first charm of chemistry and secret of the almost universal interest excited by its discoveries,' wrote Coleridge, is 'a sense of a principle of connection *given by the mind* and sanctioned by the correspondency of nature' (my italics, B.S.).[39] Objects are not discrete, separate entities; their subtle interconnections and interpenetrations are revealed in chemical analysis which is concerned with 'striving after the unity of principle through all the diversity of forms ...' In zoology the brilliant John Hunter is credited with rescuing the science from being 'weighed down and crushed' by the collection of innumerable facts, without 'any inward combination, any vital interdependence of its parts'. The concept of polarity in electricity is another example of the independent activity of mind in striving – reaching towards – the formulation of interpretative 'laws' reflecting the complexity of real phenomena; laws which are not simply given by the collection of a mass of empirical data.[40]

By at least 1819, then, and in fact earlier, Coleridge had made a clear break both with the strict materialism of his youth, and in particular with its mechanistic interpretation of relationships. By allowing the power of self-determination to the Will, and to the Imagination, the role of the subject's self-activity was given predominance, while the dialectical cast of his thought, as it now developed, allowed for movement and change in human self-development and in human beings' relations with the external world.

4

It should now be apparent why Coleridge (and Wordsworth) found the ideas and practice of contemporary rational educators so very repellent. It is not only the more extravagant ideas derived from associationist psychology and the mechanised philosophy generally, such as Tom Wedgwood's scientific procedures for the production of geniuses by isolating children in what were really padded cells to enhance the sense to touch, colour and so on, which were to them repugnant.[41] It was the whole conception of the shaping, polishing or veneering of the outer man without any recognition, far less provision for, the child's inner consciousness, his or her imagination (or even fancy in the Coleridgean sense) to which they objected; as also to the neglect of the child's *self-activity* to which Wordsworth, in *The Prelude* allows the most formative of influences, especially in relation to the world of nature, of books, and to the social activity of what today's sociologists would call peer groups – the village lads and lasses at school and at play.

Thus Wordsworth sketches the product of such an education in the passage in *The Prelude* starting:

'tis a Child, no Child
But a dwarf man; in knowledge, virtue, skill;
In what he is not, and in what he is,
The noontide shadow of the man complete; ...
He is fenced round, nay arm'd, for aught we know

In panoply complete; and fear itself,
Natural and supernatural alike,
Unless it leap upon him in a dream,
Touches him not. Briefly the moral part
Is perfect, and in learning and in books
He is a prodigy. His discourse moves slow,
Massy and ponderous as a prison door,
Tremendously embossed with terms of Art;
Rank growth of propositions overruns
The stripling's brain; the path in which he treads
Is choked with grammar ...

Later he refers to how

                              He must live
Knowing that he grows wiser every day,
Or else not live at all; and seeing, too,
Each little drop of wisdom as it falls
Into the dimpling cistern of his heart.

This, and other passages in *The Prelude* can be paralleled by
similar expressions by Coleridge; for instance, the sudden
polemic against the products of what he calls 'improved
pedagogy' at the start of *Biographia Literaria* –

modes of teaching ... by which children are to be metamorphised
into prodigies. And prodigies with a vengeance have I known thus
produced! Prodigies of self-conceit, shallowness, arrogance and
infidelity![42]

In *The Friend* (Essay X) Coleridge reverts to this theme, in
contrast with his own creative conception of education:

Alas! How many examples are now present to our memory, of
young men the most anxiously and expensively be-schoolmaster-
ed, be-tutored, anything but *educated*; who have received the arms
and ammunition, instead of skill, strength and courage; varnished
rather than polished; perilously over-civilised, and most pitiably
uncultivated.[43]

How, then, should man be educated? What is the extent of
the power of education and what are the principles underlying
it? Here we should engage in a critical analysis of Volume III
of *The Friend* – the ten Essays on the Principles of Method
which present a grand, architectonic statement of the

development of the human mind, and of the role and purpose of education, conceived of in the widest sense. Published in 1818, this was one of the very few of his works, prose or poetry, that Coleridge wished to be remembered by.[44]

But this cannot be undertaken here; the work is extraordinarily complex and raises innumerable questions. Its chief interest in our context lies in the great emphasis placed on education, properly understood, for the amelioration (and understanding) of the human condition. The Principle of Method, Coleridge says in introducing the essays, 'is the condition of all intellectual progress, and which may be said even to *constitute* the science of education, alike in the narrowest and in the most extensive sense of the word', the term 'Method' (from the Greek) implying, according to Coleridge, 'a progressive transition', 'a way' or 'a path of transit'.[45]

The general thrust of the argument lies in the critique of the empiric and the search for underlying, organic, unifying theory; hence the emphasis on the inner (Platonic) powers of the mind – what Coleridge calls Reason. A central feature of the set of essays is the ambitious attempt to fuse the Baconian approach with the Platonic, particularly in relation to the theory and philosophy of science; the whole culminating in a grand religious idea of the universe, of the relations between God and man, and so of education.

The critique of the empiricist, or positivist approaches is sustained throughout these essays, as well as the celebration of human intellectual powers – when developed – in the fields of science, humanity, religion. Here then our text on the Education of the Intellect (reproduced on pp. 129-30), stressing its potentially creative power, finds its natural place. After analysis of both Plato's and Bacon's emphasis on the role of the Intellect, Coleridge claims the authority of both as support for the importance of 'method' as he defines it:

Under the deep and solemn conviction, that without this guiding light neither can the sciences attain to their full evolution, as the organs of one vital and harmonious body, nor that most weighty and concerning of all the sciences, the science of *Education*, be understood in its first elements, much less display its powers, as the *nisus formativus* of social man, as the appointed *protoplast* of true humanity.[46]

This sets out Coleridge's position as to the potential role of a true education; and, although it really does him an injustice, the analysis must be left there – with this conception (or vision) as to what education might achieve; adding only that for Coleridge such an education must be concerned primarily with the cultivation of the mental powers, as best expressed in his encomium on Plato as educator; with the appropriation of knowledge and with its reproduction 'in fruits of its own', rather than with mere assimilation; with *self-development*, rather than the storage of information.

5

But, owing partly to the way Coleridge himself developed in the context of his time, certain sharply contradictory features in his thinking are apparent. Thus in the essays in *The Friend*, Coleridge defines education, as we have seen, as 'the *nisus formativus* of social man, as the appointed *protoplast* of true humanity'. Yet Coleridge's ordered, hierarchical conception of society, developed in middle life, led directly to his concept of the clerisy, whereby a true education, as he conceived it, was seen as the monopoly of a learned élite; while his sharp attacks at various times (but also in middle or later age) on what he called the 'plebification' of knowledge, his fears of mass education, and so on, reveal an outlook out of sympathy with the idea of social change and favouring the continued but stabilised existence of an hierarchical society as it then existed. Certainly Coleridge expressed no sympathy, as far as I know, in his middle and later life with the aspirations and efforts of the labouring poor (or working class) for knowledge, nor more generally with contemporary radical movements seeking the diffusion of knowledge, seeing education as a means to political power.[47]

Nevertheless, as argued at the start of this paper, Coleridge's view as to the purpose and methods of a true education stands in sharp contrast to present day moves to 'mechanise' the mind, and his work and outlook take on an immediate relevance to current concerns. In this connection there remains one important matter still to be elucidated. If Coleridge's central concept concerning the autonomy and independence of the Will – the 'I' – is epistemologically untenable, in that its foundation lacks a firm rationale (as Willey and Mackinnon both suggest), what degree of power remains in his analysis? An argument based on a mere assertion, or an appeal to faith (as is Coleridge's position relating to 'Reason'), loses force and rightly fails to convince.

But, as we saw earlier, Coleridge was unique in his time in the development of a philosophic outlook which attempted to subsume movement and change; a 'dynamic' philosophy, as he called it, which in this sense was reaching towards an outlook more closely adapted to the realities of human existence than could be allowed for in the contemporary mechanistic world view. Further, as already indicated, his thinking included a dialectical component in his concern with the complex interrelationships between supposedly discrete phenomena. His outlook, then, not only represents a sharp break with received views, it embodied elements both of the strengths and the weaknesses of German idealism, as it developed in the late eighteenth and early nineteenth centuries. The strength of this trend within German philosophy lay precisely in its stress on the subjective, on the activity (or, better, self-activity) of the individual, made possible only by the rejection of the strict materialist interpretation. It is precisely this issue, it is worth recalling, that Karl Marx, when himself wrestling with the problems posed both by mechanistic materialism and by German idealism, defined as crucial, in his famous Theses on Feuerbach, closely relevant to our theme.[48]

In his first thesis, Marx takes issue with the traditional, dichotomous relationship between what Coleridge called the I and the Not-I, the subject and the object, human beings and their external world. 'The chief defect of all hitherto existing materialism', writes Marx,

is that the thing, reality, sensuousness, is conceived only in the form of the *object* or of *contemplation*, but not as *human sensuous activity, practice*, not subjectively. Hence it happened that the *active* side, in contradistinction to materialism, was developed by idealism – but only abstractly, since, of course, idealism does not know real, sensuous activity as such ...

The active side of human life – human activity and its products – Marx is saying, was not and could not be developed, taken into account, within the limits set by contemporary materialism, which necessarily conceived of man as the passive product of the given external circumstances. It could, therefore, only be developed by idealism, which broke the relationship between man and his external world – in other words, set him free from constricting, determining influences over which he had no control. To place the emphasis once more on human activity was, then, the achievement of idealism, even though, as Marx suggests, only abstractly, since idealism does not (and cannot) know 'real, sensuous activity as such', that is, cannot accept the existence of human activity as a material force effecting change.

Marx himself, it is often forgotten, rejected the mechanical materialism of the eighteenth century for much the same reasons as Coleridge, in spite of his sympathetic attitude to its implications for social life. If man is formed by his circumstances and upbringing, how can changes in these circumstances be explained? Only (as he puts it) by dividing society into two parts, one of which is superior to society, in the sense that it stands apart from society, and, not itself subject to circumstances, like a *deus ex machina* changes the circumstances of others. Marx cites Robert Owen as conceiving himself (or being conceived) in this category.

Determinism, as expressed in Coleridge's 'mechanical philosophy', cannot explain change – which is yet visible all around us (perhaps particularly so in Europe in the early nineteenth century). The defect of this materialism, according to Marx, lies in the fact that this doctrine 'forgets that it is men who change circumstances and that it is essential to educate the educator himself'. And the conclusion? 'The coincidence of the changing of circumstances and of human activity (note the phrase, B.S.) can be conceived and rationally understood only as revolutionising practice.' By this Marx means that, in the actual practice (or the activity) of changing his circumstances man changes himself – his consciousness and activity are one – a unity. 'By ... acting on the external world and changing it,' Marx wrote later in a well known passage, 'he at the same time changes his own nature. He develops his slumbering powers and compels them to act in obedience to his sway.'[49]

In relating human activity to a changed external world and so to a changed self, Marx makes the connection which Coleridge sought, but ended in attributing to God. It is worth noting also that Marx, in the last quotation, does not use the term 'will', or attribute to it that autonomous power that Coleridge does (and indeed is forced to). The quotation, as also the Theses on Feuerbach (scribbled down in a notebook in the early 1840s), give a glimpse (as with the case of Coleridge) of a world outlook which Marx, of course, had then to work out in terms of history, the critique of contemporary philosophy, and so on.

6

Marx derived a central aspect of his thinking from the German idealist philosophers, and particularly from Hegel, as is well known. His fusion of dialectics with materialism remains a crucial 'moment' in the history of philosophy. Coleridge, who lived earlier, and derived from a different philosophic tradition, wrestled in his own time with some of the central issues with which Marx also was concerned. If he came up against a blind alley, and then inevitably took short cuts, finally embracing ideas that could hardly stand up to rational enquiry, that is understandable. His historic importance for English education remains his stress on human self-activity as central, and, related to this, on the autonomy and potential creativity of the individual. If his position on these matters was exaggerated, as suggested earlier, this is also understandable. But there can be no doubt that the German idealist philosophers, and Coleridge who learned from them, played an important role in shifting the emphasis from conditioning to self-activity as the means of development. And in so doing gave a new and deeper importance to what they conceived of as the essential features of a genuine education.

It is for this reason that, today, it is important to remind ourselves of Coleridge's contribution to educational thought. For this stands, as suggested at the start, in uncompromising opposition to existing, and perhaps increasingly dominant conceptions relating to the imposition of highly structured external restraints on teachers and, through them, on children; delimiting very precisely the scope for their own independent, autonomous activity, and reducing education to the assimilation of an externally determined, largely empirical content. Such an education, universally imposed, can hardly excite the 'germinal power' that Coleridge stressed as its true function. Nor can it awaken 'the principle and method of self-development'. Certainly it signals the end of any serious attempt at 'the education of the Intellect'.

Can we derive, from Coleridge, a convincing rationale for educational procedures which reject the 'mechanical' and focus on the development of the inner powers of the child? Does Coleridge provide a justification for the concept of the appropriation of knowledge rather than its assimilation? Insofar as his critique of associationism, focusing particularly on its procedures and pressing the analysis to its logical conclusion, is sharp and penetrating (even if not, perhaps, entirely original),[50] the conclusion must be positive. Associationism continued to play an important role in its relation to education throughout most of the nineteenth century, as, I hope, other papers in this volume make clear; in a modified form its value is still recognised today – as Coleridge himself continued to recognise its explanatory force. But no one now believes that it provides a complete interpretation of the operation of the human mind, as James Mill held it did. The overthrow of its mechanistic character, and of the world view derived from it, was necessary if the way was to be cleared for new conceptions of human potentiality.

It is in the formulation of these new conceptions, in particular the stress on the active role of the self, that Coleridge is important today. The limits to the scope of that activity are, of course, much disputed; but at least the *educator* today must reject the concept of the child's total determination by social or psychological factors. That human beings have the power to appropriate knowledge, and, in Coleridge's words, 'to re-produce [it] in fruits of its own' is today widely accepted, whatever may be the process by which this creative activity is brought about, and this must be a primary concern for educators. It is in this area that the humanist educator of our times must seek his or her rationale.

Notes

1. E.L. Griggs (ed.), *Collected Letters of Samuel Taylor Coleridge*, Volume 1, Oxford, 1956, p. 31. The wording of this quotation has been rationalised.
2. Frida Knight, *University Rebel, the Life of William Frend, 1757–1841*, London, 1971.
3. B.R. Schneider, *Wordsworth's Cambridge Education*, Cambridge, 1957.
4. Knight, op. cit., p. 140.
5. Schneider, op. cit., pp. 143 ff.
6. David Hartley's *Observations on Man* (2 volumes), which set out his systematisation of associationist psychology and elaborated his philosophic stance, was published in 1749. In 1775 Joseph Priestley reprinted Hartley's book with an introduction of his own.
7. See Kelvin Everest, *Coleridge's Secret Ministry*, Hassocks, 1979, for an analysis of Coleridge's early philosophic outlook. Coleridge's nostalgia for his youth is most poignantly expressed in the poem 'Youth and Age'.
8. Karl Marx, and Frederick Engels, *The Holy Family*, London, 1956, p. 176.
9. S.T. Coleridge, *The Friend*, 2 vols., Barbara Rooke (ed.), (*Collected Works*, Vol. 4, London, 1969), Vol. I, pp.472–3.
10. For example: 'A school's task is to equip pupils for adult life by developing all their qualities and talents. It does this by *delivering the curriculum* during and outside the time-tabled *periods of instruction*. The quality of what the pupils are offered depends on how good the curriculum is and on *how effectively it is conveyed* to each pupil. (My italics, B.S.). *Parental Influence at School* (Green Paper on school government), London, 1984, p. 11.
11. *Collected Letters*, Vol. II, p. 949.
12. J. Priestley, *An Examination of Dr Reid's Inquiry into the Human Mind on the Principles of Common Sense*, 1774, p. xix.
13. Ibid., p. xv.
14. James Mill's famous article on education, in the *Encylopedia Brittanica* (1818), later reprinted as a popular pamphlet (1836) contains a full exposition of Hartley's position which was fundamental to Mill's argument. 'It is astonishing', wrote Mill of Hartley, 'how many of the mental phenomena he has clearly resolved; how little, in truth, he has left about which any doubt can remain.' F.A. Cavenagh (ed.), *James and John Stuart Mill on Education*, Cambridge, 1931, p. 17.
15. S.T. Coleridge, *Biographia Literaria*, 2 Vols., James Engell and W. Jackson Bate (eds.), (*Collected Works*, Vol. 7, London, 1983), Vol. I, p. 116.
16. Ibid., pp. 118–119.
17. Ibid., p. 123.
18. Ibid., pp. 126–127.

19. Ibid., p. 105.

20. S.T. Coleridge, *The Notebooks of Samuel Taylor Coleridge*, 2 Vols., Kathleen Coburn (ed.), (*Collected Works* Vol. 3, London, 1973), Vol. I. pp. 1218ff.

21. John Cornwell, *Coleridge, Poet and Revolutionary, 1772–1804*, London, 1973, pp. 379–80.

22. Rosemary Ashton, *The German Idea*, London, 1980 (especially pp. 36–48); G.N.G. Orsini, *Coleridge and German Idealism*, Carbondale, 1969, *passim*; see also *Biographia Literaria*, Vol. I, especially pp. 153 ff.

23. Orsini, op. cit., chapters, 6, 7 and 8.

24. David Newsome, *The Parting of Friends*, London, 1966, p. 78.

25. For instance, in Orsini, op. cit., chapter 1 and Norman Fruman, *Coleridge, The Damaged Archangel*, London, 1972.

26. William Wordsworth, *The Prelude, 1799, 1805, 1850*, edited by Jonathan Wordsworth, M.H. Abrams and Stephen Gill, 1979, includes the 1799 *Prelude* with its final encomium to Coleridge. The lines which follow were included, by Wordsworth, in the Preface to *The Excursion*.

27. Ernest de Selincourt argues that Wordsworth's outlook at this stage is largely explicable on the basis of Hartleian associationism, though 'transcendentalized by Coleridge'. *The Prelude or Growth of a Poet's Mind*, Oxford, 1926, p. lvi.

28. Letter to Thomas Poole, 16 March 1801, *Collected Letters*, Vol. II, pp. 706–7; see Ashton, op. cit., p. 43.

29. Basil Willey, *Samuel Taylor Coleridge*, London, 1972, p. 195.

30. Ibid., pp. 195–6.

31. *Biographia Literaria*, Vol. I, p. 304.

32. Willey, op. cit., pp. 196–7.

33. D.M. MacKinnon, 'Coleridge and Kant', in John B. Beer (ed.), *Coleridge's Variety*, London, 1974, p. 191.

34. See Orsini, op. cit., pp. 130 ff.; Ashton, op. cit., pp. 45–6.

35. Cornwell, op. cit., pp. 20–21 (quoting J. Priestley, *An Appeal to the Serious and Candid Professors of Christianity*, 1792).

36. See Orsini, op. cit., chapter 10.

37. *The Friend*, Barbara E. Rooke (ed.), Vol. I, p. 462.

38. See Rom Harré, 'Davy and Coleridge: Romanticism in Science and the Arts', in Martin Pollock *et al* (ed.), *Common Denominators in Art and Science*, Aberdeen, 1983.

39. *The Friend*, pp. 470–1.

40. Ibid., pp. 470–8.

41. Cornwell, op. cit., pp. 177–8.

42. *Biographia Literaria*, Vol. I, pp. 12–13.

43. *The Friend*, Vol. I., p. 500.

44. Coleridge held that the Essays on Method outweighed all his other works 'in point of *value*'. *Collected Letters*, Vol. IV, p. 885.

45. *The Friend*, Vol. I, pp. 446, 457.

46. Ibid., Vol. I, pp. 493–4.

47. See, for instance, *The Friend*, Essay 3, p. 447; *Collected Letters*, Vol. III, p. 414.

48. Karl Marx and Frederick Engels, *The German Ideology*, London, 1964, pp. 651–3.

49. *Capital*, Volume One, London, 1983, p. 173.

50. The extent of Coleridge's plagiarism in *Biographia Literaria* is fully discussed in the introduction to the recent authoritative edition edited by James Engell and W. Jackson Bate (Vol. 7 of the Collected Works, 1983), pp. cxiv ff., while specific matter taken from German texts is printed alongside Coleridge's own formulations. This makes clear Coleridge's debt to J.G.E. Maass's *Versuch über die Einbildungskraft* (2nd ed. 1797) in the chapters criticising associationist psychology, and especially in his chapter (5) on the history of the theory. This hardly detracts, however, from the force or general sense of Coleridge's critique.

7

Secondary Education for All in the 1980s: The Challenge to the Comprehensive School

This lecture is designed to serve a dual purpose – both as a tribute to Raymond King, Headmaster of Wandsworth School (ILEA) for some 30 years and, as a friend who taught at that school put it recently, a hero of comprehensive education; and as a retrospective study of the whole movement for secondary education for all. This will lead me on to a look at the present challenge to comprehensive education, in terms of the realisation of the concept embodied in that historic slogan. These themes are, of course, closely interwoven, since Raymond's active life, which came to an end only this year, spanned the initial conception, gestation and finally the realisation of comprehensive education – still only partial, of course, in terms of early ideals and objectives, but now covering 90 per cent of all students of secondary school age in the maintained sector in England – rather more in Wales, and nearly 100 per cent in Scotland. In so far as Raymond devoted his energy, both as a practitioner (and a highly professional one) and as a theoretician to this cause for some 50 years, this must be assessed a considerable achievement – and a worthy memorial for one who was a leading pioneer in this whole movement. Given the criticism now being made of these, the nation's schools, often by interested parties who have their own axes to grind, this is also a convenient time to recall why

This is the Raymond King Memorial Lecture, delivered in the Festival Hall, London, in November 1983 at the invitation of the English New Education Fellowship. I have to thank Mrs Mary King for the loan of her husband's papers which were very helpful in the production of this lecture.

it was that men and women like Raymond, stemming precisely from the grammar school, selective tradition, developed, on the basis of their own experience, their own independent outlook, and so were among the first to see the need to transform these schools, serving only some 25 per cent of the secondary school population, into schools serving the entire local community.

My connection with Raymond King dates from 1958. When Robin Pedley, Jack Walton and I founded the educational journal *Forum* in that year, Raymond was one of the comprehensive school heads who agreed to join the Board, and who stuck with us through all the early difficulties. In 1964, on his retirement from Wandsworth, he became the Editorial Board's chair. This body meets three times a year, for three hours, discussing current and future numbers; discussions often tempestuous and always lively and stimulating. Raymond hardly missed a meeting – I reckon he attended some 70 or more. Always in his seat at least five minutes before the meeting was scheduled to start, he took a full part in discussions articulating his views, which changed over time, with sincerity and wisdom, and a certain impressive sonority. On closing the meeting he would always thank everyone for their attendance with great courtesy and precision, before formally declaring the meeting closed. *Forum* owes a great debt of gratitude to Raymond for his loyalty and participation as well as for the many articles he contributed over a period of 25 years. Of course, he had other fields of activity – the New Education Fellowship, of which he and his wife Mary were the heart and soul over the last 20 years and more; UNESCO, as a member of their textbook committee and in other capacities; the Rotary Club of Wandsworth, and other spheres. As far as this lecture is concerned, however, the focus must be on the general movement for secondary education for all, the transition to comprehensive education, the challenge of the present situation and Raymond's part in all this.

First a few words about Raymond's early experiences. Born on Christmas Day in 1897, his father was a railway worker in the North of England and Raymond attended a local grammar school, leaving at the age of 18, in 1916, to join the army. His record there was extraordinary considering his youth; being awarded both the Military Medal and the Distinguished Conduct Medal (neither in any sense lightly given), and in addition the Belgian Croix de Guerre presented to him by a Belgian general on the field of battle. Raymond, who, like another famous protagonist of secondary education for all, R.H. Tawney, refused to be commissioned as an officer preferring to remain among the men, finished up, at the ripe age of 20, as a Company Sergeant Major, even if designated as 'temporary'. 'I would follow King anywhere,' Mary told me, one of his men was heard to say. These early qualities of determination and courage were, in Raymond's case, to find expression in the struggle for educational reconstruction during and after the Second World War, as we shall see.

The years immediately following the First World War were years of educational ferment. In 1921 an official all party parliamentary committee concluded that 75 per cent of the nation's children were capable of profiting from secondary education, and that they should have it. In 1922 there appeared Tawney's famous pamphlet *Secondary Education for All*, perhaps the most brilliant, tightly argued, educational manifesto ever to have been published in this country. This did not, of course, propose the single secondary school, but at least it articulated a generous conception – and a clear policy – as to how *all* young people might be provided for in a variety of secondary schools, all under the *secondary* (rather than the elementary) code of regulations. The publication of this pamphlet effectively set the agenda for educational discussion and action over the next twenty years and more.

In that year, Raymond was aged 24. His war experience behind him, he was studying at Cambridge University, working for his degree, and shortly to go on to the one year course of professional training in the Education Department there. Can one doubt that Tawney's publication, and the discussions around it, already made an impression on Raymond King and his fellow students? This, in any case, was the context of his early involvement, as a would-be and trainee teacher, at a formative period of his life. And this discussion, of course, continued throughout the 1920s with the publication of the famous Hadow report of 1926, *The Education of the Adolescent*, which again argued that all pupils over eleven should experience post-primary, or secondary education.

At Cambridge from 1919, Raymond gained a first in Part I of the History Tripos two years later. He then switched to English gaining a second. At the Education Department during the next year, Raymond's total involvement and highly professional approach was clearly evident. 'He is a man of great intellectual powers, originality and force of character,' runs his final report.

> He has read widely and with discrimination. Both in English and History his teaching is thorough, modern and stimulating. He is a good athlete and throws himself into school games. He has a delicate literary taste. He is a man of good appearance who will adapt himself to any environment, but will not tolerate any injustice to himself.

Raymond's teaching practice was done as Westminster School under the supervision of the Revd H. Costly White, the headmaster, who himself has his niche in the history of education. 'His manner is stern,' he reports, 'His techniques very good. He secured the attention of a very difficult class and made them work, though they have the reputation of being the slackest class in the school. He is lucid, forcible and economical of speech and time. His knowledge and his intellectual powers are unquestionable.' As for the so-called 'Final Estimate', it reads as follows:

General Culture:
    Excellent
Industry as Student:
    Excellent
Industry as Teacher:
    Excellent
Discipline:
    Excellent
Teaching power:
    Excellent

Raymond clearly made full use of his professional training year. The final remark is:

'Can be recommended anywhere.'[1]

Raymond was appointed, in autumn that year (1923) as English and History master at Portsmouth Grammar school. Three years later, in 1926, he became head of Scarborough High (or Grammar) school, at the age of 28. He must be one of the youngest grammar school heads ever appointed. But by this time he had already a considerable and unusual experience of the world, both in peace and war. Six years later, in 1932, Raymond, appointed head of Wandsworth Grammar School, took up the post in which he was to make history some 25 years later, in one of the first grammar schools to be transformed, in a planned, rational and deliberate way, into a fully comprehensive school.

In a retrospective article written in 1979, in the 21st anniversary number of *Forum*, Raymond looks back over this period. When appointed a grammar school head in 1926, he writes, secondary schools had expanded from taking only a few children to catering for a quarter of all within the maintained system. The Hadow Committee was 'on the point of' presenting its report foreshadowing 'secondary education for all'. This was brought about by the 1944 Act, but he goes on:

> The schools which had led the great expansion drew aside from the main stream of secondary development, to their own loss and that of the nation. The local authority grammar schools, clinging to the prestige of the independent and semi-independent sector, were mostly brought in too late, too inexperienced in the new order, and too half-hearted to give any effective lead in the comprehensive system. Comprehensive education has remained incomplete, and with strong grammar school elements still outside, has not yet won the confidence of a considerable section of the indestructible middle classes.[2]

The great interest in Raymond's life (to the historian) is how it was that he, steeped as he was in the grammar school tradition, early became so convinced and resolute an exponent of the comprehensive school, as the essential organisational form through which the objective of secondary education for all must be realised. Although a few others, as we shall see, took the same road, Raymond stands out uniquely as the leader of this movement; one which, as he says in the quotation just given, was essential if comprehensive education was to be developed as a truly *national* system.

To understand this we must look back to the 1930s. The movement for the single school, then known variously as the multilateral or, more usually, the multi-bias school, dates back earlier than that, to the late 1920s. It is often forgotten that there was a groundswell of professional opinion in the 1930s in favour of the single secondary school, clearly exemplified in the evidence given to the Spens Committee, not least by the grammar school associations. The Associations of Assistant Mistresses, for instance, came down heavily for the multi-bias school, conceived as flexible, multi-track, or 'many-sided' in its internal organisation. Raymond's own association, the Incorporated Association of Head Masters (IAHM), also supported this idea, as did the National Union of Teachers. The TUC and other labour movement organisations adopted the same approach. Because of the apparent unanimity of these views, it is perhaps not surprising that the Spens Committee devoted its very first chapter to explaining why the multilateral school did *not* find favour with them (except in sparsely populated areas), so clearing the way for their recommend-ation for the establishment of secondary technical schools alongside grammar and senior (or modern) schools, though of course all under the secondary code; in fact the tripartite system with which we are all familiar.[3]

Raymond himself puts the point. In the late 1930s the grammar schools were experiencing the problem of the C stream – the alienated, early leavers who formed quite a proportion of the pupils in these schools, some of them, of course, fee payers. Outside the grammar schools were the junior technical schools, a success story, then developing appropriate curricula for students aged from 13 to 16 and apparently retaining their enthusiasm and involvement. Then again, some central and senior schools were now beginning to develop successfully five year courses, from 11 to 16. So, writes Raymond, the multilateral idea now found support from secondary, or grammar school heads.[4] Hence their evidence to Spens. Nor must we forget the radicalisation of many teachers, grammar and other, under the impact of the searing national and international events of those days – in particular, the rise of fascism in Germany and the consequent threat to democracy.

How to educate for a renewed democratic society was
undoubtedly a main motivation for the stance Raymond took
up, as we shall see.

In the late 1930s in London a group of grammar school
heads began meeting regularly to discuss education at greater
depth and with a freedom for which IAHM meetings were not
conducive. We should recall that, in 1936, when Labour first
won control of the London County Council, as it then was, a
special joint committee (elementary and secondary), presided
over by Barbara Drake (a niece of Beatrice Webb's), after very
thorough discussions, advocated, as a perspective, the
establishment of what they called 'a new type of school', large
enough to provide within its four walls most, if not all, of the
activities now carried on in existing types of post-primary
school.[5] Although under the then statutory regulations this
was impossible of achievement, from this point on the
establishment of the comprehensive secondary school was on
the agenda. Raymond's school, we should remember, was in
the LCC area.

It is at this stage, from the late 1930s, that Raymond begins
activity on this issue. Evacuated at the outbreak of war, a group
of four like-minded grammar school heads continued the
meetings begun earlier in London. As the war proceeded there
was, of course, a ferment of discussion about education,
culminating in the White Paper of 1943 and the Act of 1944.
Into this, Raymond and his three colleagues, still known at
Gordon Square (headquarters of the IAHM), as 'The Four
Horsemen of the Apocalypse' entered with vibrant energy. In
1942 their 15,000 word pamphlet, entitled *A Democratic
Reconstruction of Education*, was published and widely circulated.
This led to the foundation of an organisation – the Conference
for the Democratic Reconstruction of Education or CDRE – of
which Raymond was Chairman. At the inaugural meeting the
main speaker was H.C. Dent, then the influential editor of *The
Times Educational Supplement*. The chair of the Education
Committee of the LCC was also present. A committee was
elected including grammar school heads, teachers, professors
of education (Cavenagh and Barnard), LEA Inspectors and
others. Campaigning now got under way with a vengeance.
This, writes Raymond, 'continued from 1942 to 1946, and, as

Chairman of CDRE I found myself in lively debate in various parts of the country, most often at what proved later to be trouble spots'.[6]

What was Raymond's (and CDRE's) standpoint at that time? Democracy, he argued, is the highest form of government. But the educational system itself is highly undemocratic. Tinkering is not enough. What is required is a fundamental educational reform as the foundation of a new democracy.

The strongest criticism is reserved for the public schools. These perpetuate social schism and inequality of opportunity; they stand in the way of the construction of a truly national system. Further these schools failed the country in the inter-war period, when they signally failed to provide effective leadership. The public schools, CDRE (and Raymond) argued, should be 'absorbed' into the state system; the greater schools should be developed as vocational colleges for students over 18, the lesser brought into local systems where their boarding facilities could be used rationally and equitably. CDRE's later evidence to the Fleming Committee (on the public schools) was equally radical and just as outspoken. 'On the publication of that report (in 1944 B.S.),' Raymond wrote in 1979, 'CDRE sent its powerful and cogent counterblast to every Member of Parliament.'[7] It is salutary in these days to remember the strength of feeling on this issue, widespread at the time, and clearly articulated in these documents. Raymond never modified his outlook on this crucial question.

The second major issue dealt with was the pattern of secondary schooling as a whole. The pamphlet argued for a 'radical solution'. Secondary education should be provided for *all* from 11 to 16. Separate types of school – secondary, junior technical, trade, central and senior – should be abolished in favour of 'a new and larger secondary school for all'; this should be conceived (and this is important in all Raymond's thinking) as an 'educational community' rather than as a school. Raymond claims in his 1979 article that the pamphlet, which spelt out in some detail how such a school should be organised, was 'the first professionally conceived blueprint of what later came to be called the comprehensive school'.[8] The claim is, I think, well founded.

It is clear that a lot of thought and experience went into the design of this blueprint, relating to the curriculum in particular, to inner school organisation and structure, and to government and administration. On this latter point it is argued that the school should be an example of democracy in action; there should be much devolution to staff and students; parents and the local community must be involved and a genuinely community spirit built up – all characteristics later embodied in Wandsworth School when it went comprehensive. Interchange should be arranged with students from other countries to help further an international spirit and understanding – an activity with which Raymond had been much involved in the 1930s. Generally we see here the concept of the comprehensive school taking shape in the minds of the most advanced grammar school heads of that time – now 40 years ago.

There is so much that might be said about his period that it is really difficult to know how to proceed. This appears to be the time when Raymond first made fruitful contact with the New Education Fellowship (NEF), to which he made an enormous contribution, especially after retirement, a contribution which unfortunately lies outside the scope of this lecture. In 1941 H.G. Stead, Chief Education Officer at Chesterfield and an extraordinarily far-sighted educationalist, became secretary of the NEF; and this contributed to a shift in the focus of that organisation towards direct concern with the state system and its development (at a crucial historical moment). The NEF and CDRE now organised joint conferences on the future of education; their reactions to the White Paper (1943) and to the Fleming Committee were very similar and equally radical. In 1950 the NEF published what was, I think, the first pamphlet to be devoted entirely to 'the comprehensive school' – and this was its title. Of this pamphlet, writes Raymond, 'I was the innominate author'.

Here we should pause a moment and take stock, for this was a crucial period. On 1 August 1944 a plan for comprehensive schools was first adopted by the London County Council. Three years later, in 1947, the LCC adopted the fully elaborated *London School Plan*. This was approved by the Ministry of Education in February 1950. In an article in the first number of *Forum* in the Autumn of 1958, Raymond

writes that 'The most momentous educational feature of the
plan was the bold and imaginative conception of reorganising
secondary education in a system of comprehensive schools.'
The plan proposed a total of 103 such schools, 'of which 67
were to be planned as county high schools', the rest as the
so-called 'county complements', the London solution to the
existence of so many voluntary aided schools which, under the
Act, could not themselves be extended as fully comprehensive
schools.[9]

The adoption of the plan, according to Raymond (and I
remember this well) was accompanied by 'violent attacks,
which tended to blur the educational issues', but, he adds, the
LCC was toughened rather than tamed by this. Nevertheless
the London comprehensive schools 'have had to make their
way against much bitter opposition'.[10] In Raymond among
others, they found a formidable protagonist: highly experienced, deeply professional, articulate. Of this period Eric
Linfield writes that when a student he conceived a great
admiration for Raymond 'for his forceful presentation of the
case for comprehensive schools just after the war when I heard
him speak at the London University Institute of Education on
several occasions'.[11]

So, as London moved towards comprehensive education,
the biggest authority in the country and the most prestigious,
Raymond was fully involved. With post-war building
restrictions it was not possible to go ahead with purpose built
comprehensive schools until the early 1950s; but things were
kept moving with the establishment of eight 'interim' schools
in 1947 – with a very fine set of heads and staff that included
Margaret Clarke, Miss O'Reilly and others, and where
experience was gained in the organisation of large schools
including, usually, a fusion of selective central and modern
schools. No grammar schools were involved. Raymond,
however, formed part of this group of heads which met for
discussions since, in that year, Wandsworth was asked to take
over the London-based complement of the evacuated junior
technical section of the Brixton School of Building. Here, then,
was an earnest of what was to come. Raymond himself, anxious
to push ahead, submitted at this stage two plans to the LCC
proposing the formation of comprehensive schools through

the grouping of existing schools; due to what was then known as 'the bulge', and consequent lack of resources, neither could be implemented.

We may take the NEF 1950 pamphlet as embodying Raymond's concept of secondary education for all, within the comprehensive school – one which he later set out to implement at Wandsworth.[12] Referring to the heat and rancour of the discussion (among others he had Eric James's condemnation in mind) he argued that the comprehensive school should be considered primarily as an *educational* issue. Secondary education for all implied a revolution in English education. What was needed was a total revision of curricula (this was seen as very important) and a new spirit of enterprise and adventure among the staff.

A strong argument is developed in the pamphlet against the perpetuation of a hierarchy of schools within the state system. In place of the segregation this entails, students should be offered a common educational experience as a means to social unity. Selection, he says, implies rejection; if we get rid of this the general level of attainment will rise. Education is seen as a function of society, and Raymond develops the concept of the educative society which seems closely to follow the ideas of Fred Clarke whom, of course, he knew well through the NEF. Only the comprehensive school, he argued, can develop an organic relationship with the community which must be closely involved with the school – a concept that Raymond later realised in the school and community grouping he established at Wandsworth.

The pamphlet argues strongly for the large school, big enough to allow a variety of differentiated courses. Such schools should be established over a period by separate schools gradually growing together rather than through what he calls a 'catastrophic merger'. The first two years should form a separately organised Lower School, seen as a diagnostic period, when all follow a largely common curriculum or core. During this period there would be much flexibility of organisation and a focus on group work. Towards the end of this period the pupils would be 'self-selected' (Raymond's words) for a variety of courses in the Main School (13 to 18). Raymond's conception of this was of a school in which there would be no segregation by 'types' – that is, he rejected the multilateral idea; instead all students would follow a common core of studies offered within a wide variety of courses. The common core would be constructed around first, areas relating to the individual's personal needs, and second, those relating to the claims of society. For students aged 13 to 15 streaming was rejected in favour of banding and setting related to the variety of courses and directions offered. Technical education should be embodied in the curriculum for all, conceived as a component of a liberal culture rather than as a utilitarian study. Sixth form studies should be broadened and liberalised comprising three elements; first, study of specific disciplines, second, general studies, and third general background, or what he called 'recognition' knowledge.

As far as social organisation is concerned, Raymond had already pioneered the tutor system when at Scarborough in the 1920s, and later wrote much on this topic. The pamphlet argues the case for tutor groups across ages and for houses within the school, a pattern which has, of course, become very familiar. The pamphlet finishes with a section on the school directorate which percipiently identifies the new role of the head of such a school – the need for delegation, team work and co-operation; the respective roles of the Staff Council and what he called 'the Cabinet', and the nature of student participation. The comprehensive school, Raymond concludes, may not be the final solution; eventually we may arrive at a new conception of the school as a function of the community. It could be seen, however, as a step along that road.

Can we now turn to the transition to comprehensive education at Wandsworth itself? This was a planned and deliberate *process* which was spread over several years until, as Raymond put it later, the new, fully comprehensive school 'slipped into gear from the first morning' in its new, purpose-built buildings in the Autumn of 1956. Raymond always paid tribute to the LCC for the great degree of autonomy it allowed its heads. 'No doctrine', he wrote, on his retirement in 1964,

No blue print, no directives – apart from the initial conditions

('Unselected entry', 'Balanced Intake', 'Delimited Area') conditions designed to make the new schools as comprehensive as
possible in a non-comprehensive field.

It was

> the highest tribute ever paid by an education authority to its
> teachers: to leave them virtually free to build up the great
> comprehensives in the way they judged best. Hence the exciting
> variety of organisational pattern, both scholastic and social, in the
> London schools, and the immense range of experience they have
> collectively accumulated in the last ten years.

In reply to an enquiry from the secretary of his professional
organisation in the same year (1964), Raymond again stressed
this point, adding that he had, of course, the option of
objecting to the plans for his school; that he also could have
deliberately stirred up parental and local feeling in a campaign
to 'save the grammar school', and that, had he done so, the
Ministry of Education would have backed him, as had been the
case with the Eltham Hill Girls High School, Bec Grammar
School and Strand. The early 1950s was, of course, a time when
opposition to comprehensive education under that precise
slogan was widespread, the Minister herself, Florence
Horsbrough, disallowing the integration of a maintained local
authority grammar school as part of Kidbrooke, London's first
purpose built comprehensive school. Some will remember the
hullabaloo over the Bec and Strand proposals, both also
rendered nugatory in this manner. This is partly the historic
importance of schools like Wandsworth, its sister school
Mayfield under Margaret Miles, Holloway, Parliament Hill
and Sydenham which were the first London grammar schools
to take this road. This was the time when London certainly led
the country in the transition to comprehensive education.

But, Raymond goes on in his long memo to the official, he
did not take that road. On the contrary, as early as 1947 he had
agreed to take over the junior technical branch of the Brixton
School of Building 'voluntarily, and not under pressure'. From
1948 he had agreed to a gradual expansion by recruiting first
one, then two, and finally in 1955 three non-grammar forms at
11 plus, and re-planning the technical branch as a two form
entry instead of the original four to accommodate the new 11

plus entry. All this, he writes, 'was my own plan, not enforced, or even suggested, by County Hall'. He also planned the courses – a total of 14 with 8 languages; set up the tutorial and house forms of social organisation (Mayfield used the form and year system, he pointed out), and designed the new management hierarchy consisting of a deputy head and four 'Principal Masters'. Further, though against LCC policy, he established his separate 11 to 13 Lower School, brought in a building and engineering bias in the third year (the LCC plan was for no such biases until the fourth year), and persuaded the authority to modify the recruitment scheme so that the three schools serving the local area, Mayfield, Wandsworth and Elliott, were available to all by choice, so giving the option of a girls', a boys' and a mixed school. True to his ideals, Raymond took the initiative in 1955, when the three comprehensives were on the point of opening, of gaining community involvement through setting up his 'School and Community' organisation involving parents and many interested local people and organisations. He wrote, in 1979, 'Parental opinion had been carried with us over the gradual expansion; so that when the anti-comprehensive movement started up in Wandsworth, it fell completely flat.'[13]

'The grammar school which had expanded to become comprehensive,' Raymond wrote in 1958, 'now finds itself where it should be: it is an integral part of a complete secondary service providing wider opportunities for its pupils without any deterioration in standards.' The comprehensive school involves 'far-reaching changes, not only in administration and organisation, but in the whole conception of the nature and purposes of education at the secondary stage'. 'To teach in a London comprehensive,' he added, 'is an exhilarating and, it must be added, a strenuous experience.'[14]

This may be seen now as the heroic period of the London comprehensives. The new system was on the point of beginning its breakthrough. In Coventry, Glasgow, Anglesey; in the new towns, and in isolated areas all over the country the new schools were getting off the ground. In 1957 the Leicestershire Plan was launched in two areas in the country, providing a new model of the two-tier school. All over the country local authorities were now discussing or planning the

transition, though with no encouragement either from the
Ministry or the government of the day – rather the opposite.
Wandsworth, like others, was overwhelmed with visitors. Within
the school the excitement of the new venture was everywhere
apparent. Roy Waters, appointed to Wandsworth in 1954
remembers, in his appreciation of Raymond, 'the staffroom
frequently half full of young teachers excitedly talking shop at
six in the evening when the school keeper (an appointment as
happy as that of most of the teaching staff) came round to chivvy
us out.'[15] Such was the feeling in those days.

The opposition, however, was unrelenting – particularly at
about this time; and this must be remembered in evaluating
the comprehensive school. Raymond's files bring back
memories. There is the statement by the Joint Four, as the
secondary teachers' associations were called, of 1959. Entitled
The Organisation of Secondary Education it consists of a sustained
polemic against the comprehensive and for the grammar
school. A year earlier Raymond's own association, the IAHM,
issued a statement entitled *The Grammar School: a Reply to the
Labour Party's Educational Proposals*. Scored, queried, and
sharply commented on in the margins by Raymond, it argues
that the grammar schools must remain inviolate. The IAAM
(Assistant Masters), in a leaflet entitled *Comprehensive Secondary
Education*, issued at the same time, concludes that the nation
should resolutely resist any development which might destroy
or damage the grammar school. Of course it was always
Raymond's contention that far from destroying the grammar
schools, the transition to comprehensive education meant the
extension and transformation of these schools to meet the
needs, and the nature, of the entire secondary school
population. In allying himself so totally with the movement to
comprehensive education, Raymond, a leading grammar
school head, gave the lie to these charges in his own person.

At Wandsworth Raymond developed an organisational
pattern which he felt to be appropriate to the abilities and
interests of his comprehensive intake. Eight teachers
comprised a remedial department for what are now known as
the slow learners; projects and activities, some very
imaginative, formed the staple of the educational experiences
of 'the next 20 per cent' (in Raymond's words).[16] The variety of

courses offered in the main school covered what he then saw as five levels of ability and comprised a variety of directions. In the tutorial groups and houses, in games and athletics, in the famous Wandsworth School choir, in dramatic activities which Raymond encouraged, all the students mixed together, whatever their courses and direction. Standards were raised, as Raymond predicted they would be. In September 1956, he wrote 6 years later,

> By unselective entry 410 boys of 11 plus were admitted to Wandsworth school in London. In September 1961, 130 of them entered the sixth form, a proportion which a few years ago would have been respectable in a grammar school ... Boys from every one of the 14 forms of 1956 entrants reached the sixth and from nine of these fourteen forms the academic sixth.

Only 62 of the original 410 entrants had the IQ of 115 or over that distinguishes the grammar category. 'And yet just over 70 per cent not only stayed beyond the compulsory age but continued into and mostly completed a fifth year.' No wonder he titled the article: 'Comprehensive School – a Pattern of Achievement'.[17]

Such, then, was Raymond's contribution to the concept of the comprehensive school, as realised in his own school in the late 1950s and early 1960s. In the twenty years which followed his retirement, when chairing the *Forum* Editorial Board, his thinking did not stand still – indeed he was one of those rare people who seemed to get more radical as he grew older, certainly he did not ossify. He took the chair, for instance, at the massively popular conference *Forum* organised in 1966 on the whole issue of non-streaming – or mixed ability grouping – in comprehensive schools; a movement which some saw as a logical development from comprehensive reorganisation. He was profoundly interested in the new models developing outside London, for instance Countesthorpe in Leicestershire whose successive heads, Tim McMullen and John Watts, contributed their thinking to *Forum*, based on what many would regard as a development of Raymond's original ideas and model. He certainly recognised the need for new approaches to hold the interest and ensure the involvement of new generations of students, subject to new influences and so generating a new outlook on the world. Although fully comprehensive in its intake (though for boys only), Wandsworth was not, of course, an inner-city school and Raymond certainly realised that the problems these schools face today require new solutions.

Having traced the movement to comprehensive education through the thinking and experience of Raymond King, what, now, of the challenge to comprehensive education in the 1980s, in the unending struggle to realise secondary education for all? Although the times are not propitious, circumstances can change, and be changed through our action. It is as well, therefore, that those closely involved in this issue should define, and redefine objectives. Only so can we hope to hold, or to regain, the initiative.

First, then, what comprehensive schools? Raymond's whole life struggle was directed to attempting to ensure that we in this country would construct a school system that was truly *national* in its scope and structure. That was why he was and remained so sharply opposed to the maintenance of an independent system of fee-paying schools quite outside local authority systems; and that was why he deliberately and systematically set out to transform his own school as a comprehensive school – a model in miniature, as he hoped, of what might be a national system.

The creation of a truly national system of education through the conscious development of comprehensive schooling, must surely remain the objective – as opposed to current policy which, through the assisted places scheme and in other ways, attempts deliberately to shore up the private sector at the expense of the public, or maintained system of schools, quite apart from more 'radical' talk and rumours of wholesale privatisation. In all sorts of ways, comprehensive systems are now under attack. Raymond's policy in the present circumstances (and I am sure I can speak for him here) would be not only that of strengthening the defence of existing systems – of all that has been gained over the last 20 years and more – but to take the struggle into what might be called enemy territory, and work for the *extension* of comprehensive systems until they genuinely form a *national* system of education. We need again, as he said to London teachers, when discussing this issue in 1964, 'a revival of the spirit of 1942'. This was a time when just such perspectives were being advanced with wide popular support. In this connection we may surely take heart from the events at Solihull, where deliberate attempts to put the clock back 50 years have met with strong resistance from parents, teachers and others, determined to retain their comprehensive system.

Second, a re-think of the nature of nature of comprehensive education is urgently necessary, together with structural changes, especially in the examination system which still reflects the divisive and élitist structures of the past. This re-thinking is, of course, being undertaken in London by the Hargreaves Committee (ILEA). Comprehensive schools must cater for *all* students, whatever their gender, ethnic or class differences. All need assistance to develop not only the basic skills in literacy and numeracy, but also to gain access to that selection from our culture which holds the key to knowledge and so to autonomous and effective action and living in the contemporary world.

This re-thinking is a major undertaking, and the sharpness of the problems involved, particularly in our inner cities, cannot be under-estimated. How can we establish a common curriculum, or core, appropriate to young people at the turn of the century? How far do we need national or local authority guidelines – and by what democratic means should these be established? How far should it be left to individual schools to establish their own curricula in the light of such guidelines? Malcolm Skilbeck, now Chair of the World Education Fellowship, has recently argued for the establishment of a national forum to hammer out these questions, now that the Schools Council has been summarily abolished. The challenge to educators, Skilbeck argues, 'is to locate core curriculum analysis in terms, not just of *areas* of experience, but of learning *processes* and the type of learning *environments* which may best sustain those processes'.[18] If we think in terms of a common core in this sense for all between the ages of 11 and 15 or 16; if schools are left free to adapt this to local circumstances and interests so that the activities and learning undertaken have meaning and relevance for students in specific areas and conditions; if we can transform the assessment system so that it reinforces such learning instead of distorting it (as at present), then we can surely find the way forward – as indeed many schools are already – in spite of all the constraints still existing. Here, then, is the major challenge to the comprehensive school.

Linked with this is the perspective, seen as crucial since the inception of the movement, of reducing and so far as possible abolishing internal differentiation processes within schools; at least, such differentiation as leads to qualitatively different educational experiences for whole groups of pupils, as the obsolete system of streaming certainly did and as the new Technical and Vocational Education Initiative threatens to do. When we argue for a common core we are not arguing for the imposition of the same curriculum for everyone either in the system as a whole or within individual schools. We are arguing that all should have access to the knowledge, culture and skills all require in contemporary society. There is room, in such a system, as many schools are showing, for individual students to find their own direction with the help and guidance of teachers. Such individualisation, within a common perspective, may be the way forward; though I personally agree with David Hargreaves that our system has made too great a fetish of individualism and that what is needed now is a more organic approach involving groups of students working together on common problems rather than the totally individualised work-sheet approach on common problems which, I hope, has had its day.[19] Linked with this perspective is our heightened awareness of the dangers of gender and ethnic discrimination, and the clear and evident need consciously to overcome practices of the past which have narrowed the opportunities offered to female students in particular (but in some areas also to males) and particularly to members of ethnic minorities.

There are two other points, both issues on which Raymond felt strongly. First, the development of comprehensive schools as communities, and, taking it further, as community schools. As mentioned earlier, Raymond saw the comprehensive school possibly as leading to the school as a community function. The movement to comprehensive education was, in fact, a grass-roots movement, at least at its inception. It still has the potential of recapturing that characteristic, and, I suggest, this is the direction it should go, as indeed it is in various parts of the country. This opens out the possibility of transforming the system into a truly popular system of comprehensive schools, serving and controlled by local communities within local authority systems. We need, I suggest, to gather and evaluate the experiences of community schools in different parts of the country, and so find the way to enhance local and popular control of schooling. Schools can only gain strength from such contact; once the school is isolated from the community it becomes immediately vulnerable to forces which do not and cannot have popular objectives in mind.

The second point is linked with this – democratisation, both within the school, and in terms of its external control. If our objective is popular community control, then within the school there is the need to enhance opportunities for participation in decision making to the staff as a whole (including the younger and newer recruits) and also involving the students; that is, moving in a collegial direction. There have been a number of striking developments here over the last few years, but progress in general remains slow. There is an enormous fund of professional expertise among the teachers, and forms of control must tap this source of energy and innovation rather than inhibit it. Admittedly there are difficulties here, especially in the larger urban schools. But, if we are bracing ourselves for a new leap forward, then it is necessary to harness all the energy and enthusiasm that can be found to gain the force and power to make the changes that are so urgently needed today.

Such, then, is our perspective, based very much on Raymond's thinking, and on its development after retirement. The comprehensive system as a national system; a restructured common core of activities for all between the ages of 11 and 15 or 16; the abolition of all forms of segregation within the school relating to so-called 'abilities', or to gender and ethnic differences; the development of the comprehensive school as a community school or function; democratisation of control both externally and within the school. These are all objectives that Raymond strove for and sought to achieve. Single-minded, sure-footed (his own term), *resolute*, Raymond pioneered the road in a way few could equal. 'I am not alone in believing Raymond King to have possessed greater intellectual and moral stature than anyone else I have known', writes Roy Waters, members of his staff at Wandsworth, a London head and later a district inspector for the ILEA. 'Nor will I be alone in remembering his encouragement and deep kindness. I heard of his death with sorrow; but I rejoice in having known him.'[20] He surely deserved the description I quoted at the start. He was a true hero of comprehensive education.

Notes

1. I am indebted to Dr Peter Searby, of the Cambridge University Department of Education, for this information.
2. *Forum*, Vol. 22, No. 1, Autumn 1979.
3. Brian Simon, *The Politics of Educational Reform, 1920 to 1940*, London, 1974, pp. 257–60.
4. *Forum*, loc. cit.
5. Simon, op. cit., p. 195.
6. *Forum*, loc. cit.
7. Ibid.
8. Ibid.
9. *Forum*, Vol. 1, No. 1, Autumn 1958.
10. Ibid.
11. Personal letter to the author.
12. *The Comprehensive School* (nd 1950), published by the NEF.
13. *Forum*, Vol. 22, No. 1.
14. *Forum*, Vol. 1, No. 1.
15. *Forum*, Vol. 26, No. 1, Autumn 1983.
16. In 'Educating the Non-Scholastic', *Forum*, Vol. 4, No. 1, Autumn 1961, Raymond King described vividly some of the work done with this group.
17. *Forum*, Vol. 5, No. 1, Autumn 1962.
18. Malcolm Skilbeck, 'Core Curriculum Revisited', *Forum*, Vol. 26, No. 1.
19. David Hargreaves, *The Challenge for the Comprehensive School*, 1982.
20. *Forum*, Vol. 26, No. 1.

8

Marx and the Crisis in Education

In November 1976 the then Prime Minister, Jim Callaghan, in a speech (significantly) at Ruskin College, Oxford, initiated what came to be called the 'Great Debate' on education. I use the word 'significantly' because it was, of course, at Ruskin College that there took place one of the classic ideological struggles over the content of education – back in 1909. The great issue was whether economics should be taught from the angle of the working class – that is, from that of Marxism – or whether the economic theory purveyed to the adult, mature students from the trade union movement should consist entirely of bourgeois apologetics. The struggle escalated to raise sharply the question of control – whose college was it and who should run it? The outcome is, of course, well known. Following the students' strike there followed, first, the formation of the Plebs League, then the establishment of the Central Labour College, from all of which emerged the National Council of Labour Colleges, which played an important part in labour movement education for very many years.

It is appropriate, then, that Marx himself should intervene in this debate, if only, of necessity, in surrogate form. We meet today to discuss the question of the crisis in education on the anniversary of Karl Marx's death, and it is clear that circumstances have made it an appropriate choice for the Memorial Lecture. Perhaps we can use this opportunity to stand back a little from immediate pressures, to go back to

---

The Marx Memorial Lecture for 1977.

Marx himself to see how he dealt with related issues in his time, and to consider what guidelines we can find applicable to our present predicament.

While it is true that Marx wrote little specifically about education as such – in the sense of analysis and interpretation of institutionalised education – it is certainly the case that Marx's analysis in the fields of economics and politics, of the role of classes and class conflict in social evolution; his formulation, and application, of the principles of historical materialism, as well as of the basic principles of dialectics, and above all his analysis of the nature of man and his potentialities – all this and more bears directly on the field of education which, especially in advanced industrial countries, fulfils profoundly important social functions. Marx's works and his activities, therefore, provide us with a standpoint from which an evaluation of the current situation can be made.

But two points should be made at the start. In a short article like this, only certain issues can be tackled. It is necessary to select those aspects of Marx's thinking that appear most directly relevant to contemporary educational issues, leaving many others aside for want of space. Second, I am conscious, given the wealth of material only now becoming easily available with the publication of the *Collected Works* in English, of my inadequacy to take on this task, which can only be regarded as a preliminary clearing of the ground. I very much hope, and indeed it is essential, that these and other aspects of Marx's approach to education will be taken up and developed in a more penetrating way by others in the future.

1

Is there a crisis in education? I suggest there is. It finds expression in three areas. First, in what might be termed the economic, fiscal and administrative area. Second, in the field of ideology; and third, arising from these, in what might generally be termed the political arena – I refer here particularly to the question of control – who does, or should control the schools? Or to put it another way, *To Whom Do Schools Belong?* – the title, incidentally, of a book written 30 years ago by an experienced Director of Education who was also a historian.

The instability of capitalism, the impossibility of planning in the light of domination by the market and the anarchic conditions of production, the consequent lack of any overall perspective in terms of social development – all this is reflected in the field of education which is particularly vulnerable to succeeding economic crises. Today the insistent pressure from central and some areas of local government radically to reduce expenditure on education is a direct reflection of the current economic crisis of capitalism – one experienced with special sharpness in this country.

Related to this is the fiscal crisis – epitomised in the financial problems facing local authorities, due partly to the inadequacy of the rate support grant – the central government's component of educational and other expenditure in support of moneys raised from the rates – which has recently been very substantially reduced. Hence the massive cuts being effected by local authorities in their educational budgets; cuts which, it is estimated, 'will have catastrophic effects on public services and education in particular'.[1]

These cuts are felt in the schools and colleges in the form of increased pupil-teacher ratios (or larger classes), reduced capitation grants (covering books, paper, and other resources essential to teaching), reduced welfare services (school meals and milk), and so on. All this is a direct reflection of the instability of capitalism, as well as of its lack of serious concern for the educational welfare of the people.

But this economic and fiscal crisis is compounded by the effects of local government reorganisation and by the corporate management techniques that came with it. Conceived, perhaps laudably, as a means of ensuring rational use of resources, its objective significance has been to downgrade education and leave it especially vulnerable to further economies and cuts on the part of local Pecksniffs who have always wanted to cut the publicly maintained system of education down to size. There is little doubt that this was its deliberate objective, and that this also was seen as one of the means by which educational development could be curbed. Whatever the truth of that, the system has certainly led to confusion and inefficiency, highlighted in the resignation of the Avon Director of Education on this specific issue late in 1976.

A group of experienced and leading directors have sharply raised the question as to whether, given these developments, local government can continue to run school systems, and are actively searching for new, to them more satisfactory, means of control which allow for positive developments and responsible democratic management. The labour movement should take note of this as it is an important issue, but the point to stress here is that the combination of economic and fiscal crisis with the effects of local government reorganisation enhances the crisis facing education as a whole.

This is the context of the crisis – but it goes deeper than this. There have always been ideological disputes in the field of education and, given its importance as a social function, there are always bound to be. But over the last few years these have reached a new level. A characteristic aspect of this is the involvement of the mass media (the popular press and television) in a big way in what are basically ideological issues, though with clear political overtones. I refer as examples not only to the Black Paper phenomenon (which is specifically ideological), nor to the massive exploitation of Jensen and Eysenck's fundamentally reactionary ideas on intelligence, race and class, but also to the way the mass media exploited the small-scale research project carried through at Lancaster University by Neville Bennett,[2] and to the exploitation by the press of the Tyndale dispute in London.

These indicate that there is today a sharp conflict over the nature of education and its processes, covering both the content of education and its methodology, as well as its control. At the height of the hysteria triggered off by the exploitation of the Bennett research and the Auld report on Tyndale, that responsible journal of the establishment, *The Times*, talked of the 'wild men of the classroom' who must be brought to heel, implicitly labelling all primary school teachers in this way. In the privileged and sombre recesses of that obsolete institution, the House of Lords, Noel Annan released a flood of vituperation against one of the Tyndale teachers, describing him as an evil man whose uncontrolled activities – if allowed wider scope – could lead to disaster. All this lay behind the Prime Minister's Ruskin speech and sparked the so-called 'Great Debate'. This ideological conflict raises fundamental questions as · to the nature and purpose of schooling in capitalist society. The economic and fiscal crisis, then, is compounded by an ideological crisis.

If we place the present crisis in its recent historical setting it may help us to orientate ourselves. One aspect is certainly disenchantment on the part of the ruling forces in society with the efficacy of purely educational measures in softening deep-seated social and economic conflicts. This was highlighted in particular in the United States with the supposed failure of the Headstart and Follow Through programmes which (according to some) did not achieve the objectives of overcoming, through education, the social and economic disadvantages of the poorest sections of the community (predominantly blacks). This somewhat premature conclusion was compounded by large-scale educational surveys which purported to show that 'schools make no difference' – a convenient doctrine for those who wish to cut back on education, whether for economic or political seasons, and one which prepared the way for the economic attacks on education.

In this country the so-called boom period of the 1960s presaged by Wilson's 'white hot revolution', led to the expansion of higher education with government support, to the partial establishment of comprehensive secondary education with at least, for the first time, some official support so that it broke through to become, by now, the leading system in the maintained sector; and to the modification of the rigid inner school streaming and differentiating systems inherited from the past. It has been following this period of relative advance that, in the 1970s, have succeeded the increasingly sharp economic and ideological attacks referred to at the start.

These latter advances, the impetus for which, it is worth recalling, seldom came from above (from the government), but from below, particularly in the insistent pressure of the labour movement determined to achieve comprehensive education, and from teachers and others who, through their own experience, increasingly abandoned streaming and differentiating systems within the schools, carried the perspective of further radical changes. It is fear of this advance, I suggest, which lies at the basis of the current crisis, and which gives it its overwhelmingly political form today. As the lid comes down, aspirations which were beginning to find realisation in the school system are suppressed – more or less forcibly. So the conflict is necessarily sharpened, raising as the fundamental question – that I mentioned at the start – to whom *do* schools belong?

If the attempt is now being made to establish central control from above, then for the labour movement and its allies is not the crucial question now *how to enter effectively into the system and transform it?* And this raises the question as to what scope there is in modern capitalist society to do just this? What is the relation between education and the state? These are important issues, basically political in character. It is here particularly that I want to look at how Marx dealt with such questions in his day. Because for Marx also, when he turned his attention to education, it was these questions that he regarded as of paramount importance.

2

The first point to clarify is precisely this: what was Marx's own attitude to the public provision of education, and what was his view as to the role of the state in making this provision? These are both issues on which, fortunately, we have a clear expression of Marx's views, and shortly I will turn to these.

But first it will help us to orientate ourelves to this topic if we look first, briefly, at Marx's attitude to a closely related question; that is, to the contemporary struggle for the shortening of the working day – itself a precondition for the wider provision of education. As is well known and fully documented, Marx stood very firmly in favour, and fully supported, the long-drawn struggle for the limitation of the hours of labour, first to 10 hours, and later for the eight-hour day (all this is fully documented in the chapters on the Factory Acts in *Capital*). In his well-known Instructions for the delegates to the Geneva Congress of the International Working Man's Association in 1867, Marx spelt this out as imperative, 'a preliminary condition', as he wrote, 'without which all further attempts at improvement and emancipation must prove abortive'. The limitation of the working day, he insisted, 'is needed to restore the health and physical energies of the working class, that is, the great body of the nation, as well' (and I stress this) 'as well as to secure for them the possibility of intellectual development, sociable intercourse, social and political action'.[3]

The achievement of this measure he saw as a practical possibility in the conditions of class struggle. By carrying through a mass movement with this as its objective, Marx understood that the organised working class had shown itself capable of grasping a specific issue and, in fighting for it, of bringing about a transformation of the situation which itself opened the way for further advance. How else do we interpret Marx's famous assessment that the winning of the Ten Hours Act in 1846 was 'the victory of a principle'; that this was 'the first time that in broad daylight the political economy of the middle class succumbed to the political economy of the working class'.[4]

In just the same way, and on the same occasion, Marx argued strongly for the provision of mass, popular education – that provision (and I stress the word provision) to be made through the state. 'The more enlightened part of the working class,' he wrote in 1867, 'fully understands that the future of its class, and, therefore, of mankind, altogether depends upon the formation of the rising working generation.' 'They know that, before everything else, the children and juveniles must be saved from the crushing effects of the present system.'

'This can only be effected by converting *social reason* into *social force*, and, under the given circumstances, there exists no other method of doing so, than through *general laws*, enforced by the power of the state. In enforcing such laws, the working class do not fortify government power. On the contrary, they transform that power, now used against them, into their own agency. They effect by a general act what they would vainly attempt by a multitude of isolated individual efforts.'[5] Here again, then, we have the concept of *transformation* through struggle.

There can be no doubt whatever that Marx (and for that matter, also Engels) placed great importance on the struggle of the working class for the means to education for their children. No one who has seriously studied Marx's work, for instance

Capital, can doubt this. But the question is, how did Marx envisage that such education could be provided, and, above all, what was his view as to the control of education?

Marx realised, as we have seen, that the only means by which effective public provision could be made was by utilising the power of the state. He develops this approach very clearly in the section on education in the *Critique of the Gotha Programme* – a section, incidentally, which occurs centrally in that dealing with the state where he held that the programme was sadly deficient.

Marx thoroughly objected to the formulation in the programme which demanded the provision of 'elementary education *by* the state'. This, for Marx, was 'completely objectionable'. The programme of the Social Democratic Party should demand that the state provide the *means* to education – not the education itself. This is the essence of Marx's point, and it is completely consistent with the viewpoint expressed earlier, to the delegates to the International.

The state is the appropriate body to define and even enforce certain regulations; for example, qualifications of the teaching staff, the subjects to be taught, and so on. It should also employ inspectors 'to supervise the observance of these regulations' (as Marx put it); but this, said Marx, is something quite different from appointing the state as 'educator of the people'. Rather (he adds) 'government and church should alike be excluded from all influence in the schools'. Far from the state educating the children, it is inversely 'the state that could do with a rude education by the people'.[6]

Here we have the essence of Marx's demand; and his standpoint in relation to the education of the people. The means for this education can only and must be provided by the state. It is in line with this thinking that, having achieved the means to elementary education, the working class is also right to fight for the extension of this provision into secondary and higher education. But it is certainly not enough to do this alone; to rest satisfied with the gradual extension of the means to education – as some on the left have done and do today. There is also the question of control, and so of the nature and general tendency of the system of education that is brought into being.

Marx held the view that it was entirely objectionable (from the standpoint of the working class) if the state in capitalist society arrogated to itself the right directly to control the education of the workers. This was his main point of criticism of the Gotha programme. To ensure that the means of education are provided by a general law, he wrote, 'is something quite different from appointing the state as educator of the people'. By framing the question in this way, Marx is directing attention precisely to the question of control.

Marx did not develop this theme so far as I am aware, and we must be wary of putting words into his mouth, but is it not evident that Marx envisaged some form of popular, perhaps local and democratic, control over education? His specific references in this context to the United States and Switzerland, where at this time education was not provided by the state, but through locally elected school boards and similar organis- ations, is a clear indication of this. What he was objecting to was the proposition in the Gotha programme that laid the way open to supporting state control in the highly centralised Prusso-German state (as he put it) which was the reality the German Social Democrats faced.

This is how Marx dealt with the question in his day. And if we analyse objectively the position in Britain today, it is evident that the state, as such, does not control education in this sense – or at least does not as yet do so. The system of education is directly administered by authorities elected locally, each with its own administrative staff, within the administrative and statutory structure determined by law (through Parliament). The teachers are employed by these authorities – they are not employed directly by the state nor by the central government. Neither state nor central government lays down by law what should be taught, nor how it should be taught.

Nevertheless – and this is the point I want to stress – powerful voices are now being raised (taking advantage of the current crisis) to demand just that centralisation of power over the process of education that Marx warned most strongly against. To some extent, it could be argued, the crisis is being deliberately fuelled with this as the desired outcome. Those who support this proposal, and they include leading officials in the Department of Education and Science itself, are clearly making a bid to bring education more directly under the immediate control of the state. We should recognise that this is the objective significance of such demands. And, if we are to be guided by examining how Marx dealt with the same issue in his day, then, like him, we should strongly and consistently oppose any such tendencies.

3

It is, of course, the case that, since Marx wrote on the subject roughly 100 years ago, there has been a considerable expansion of the state's bureaucratic apparatus concerning education – as well as a constant and discernible move towards centralisation. But is it right to go as far as many do today, sometimes claiming to speak as Marxists, in the evaluation of the whole system of education as a function controlled by the state, and reducible to the simple reproduction of existing social relations? Or is it right, from a Marxist standpoint, to characterise the existing system and all previous systems as operating solely to legitimise the status quo?

Are the Althusserians right when they define education as the means by which the ideology of the ruling class is assimilated by the rising generation – as, as Althusser puts it, an Ideological State Apparatus (ISA), and leave it at that? Are these people right when they tell teachers and others that, whatever forms or procedures they adopt in school or classroom, they can do *nothing* to transform the situation? That they are, in fact, mere cogs in an other-directed machine?

In my view, interpretations of this kind, popular among academic sociologists, but having a certain influence and presented under the banner of Marxism, have little in common with Marx's own views on these questions. There is nothing in Marx's writing, so far as I am aware, which indicates that he would 'place' education as part of the oppressive apparatus of the state, not open to any influences which could bring about its transformation – given that the external conditions are ripe. In any case this kind of thinking and interpretation seems alien to Marx's whole approach, particularly in that it ignores the dialectical, and, one might add, the historical nature of his thinking and analysis.

We could consider this both from the angle of the structure of educational systems, and from that of their content and ethos. As far as structure is concerned, Marx's social and political analysis would lead us to suppose that educational systems reflect class differences – to put it briefly (and certainly my own work in the history of education indicates that this is the case). But what is there fixed and final about that?

Marx also showed that the relations between different social classes change as a result of human action conditioned by economic and technological development. Indeed Marx's whole thinking and analysis of capitalist society led him to the conclusion that revolutionary change is not only possible but, given the conditions (both economic and political), inevitable.

The hegemony of one class (or alliance of classes) gives way to that of another; and in the course of such revolutionary change the previously oppressed class becomes dominant, ushering in a new economic-social formation – that is, socialism.

If that is your perspective as a Marxist, how can you hold and propagate the view that the working class and its allies have not the power, the ability and the potential force to transform social institutions? To represent the working class or labour movement as cribbed, cabined and confined for all time within the rigid bonds of class structuring and dominant ISAs is not only to disarm the working class in this struggle, it is to distort Marx's main and most important teaching about the nature of society and the means and possibilities of change.

Far from seeing the working class as the passive subjects (as it were) of a system of education provided and controlled by the state (representing the bourgeoisie) – the picture presented by some analysts – Marx clearly entertained (and promulgated) the perspective of *control over the system by the working class and its allies.* He clearly held the view that the working class and its allies must make use of the means to education provided by the state – must enter and transform the system so that it directly meets their own needs. That is the clear implication of his insistence that neither government nor church should control the system of education itself. And this is surely the lesson for us today. And in parenthesis one might add that the last thing the working class and its allies must do is to follow the advice of Ivan Illich and others and set out to destroy the school system as the first step in introducing the convivial utopia they claim would follow. From the Marxist angle this is very clearly the wrong target.

Much the same analysis is relevant to the problem of the nature or content of education – its general ethos and direction. This is a difficult question to deal with briefly and I must confine myself to some leading points. In his Instructions to the Delegates at the Geneva Congress Marx set out briefly his ideas on this topic. 'By education', he said, 'we understand three things', first 'mental education', second 'bodily' or what we would now call physical education, and thirdly tech- nological training which, he said, 'imparts the general principles of all processes of production, and simultaneously initiates the child and young persons in the practical use and handling of the elementary instruments of all trades'. 'The combination,' he adds, 'of paid productive labour, mental education, bodily exercise and polytechnic training will raise the working class far above the level of the higher and middle classes.'[7]

These ideas, put briefly here – almost in a kind of shorthand – cannot be dismissed as anachronistic, even if circumstances have changed considerably since they were formulated. They arise logically from Marx's whole analysis and interpretation of human social evolution. Marx saw human development as the product of labour on the one hand, and of knowledge on the other.

It is through social productive labour that human beings develop their specifically human qualities – speech and the capacity for thought and planning, the many-sided skills and abilities that developed in close relation with their increasing penetration both into nature and society – that is, knowledge. Hence the emphasis on productive labour and polytechnical education as essential aspects of education. 'There can be no doubt,' wrote Marx in *Capital*, 'that when the working class comes to power, as inevitably it must, technical instruction, both theoretical and practical, will take its proper place in the working-class schools.'[8] It is also worth noting the stress on physical education, which Marx shared with Robert Owen, whose educational practice he holds up as a model in *Capital*.

But what of the content of what Marx defined as 'mental education'? We cannot know precisely what Marx meant by this, since he does not elaborate on it, but presumably he had in mind what we would now call cognitive development – the development of the capacity for systematic, generalised thought, of human beings' highest mental characteristics. Marx says nothing about the content of this education (apart from the insistence on polytechnical education) which must, in any case, be determined in the light of contemporary knowledge in the natural sciences, the social sciences and the humanities, as well as in the field of technology. And this raises the question of the ideological (in the sense of distorting) components of that knowledge.

It is perfectly true that Marx held that the dominant ideas in any epoch are the ideas of the dominant class; if this is accepted it follows that such ideas inevitably penetrate education. But does this mean that, equally inevitably, the ideas of the dominant class must *always* dominate in the field of education? Clearly this depends on under whose control the educational process is carried on – hence, surely, the extreme importance (and primary significance) of Marx's position on this latter question already discussed.

But we should also remember that Marx warned specifically (as did Engels later) against too mechanical (or 'technicist') a view of the relations between superstructure and base. He recognised (as after all he was in a good position to) that the class struggle is reflected in ideological struggle; that new classes develop their own ideological outlook and fight to achieve hegemony, just as the French Encylopaedists did before the French revolution and the Marxists did in Russia before 1917. Indeed, we saw a good example of this at the start of this lecture in the struggle over the content of education at Ruskin College leading to the Ruskin strike and formation of the Plebs League.

So again the conclusion is that there is nothing fixed and determined in this field either – that the dominant ideology (or ISA), representing the interests of the dominant class in capitalist society, can be challenged, and challenged successfully, given the conditions – the general political and social context.

And it is precisely to transform the nature of the education given in the public system – its content and ethos – that must be a primary objective of the labour movement.

This involves a critical analysis of the ideological components of knowledge – particularly in the social sciences – which form the subject matter of school education and so the material in terms of which mental development takes place, and an insistence that this subject matter should be cleansed, so far as possible, from ideological components in order to present to pupils and students a correct reflection of reality rather than a distorted view whose object is to buttress existing class interests and relations. The aim must be to define a content of education which both provides access to knowledge (involving a grasp of symbolic systems necessary for all – especially language and mathematics), and which systematically encourages mental development through promoting an understanding of both nature and society as they really are.

4

Since this is the Marx Memorial Lecture, it is worth developing this theme with a reference to Marx's own self-education – not necessarily as a model of what he would wish for others, but as indicating what he held to be of value. In his well-known speech to the Youth Leagues on education, where he stressed the need for the working class 'to take for ourselves the sum total of human knowledge', Lenin stressed the fact that Marx himself developed 'Communist theory, the science of Communism' because he 'took his stand on the firm foundations of human knowledge which had been gained under capitalism'. Lenin refers to the fact that Marx's elucidation of the laws of development of human society was based on

the most exact, most detailed, most profound study of capitalist society with the aid of preceding knowledge, which he had thoroughly assimilated. He critically studied all that had been created by human society, and did not ignore a single point of it.[9]

This, of course, is certainly the case. The three main sources of Marx's outlook (and method) were identified by Lenin as German philosophy, English political economy and French socialism. But quite apart from his immensely wide reading and study in these and related fields, Marx had a fascinated interest and love for world literature and had himself been brought up a classical scholar. 'Just as his own scientific work mirrored a whole epoch,' writes his biographer, Franz Mehring, 'so his literary favourites were those whose creations also mirrored their epoch; from Aeschylus and Homer to Dante, Shakespeare, Cervantes and Goethe.' According to his son-in-law, Lafargue, Marx read Aeschylus in the original Greek at least once a year. 'He was always a faithful lover of the ancient Greeks,' writes Mehring, adding that he would have scourged those contemptible souls from the temple who would have prevented the workers from appreciating the culture of the classic world.

Lafargue wrote of Marx that he could read all the leading European languages and write in three (German, French, English), seeing a foreign language as 'a weapon in the struggle for life'; at fifty Marx learned Russian in order to read Pushkin, Gogol, Shchedrin. Late in life he made a detailed study of Shakespeare's use of language. Marx was able to recite whole scenes from Shakespeare from memory, as well as long passages from the *Divine Comedy*, 'of which', according to Liebknecht, 'he knew almost the whole by heart'.[10]

These points are made since they are relevant here; they help to establish, or give body to, Marx's outlook on science, culture and knowledge generally – the extent to which he himself 'appropriated' human knowledge, how he prepared himself to obtain access to 'the sum total of human knowledge', as Lenin put it. To some extent they indicate his attitude to education and its function – to what he meant by the simple phrase 'mental development'.

If Marx would have 'scourged from the temple' anyone seeking to deprive the working class from access to the culture of classical antiquity, this can be taken, in the modern context, to imply that Marx would have taken the same attitude to proposals (widespread among some wearing 'radical' garments today) that the working class, or their children, should be denied access to the most valuable, important and precious aspects of science and culture, to be fobbed off with entertainment and anodynes or firmly kept within their own immediate environment, cultural or material – a standpoint rationalised by a crude relativist view as to the nature of culture and knowledge.

I believe that the way Marx dealt with this question also in his day is highly relevant to this key issue today – how and in what direction should the nature of education be transformed so that it begins genuinely to meet the interests and needs of the working class and to provide full scope for mental development.

5

I have dealt so far with Marx's attitude to the provision of education for the working class, and with its content, bringing out Marx's view as to the role of the state in the provision of the means to education, of the importance of democratic control, as well as discussing Marx's own views as to the nature of education.

But what, now, of the power of education to bring about human change, and what of the nature of the educational process itself? What was Marx's attitude to these crucial theoretical questions, now regarded as highly controversial? It must already be clear that Marx placed immense importance on education in terms of human development – I have already quoted his statement that the future of the working class, 'and therefore of mankind, altogether depends upon the formation of the rising working generation', and his statement that, if the kind of education he outlined could be won – that is, an all-round education linked closely to life (one in sharp contrast to the narrow academic abstracted type of education typical of bourgeois conceptions and practice at that time) – that such an education would 'raise the working class far above the level of the higher and middle classes'. These are already clear statements of Marx's belief in the power of education to effect human change.

In taking this standpoint, Marx was in the classic tradition of English materialist philosophy. It was John Locke who held that nine parts in ten of what someone becomes is due to his or her education, basing himself, of course, on a materialist interpretation, as set out in his *Essay on Human Understanding*, as to how man's knowledge, attitude and, indeed, character are formed through the impact of the external world on the senses. Here lies the basis of the Marxist theory of reflection, elaborated, following the work of Locke, and particularly Hobbes, through the crucial formulation of associationist theory by David Hartley, to the outlook of a Joseph Priestley and particularly of the French Encyclopaedists, or *philosophes*, such as Helvétius.

It was this outlook and its implications for human and social development that is so effectively summarised by Marx in *The Holy Family*. Here he spells out the perspective of building the educative society deriving from this view of the relation of men to society – and to the external world.[11] The early Utopian socialists, both French and English, assimilated and developed this standpoint while Robert Owen, of course, attempted to create just such a formative society in his co-operative communities.

But Marx went further than this, and this is where his importance lies in any consideration of education as a process. It was precisely the mechanistic character of classical materialism that Marx saw as defective – the fact that, according to this interpretation, man was seen as the passive product of external circumstances, the recipient of external stimuli which formed his knowledge and character. This indeed was the view of Robert Owen, expressed in his famous slogan 'Circumstances Make Man', as of the utilitarians (or philosophic radicals), Jeremy Bentham and James Mill, the former of whom held that children could be moulded 'like wet clay in the plastic hand'. The defect of this materialism, said Marx, lay in its inability to subsume the *active* side of human development, and its consequent failure to provide any consistent explanation of human and social change. In his Theses on Feuerbach, Marx notes – and here he points to his own solution – that:

> The materialist doctrine that men are products of circumstances and upbringing, and that, therefore, changed men are products of other circumstances and changed upbringing, forgets that it is men that change circumstances and that the educator must himself be educated.[12]

As is well known, Marx expressed his synthesis, or seized the contradiction, thus: 'The coincidence of the changing of circumstances and of human activity,' he wrote, 'can be conceived and rationally understood only as revolutionising practice.'[13] Human beings, through their own activity, *in the process of their activity*, both change their external circumstances and change themselves. People's consciousness and their activity are one – a unity. And activity implies both a changing consciousness and a changed external world.

Here we have the kernel of the Marxist outlook – one which links together both dialectics and materialism in the explanation of human social evolution, and of human development as such.

I will come back to a consideration of the implications of Marx's thinking as expressed here for child development – the development of abilities and skills in the process of education – very shortly, since it must surely be clear that here we have a key of profound importance for teachers and educators primarily concerned with just these aspects of human development. But first I must refer, if briefly, to a closely related matter, that is, to Marx's view as to the relationship between consciousness and language, which also has profound significance for education.

'Language,' he wrote in *The German Ideology*,

> is as old as consciousness, language *is* practical, real consciousness … language, like consciousness, only arises from the need, the necessity, of intercourse with other men.[14]

And here it is appropriate to pay tribute to the brilliant group of psychologists in the Soviet Union, pupils of Lev Vygotski, who have consciously developed Marx's approach and related it so fruitfully both to psychology and to education.

I refer in particular to the work of Professor Luria, Professor Leontiev and others who have clearly brought out in their theoretical, scientific and experimental work, both the central role played by language in mental development, and the importance of the child's activity in the formation of abilities.[15] This is to elaborate a specifically *Marxist* standpoint on education. it leads logically to emphasising the role of the teacher as educator, responsible for structuring the child's activity, and so his or her learning and development.

Hence the positive approach, in the work of Luria and others, to the development of children's abilities, mathematical, scientific, musical, artistic, provided always that the proper conditions can be created. From all this arises the firm standpoint of Marxists as to the power of education in effecting human change and development. In the first place this is based on a recognition that human development cannot be explained simply in terms of biological laws.

Human beings differ from the rest of the animal world specifically through the development of speech with its power of abstraction and generalisation. Through the use of language human beings' entire social and cultural inheritance can be passed on from generation to generation in quite a different way from the laws governing heritability in the animal world. This is clearly a matter of key importance. But in the second place, acceptance of the power of education is firmly grounded scientifically and experimentally, since Marx's day, in the empirical work of psychologists and educators both in the Soviet Union and elsewhere.

In particular this aproach forms the rational basis for the rejection of all fatalistic theories as to the limits of development characteristic, for instance, of the pseudo-science of intelligence testing (with its recent expressions of racist and class prejudice), although this also depends, of course, on a critical analysis of the unexpressed assumptions embodied in the technologies supporting these anti-human theories – and, one might add, in view of recent revelations, in a hard, cold look at the actual data adduced in their support.

With this as a basis we may touch briefly on some matters relevant to current ideological controversies in education. If it is through his or her activity that the child's consciousness is formed – the material substructure of which lies in what Luria calls 'complex functional systems' built up in the child's brain and higher nervous system – then it is the educator's responsibility both to provide for that activity and to guide it so that learning and development can most effectively take place.

The child's activity may be both physical and mental; indeed the two often stand in a close dialectical relationship with each other, as research has shown; in forming concepts of number, for instance, the actual physical movements of the hand and arm may play a decisive part at a specific stage. Again, such activity may be based not only on the manipulation of objects but also utilise visual and verbal presentations – again at different times. All this is a matter for research. But one thing is clear; learning on the part of the child can and must logically be separated from teaching – even if the role of the teacher, as already argued, is highly important. The teacher who adopts the approach that he or she alone, as the teacher, must be active – the children passive, recipient of stimuli emanating from the teacher, is falling into the old error of the mechanical materialists of the past (an error on which much of existing practice in the schools is certainly still based).

Such an approach is more likely, if one can generalise, to turn off the pupil or student than to involve him directly in the learning process. Rather the teacher's role is so to structure the child's activity as to maximise learning on the part of the child. With large classes, and lacking the necessary resources, that is difficult; hence the need to provide the teacher with the conditions necessary and with the tools of the trade. But certainly this is the approach most directly in line with the Marxist approach to teaching and learning.

It is not enough, therefore, for those who speak in the name of Marx and Marxism, to dismiss with contempt those who are seeking the way to activise the child's learning as 'trendies', nor to hold up to ridicule those who are attempting, without sufficient theoretical or practical assistance, to break away from the rigid and arid approaches of the past. Nor is it enough, to go to the other end of the spectrum, to deny altogether the need for structure or even 'interference' by the teacher in the supposed 'spontaneous' development of the child.

The first of these standpoints expresses no more than a philistine ignorance both of Marxism and of modern developments in the field of education and psychology. The second, in sacrificing all such knowledge on the altar of the child's spontaneity, leads to a kind of mushy liberalism which only adds to the confusion. Neither approach has anything to do with Marxism, as must be evident.

All this is directly relevant to the controversy over teaching styles, or ways of teaching, referred to at the start of this lecture in the way the mass media exploited Bennett's research. This was seized on by Black Paper and conservative educationists to demand a return to rigid authoritarian methods which have already shown their educational ineffectiveness and are, in effect, being proposed as a means of social control – through fear of a break out.

If we are concerned, with the *transformation* of the school, as I think we are, and as Marx conceived the problem – a transformation which bends the school system in such a way that it can act as a release of the potential energies and abilities of children in general – then I suggest we need to take up and develop in a rigorous way the clear pointers that Marx outlined in this field. The richness of Marx's ideas on this issue, their applicability to education, stand in sharp contrast to the direction of much psychological and sociological theorising today in the field of education. It is this heritage, I suggest, that has been neglected in this country, even by Marxists, and that urgently needs development.

6

This paper started by delineating the current crisis in education and analysing, briefly, its form. While it is consistently suggested (officially) that the economic difficulties facing education are the direct result of Britain's more general economic problems – in that the cut-back in educational expenditure will somehow act to improve Britain's balance of payments, free resources for profitable investment, and so on, I want to repeat my earlier suggestion that a deeper (and more accurate) interpretation lies in a *fear of education*, of its power and implications, so clearly brought out in Marx's thinking and his proposals as to the importance for the working class of educational advance. There are many indications that such a fear motivates the attacks on comprehensive education, on the move to non-streaming which opens up the school system as a whole in a new way, on the extent of teachers' freedom (in this country) to determine the content and methods of education within the primary, as also in the secondary school; many other examples could be given.

These and other movements or trends within the school system represent a genuine, if perhaps a long-term, threat in their potential development, so that what we are experiencing, I suggest, are the opening shots in what may prove to be a sharp, and possibly decisive, struggle not only to cut back the system, but to bring it more stringently, more minutely, under control from the centre – that is, *by* the state. The hysteria (that is not too strong a word) developed recently, leading to Jim Callaghan's speech and the so-called 'Great Debate' (though many feel that precise measures have already been decided on), can be seen as deliberately prepared and fanned (partly by the mass media) in order to prepare the atmosphere which could allow a takeover bid to succeed.[16]

If this is a correct interpretation, then clearly the labour movement needs to grasp its implications and take up the challenge. In these circumstances the stance of the labour movement is surely clear – and in accordance with its traditions.

First then, we should accord to the power of education that attributed to it by Marx himself, and insist on its extension in the interests of the working class and its allies.

Second, there is the question of the transformation of the system, both as regards structure and content. I have argued that this is not only a possibility but even a necessity. The labour movement should certainly reject all fatalistic ideas, derived from whatever source, as to the impossibility of such action. There can be no question that today the labour movement has such power, and this can and must be exerted in the field of education as well as elsewhere. In co-operation with the teachers, who are part of the labour movement, the need is to bring about a transformation both of the content of the educational process (what is taught) and of the methodology (how this is taught) on lines already outlined, derived directly from Marx's thinking and analysis.

Finally, and this follows from the last point, there is the question of the control of education of which Marx spoke so clearly. This points to the need to strengthen democratic systems of control without which, in any case, there can be no transformation of the schools. Local systems of education are still nominally under the control of local authorities, as I mentioned earlier. But recent events have induced a crisis in these systems, while at the same time centralising and bureaucratising tendencies are given free rein.

It is essential to counter this policy, the objectives of which are all too clear, and indeed to launch a counter-offensive against current tendencies. This means that every means must be found to strengthen local democratic control of the schools and school systems, and to provide scope for teachers, parents and school students to participate effectively in the government and control of the schools. It is impossible now to spell out what steps need to be taken to ensure this is done, nor would it be appropriate in a paper of this kind. What can be done is to point to the necessity for such action, and to the importance of pursuing an active policy in this direction.

So I conclude that a study of Marx's writings, and his actions, in one specific field can, nearly 100 years later, still provide us with an all-round understanding and with a guide to action relevant to our problems today. In other areas, to which Marx devoted much more attention, the same is certainly true. We are surely right, then, to pay tribute to his genius in the clear and penetrating analysis he was able to make in areas of fundamental significance for man's present life, and for his future. Because in a very real sense, Marx's central concern throughout his life was with human development, seen as a whole – with the evolution of human societies in the past, the present and the future. Above all, he wished to find the form of social organisation which would enable people to develop what he called their 'slumbering powers'; to shake off all one-sidedness and distortion, to develop their full humanity as all-round people; to create new forms of social living allowing the emergence of new characteristics; to enable people to enter into direct relations one with another in place of the alienation and exploitation which now separates people from one another. Such was his life's effort.

In one sense his central concern was, therefore, with the formation – the education – of humankind. If that is the overall significance of the totality of his life's work, then I suggest we need to pay very special attention to his concept of an all-round education for all closely linked to life, and to endeavour to begin to realise it through the transformation of the school, linking this integrally with the struggle in other areas, economic, industrial and political, for the transformation of society as a whole.

'Does not the true character of each epoch,' Marx once wrote, 'come alive in the nature of its children?'[17] And was not Marx's primary concern to transform capitalist society in such a way as to provide for the fullest development of human potential – children as well as adults? But for Marx, as we know, analysis was not enough; action was also necessary. Previous philosophers, if I may conclude with a well-known quotation, 'have only *interpreted* the world in different ways; the point is to change it'.

Notes

1. *NATFHE Journal*, 24 November 1976.
2. See Neville Bennett *et al.*, *Teaching Styles and Pupil Progress*, London, 1976.
3. David Fernbach (ed.), *The First International and After*, Harmondsworth, 1974, p. 87.
4. Marx's 'Inaugural Address of the International Working Men's Association', ibid., p. 79.
5. Ibid., p. 89.
6. Ibid., p. 357.
7. Ibid., p. 89.
8. *Capital*, Vol. I, London, 1977, p. 458.
9. Lenin, *Collected Works*, Vol. 31, London, 1966.
10. These quotations are taken from a volume of selections from the writings of Marx and Engels on *Literature and Art*, New York, 1947.
11. See the essay on Coleridge, p. 000.
12. Engels, *Ludwig Feuerbach*, London, 1947, p. 76.
13. Ibid., pp. 75–6.
14. Karl Marx and Frederick Engels, *Collected Works*, Vol. 5, Lawrence & Wishart, London, 1970, p. 44.
15. See, for example, A.R. Luria and F. Ia. Yudovich, *Speech and the Development of Mental Processes in the Child*, edited and translated by Joan Simon, Harmondsworth, 1971.
16. See 'Breaking School Rules', p. 221ff, where this analysis is developed.
17. Karl Marx, *Grundrisse*, Harmondsworth, 1973, p. 111.

9

Education and the Right Offensive

It is now generally agreed among the Left that the return of the Thatcher government marks a new phase in British political developments. 'Thatcherism', as Martin Jacques put it in his analysis, 'represents a new kind of global rightism. Its offensive impinges on most areas of society.'[1] The nature, rise, and above all the ideology of 'the new Right' as 'the seedbed from which Thatcherism has grown' has been acutely analysed by Andrew Gamble.[2] Gamble isolates two strands in its composition; first, the concept of the social market economy as a primary objective, involving the abandonment of government interventionism and reliance on primary market forces in determining economic development, and second, 'the new populism' – focusing on 'issues like immigration, crime and punishment, strikes, social security abuse and permissiveness'. In this connection Gamble refers to the great variety of new right-wing pressure groups which have germinated 'like dragons' teeth for the last 15 years'.

Thatcher's return was, of course, facilitated by the convergence of a number of factors following an aggressive campaign and ideological stance appealing to individualist, rather than social values. On the side of Labour the lack of any kind of socialist perspective meant that the Thatcher campaign won by default. Gamble is right in saying that the new, populist campaign and propaganda had been under way over the last 15 years – and steadily gaining in momentum. A good example of Labour's loss of the initiative, on an important social and political issue over these years is that of education. This also is the scene of a successful rightist ideological campaign initiated by the series of Black Papers from 1969,

Reprinted from *Marxism Today*, February 1980.

and cleverly exploited by the maverick populist agitator Rhodes Boyson, rewarded by appointment as a Minister of State for Education. There is no doubt whatsoever that this is an area that gained the Tories many votes, and contributed handsomely to their electoral victory. As an important area both in its own right, and in terms of educational and political strategy and tactics, these developments deserve analysis, in the attempt both to determine what went wrong and why, and to contribute towards discussion of a new perspective for the Left around which a wide popular movement may be developed.

1

In a nutshell, it is now clearly apparent that, from the early 1970s at least, Labour's educational policy, together with its supporting ideology, lost momentum and popular appeal. This, of course, was not peculiar to this particular field – it was the same in other fields of social policy (for instance, health), as well as in economic and political policy generally. In effect the crucial issue was the failure to adopt socialist policies, or policies that could clearly and definitely be presented as linking educational measures with socialist political perspectives. Instead, Labour pinned its policy to an illusory belief that persistent economic growth would allow a continuous increase in public expenditure within a mixed economy and, on this basis, espoused an egalitarian ideology rather than a socialist one. Hence the partially successful transformation to comprehensive secondary education was pursued not so much for its class significance, in terms of breaking down minority privileges and opening the perspective of more radical change, but more particularly as a limited reform motivated by Labour's objective of 'modernisation' within a mixed economy, leaving power relations unchanged.

The dominant Labour ideology motivating this reform lay in the social engineering theories of Anthony Crosland and Shirley Williams whose objectives comprised the efficient functioning of a mixed economy, requiring assimilation of the workforce to acceptance of capitalist social relations. Hence the emphasis on the need for social harmony, to be achieved by a common experience of schooling, spiced with an 'egalitarian' rhetoric. As greater proportions of the secondary school population in maintained schools were reorganised into comprehensive schools (30 per cent at the end of Labour's 1960s governments, 60 per cent at the end of Thatcher's four years at the Department of Education and Science to 1974, and 82 per cent in 1979), and as initial enthusiasm and public support began to wane, no new perspectives for more radical educational change linked to social change were, or, within this ideology, could be advanced. It was into the vacuum created by this situation that the Tory populist assault was mounted, not only on comprehensive education, but also on a whole number of related issues ('progressive' education, authority and discipline, and in particular educational 'standards') on which the Left was divided or confused. In the circumstances, this campaign proved highly successful. There are many lessons here for the Left.

A few words may be said to remind ourselves of the kind of issues which fuelled the New Right in education, and the circumstances which gave it its opportunity. The early 1960s saw a developing consensus between the more advanced (or 'progressive') Tories (epitomised by Edward Boyle) and the Labour leadership as to the necessity for educational advance, the basis of which lay both in the degree of economic growth and technological advance then experienced, and in the need for higher educational levels to meet this situation. It was a Tory Prime Minister (Home) who, on the day the Robbins report was published in 1963, announced to the country on television that the Tory government would implement the full recommendations. The Tory Minister (Boyle) steered an Education Act through Parliament in 1964 which was specifically designed to ease the transition to comprehensive education in urban areas. The leadership of both parties at this stage were concerned to encourage 'modernisation' of the educational structure while, of course, preserving the independent sector ('public' schools) inviolate. It was at this point also that considerable resources were devoted to modernisation of the curriculum through massive funding, first by the Nuffield Foundation and then by the newly formed Schools Council, of curriculum reform projects in the sciences, mathematics, etc. Through the period of Labour's 1960s governments (1964–70) comprehensive secondary education was encouraged, higher education expanded (especially teacher training), while even the neglected primary sector received a degree of attention and support reflected in the setting up of the Plowden Committee (by Boyle in 1963) which reported in a highly 'progressive' vein four years later (January 1967). Indeed that report epitomised, in a sense, Labour's dilemma. Predicating the inevitable continuance of full employment, increasing affluence, the abolition of poverty, and a constantly rising level of public expenditure, it was probably the last semi-official statement of the then popular and widespread view of continuous social/economic advance within a capitalist system, but one comprising a public sector of considerable significance. Less than a year later the harsh economic climate of the late 1960s had already called this illusory perspective into question.

It is worth recalling that, just as the *first* action of the Thatcher government of 1979 was to pass an Act repealing Labour's 1976 measure aimed at bringing recalcitrant local authorities into line on comprehensive reorganisation, so the *first* action of the Heath government of 1970 was to 'withdraw' Labour's Circular of 1965 (10/65) which pressured local authorities to introduce comprehensive reorganisation. As Secretary of State for Education, Thatcher, already emerging as a doctrinaire rightist politician, took this action (in 1970) to 'free' local authorities (as she put it), and did her best over the next four years to slow down the rate of advance towards comprehensive education. But she was quite unable to stop it, as the figures given earlier show. In fact the rate of advance, in terms of the numbers of schools and pupils, was greater under Thatcher than under the previous Labour administration. By this time comprehensive education had become a 'rolling reform'; plans made under the Labour government were coming to fruition and many Tory authorities (for instance, Leicestershire) were enthusiasticaly developing their local systems (this pride in local achievement, incidentally, should by no means be ignored).

However it was in this period that the profound world economic recession, magnified in Britain as a result of the increasingly serious weakness of our economic and industrial base, resulted in a policy of massive cuts in projected public expenditure including education. This process had already started under Labour – in 1968, for instance, the projected (and promised) raising of the school leaving age was postponed, to be implemented, incidentally, by the Tories in 1972. So the position was ambivalent, showing contradictory tendencies; Tory educational policy, involving strict control and financial retrenchment, was announced in a White Paper characteristically entitled *Framework for Expansion* (1972), and this pledged the Tories to a massive expansion of the nursery sector as proposed by the Plowden Committee (a policy that was never implemented).

In this 'betwixt and between period' (early 1970s) a general disenchantment with education as *the* palliative for social ills and discontent spread from the United States across the Atlantic; the Coleman and Jencks reports of 1966 and 1970 both supported the conclusion that schools 'made no difference' to the distribution of wealth and income, i.e. that education could not effectively bring about social change in terms of a more egalitarian – but capitalist – society. At the same time the well-known 'Headstart' programmes in the United States, which aimed to enrich the early education of the poorest sections of the population, were (prematurely) declared a failure. All this contributed to an atmosphere of lack of confidence in the value of educational reform and change which was quickly exploited by the New Right in this country who, for instance, in whipping up parental support for the defence of selective schools in areas undergoing reorganisation, had already developed something of a populist basis (particularly among the lower middle class) for their attacks on comprehensive education, as well as on 'progressive' methods, new 'integrated' curricula, non-streaming and other developments which they identified (often wrongly) with the transition to the single secondary school.

This movement received an enormous fillip from the Tyndale affair of 1975–76, when a group of teachers who espoused an extreme version of 'progressive' teaching techniques were exposed to intense mass media attacks and widespread criticism over several months or even years. The real issue at stake here, it soon became apparent, was that of control: who, in fact, is or should be responsible for what goes on inside schools – the teachers, the parents, the local authority or the state? Although the issues were confused, Tyndale provided fertile ground for the promotion of the ideological cohesion of the New Right, epitomised in the outlook expressed in the leader columns of the *Telegraph, Mirror* and *Sun* as well as *The Times*, as also on television. Indeed the whole question of control and authority in the schools was highlighted in a series of television programmes, including one presenting what was later admitted to be a very slanted view of a single comprehensive school, introduced as 'typical' of all such schools by the BBC. (The role of the mass media in this whole movement is worth investigation.)

The critique of contemporary educational developments reached a climax with the publication of the so-called 'Bennett report' in May 1976.[3] This was interpreted on television and in the press as showing that 'traditional', 'authoritarian' teachers who used methods of which the Plowden Committee, for instance, thoroughly disapproved, achieved generally better results than 'progressive' or 'informal' teachers using modern methods. (It is worth noting that this is how the results were presented by the mass media, which gave the research immense and unusual coverage, in spite of the fact that the teacher achieving the 'best' results used 'informal' or 'progressive' techniques.) This formed the background to the then Prime Minister, Jim Callaghan's Ruskin speech (October 1976), the so-called 'Great Debate' on education promulgated by Shirley Williams, and later developments – a clear but belated (and largely ineffective) attempt by Labour to steal the Tory ('New Right's') clothes and regain the initiative. That this was largely ineffective was because Labour had no clear answers to the questions raised, and no clear perspective as to the direction of development. Their reaction was to play for time, try to upset no one, and go on in the old way.

But it is not only Labour which may be criticised; the Left as a whole, fragmented (particularly in education), failed to develop agreed alternative policies uniting the struggle for educational change with relevant and realisable political perspectives. This is undoubtedly partly due to the failure of the Left to tackle theoretical or ideological issues affecting both the content and the process of education itself, and its relation to social and political change. In this context the Left in education includes the various socialist and radical groupings of teachers around such journals as *Socialist Teacher, Radical Education, Rank and File, Socialism and Education* (Labour teachers) as well as the Labour left and the Communist Party. The whole, potentially strong movement represented by these groupings, was itself split down the middle on the issues raised by the Tyndale affair relating to the control of schools and the professional rights of teachers, e.g. how far teacher control is legitimate. It was similarly split on the issue of teaching methods, or rather on the whole approach to teaching and learning, tending to accept the current dichotomies of 'progressive/traditional', 'formal/informal', and siding with one side or the other, in spite of the clear conclusion of Marxist educators, e.g. Lenin and Gramsci, on the need for structure, clarity of purpose, and the *formative* power of education. That the Tories, or rather the New Right could make the fight for 'standards' a rallying cry winning mass support is itself a criticism of Labour and the Left generally in that the ground was left open to the Right to exploit this initiative.

A political movement representing the interests of the mass of the people, as the labour movement and the Left generally does, must be concerned with standards – with ensuring at least minimum levels of literacy and numeracy – since both cover symbolic systems which are the key to all learning and culture. Yet the way was left clear for a mass, popular campaign *by the Tories* on this specific issue, even though it is apparent, from their actions since taking office, that this interest in 'standards' was largely rhetorical. Nevertheless the agitation on standards was a popular agitation which gained mass support; this was the context of the rise of Rhodes Boyson who boasted, correctly, that he could fill any hall in the country, and who, with his idiosyncratic personality and experience as a comprehensive head, was able fully to exploit the situation in the interests of the Tory backlash. It is true that every kind of fraudulent technique was used in this campaign, beginning with Cyril Burt's fictitious 'data' in Black Paper II purporting to prove a sharp decline in literacy over the last 50 years – a totally fraudulent claim but one given enormous coverage (and support) by the media. But this hardly exonerates the Left from responsibility for the failure to tangle effectively with these issues, to adopt a clear, rationally based and theoretically valid position and to make that position widely known. There is now a new opportunity, indeed necessity, to do precisely this. In the next section the nature and impact of Tory policy will be analysed before discussing the new perspective for the transformation of education as an essential aspect of the transition to socialism.

2

There is no question that the ideological assault mounted by the Tories on contemporary educational trends and developments – particularly the critique concerning 'standards', permissive methods and practices in the schools, and the like – contributed significantly to their return with a largely increased vote. It also provided the ideological base for the series of actions taken by the government since its election in May 1979. It is now clearly apparent that the main objectives of government policy are to strengthen the independent sector and to downgrade the public sector in education and starve it of resources. In particular the intention is to halt the advance to the establishment of a fully comprehensive system of secondary education and to turn back the clock. Each action of the government ties in with this general objective, and indeed the attack on education, with the aim of bringing about a decisive change to a new direction, was, significantly, given top priority with the introduction of *two* Bills on the issue within the first six months of office.

The first Bill, as already mentioned, which received Royal Assent in July 1979, declared in effect that comprehensive education was no longer 'national policy' by repealing the 1976 Act, so allowing reactionary local authorities not only *not* to reorganise their schools as comprehensive systems, but to go further and split up existing comprehensive schools to bring back the grammar/secondary modern division. Thus large authorities such as Essex and Kent withdrew proposals to go comprehensive submitted under the 1976 Act and proposed to retain their existing divided systems in wide areas of the counties concerned, while urban authorities such as Bolton and Kingston-on-Thames took similar action. The importance of this is not only that selection is retained in important areas of the country (500,000 children were still in secondary modern schools in 1977), but that it keeps the option open of a massive *reversion* to selective systems if and when this is thought to be politically (and socially) desirable. The option of splitting existing comprehensive schools into grammar and modern was, in 1980, under consideration by at least one local authority, and this course also may be encouraged.

Further actions taken by the government over the summer of 1979 were also directed at halting the movement towards comprehensive education and strengthening the independent sector. First, there was the decision, announced by the Secretary of State in June, that the proposal originally made by the Schools Council for the substitution of a single examination at 16 plus, in place of the divisive, double examinations (GCE and CSE) would not be implemented, thus actively preventing schools from developing unified and integrated courses for *all* their students between the ages of 11 and 16, when the examinations are taken. The Labour government itself had, typically, prevaricated on this issue, which has massive support in the teacher unions, setting up a committee to assess its feasibility (the Waddell committee). This committee finally reported in *favour* of the move shortly before the election. The Tory decision to retain the obsolete system inherited from the past and devised in the context of the divided system before comprehensive reorganisation is clearly directed to forcing comprehensive schools to continue operating internal systems of differentiation between pupils at the ages of 13 or 14. It is, therefore, logically in line with their whole policy.[4]

Second, the Government issued new regulations in July permitting local authorities to finance pupils (out of the rates) to attend independent schools. This was an area where Labour had been operating, to some effect, to put an end to this practice, which is a means both of retaining and reinforcing selective processes in the schools, and of shoring up independent schools. By pursuing this policy with energy, Tory dominated local authorities will be able to use public money to strengthen the independent sector, quite apart from or in addition to, the support accorded to the independent sector from the Assisted Places Scheme, analysed below.

Third, since we are dealing with these matters chronologically, the massive 'real' cuts in the rate support grant (RSG), in line with the Thatcher government's overall strategy relating to public expenditure, mean that the publicly provided system of education, in contradistinction to the private or 'independent' sector, is to be, or is already being, starved of resources – of the funds needed to carry on and improve its work. The Secretary of State argues that these cuts will not affect 'standards'; their primary targets lie in school meals and transport. But even if this is accepted, the cuts being demanded of local authorities, particularly those planned for next year and the year after, means cuts in the teaching force on a massive scale as well as in capitation grants – that is, on the money available to schools for books, paper and resources generally – that are already biting deep. Thus while the independent sector is to be reinforced financially, the public sector – where the mass of the nation's children are educated – is already being severely pruned, though this might be no more than a foretaste of what may come.

Fourth, and from the point of view of overall strategy the most important of these measures, there is the so-called 'Assisted Places Scheme' (APS) brought in in the Education Bill presented to Parliament early in 1980. This is a scheme to build a selective system in 'independent' schools by the infusion of £70 million of public money per annum – money saved from, and therefore taken from, the publicly maintained system. The scheme is to be brought in on the specious grounds that the former are, and the latter are not, capable of giving an effective education to the most advanced students.

The 12,000 to 15,000 children who will be selected *each year* for this treatment form from 2 per cent to 3 per cent of an age group, but Peter Newsam, then Director of Education for the ILEA, calculated that they form some 20 per cent of that proportion of an age group that stay on at school to study in sixth forms or colleges for 2 or more A Levels. In this sense alone the scheme comprises an extremely serious threat to the viability of advanced work in the publicly maintained system as a whole. But Newsam argues further that this proportion may turn out to be considerably higher, and this for three reasons. First, as part of the APS it is suggested that additional transfers to independent schools be arranged to take place at sixth form level (from age 16); second, local assisted places schemes such as that already being operated by the Greater Manchester Council (a Tory authority) may well multiply, whereby local authorities covering wide areas but *without* educational responsibilities set up trust funds financed from the rates and use the income to subsidise pupils at independent schools; and third, the tax rebates given to high income groups may result in greater demand for places in independent, as opposed to maintained, schools. If all these factors operate, as they well may, Newsam predicts that the consequences for advanced work (at A Level) in the maintained sector 'would be profound'. In general, within a static or declining total of resources available to education, these measures, he claims, reflect 'a shift in the balance of expenditure towards independent schools'.[5] This is certainly the case. There is little wonder, then, that this clear and vindictive attack on local maintained systems of education has aroused strong outspoken opposition on the part of the Society of Education Officers, representative of Directors of Education and Chief Education Officers throughout the country. In an unusually outspoken comment submitted to the Secretary of State they say that 'the picture of LEAs running establishments little better than good secondary modern schools, while their able children go to independent schools, is unacceptable'.[6]

But Education Bill No. 2 (now an Act) goes much further than this. Quite apart from the clauses on the Assisted Places Scheme it contains a group of clauses designed to undermine existing local comprehensive systems – to turn them into covertly selective systems giving special advantages to middle-class children whose parents are able to play the system. The technique here is to extend the scope of 'parental choice' and give it statutory backing in such a way as to ensure that 'popular' schools become middle-class enclaves while inner city schools catering for the working class go to the wall. As

Caroline Benn puts it, the 'new 11 plus' is based on the opting out of comprehensive education of the selected; the new 11 plus is 'covert, restricted, optional and socially based' – delegated (through 'parental choice') 'to individual head teachers of grammar, aided and feepaying schools'. Under the banner of slogans about 'choice' new, socially based, differentiating structures are being built into the publicly provided schools system. Through measures such as these the ground is being prepared for a decisive turn in the structure and function of the education system.[7]

No attempt will be made here to record or evaluate the total impact of government policy on education. The severe cut-back in university and higher educational finance generally (which has led to strongly worded protests by the Vice-Chancellors Committee among others), in adult education, in the Youth Opportunities and other schemes is already well known. Attention here is directed specifically to the schools. One general point may be reiterated: the claim that all these measures will not affect 'standards' in the publicly maintained sector can be seen as entirely specious. As indicated earlier, the fight on 'standards' now stands revealed as no more than a populist, rhetorical device in the fight for political power. The Tory government is not concerned with standards, but with the exercise of *control*; and this in order to remodel the educational system so that it overtly reinforces social, or class stratification.

This is entirely consistent with Tory educational policies over the last fifty years and more, though, perhaps as a result of the increasing democratic challenge in education, the policy is now being pursued with an assertiveness and vigour beyond what has been attempted in the past. There is, however, a clear parallel between current Tory policy and intentions and the actions of the Tory administration in the years 1895 to 1905. This was a decisive period in the structuring of the English educational system, when a reactionary Tory administration successfully halted a broad movement for educational advance based on democratic, locally elected School Boards, and instead imposed the selective, hierarchic system which only began to be effectively challenged in the 1960s. The democratic movement in education, in effect, then suffered a severe setback from which it took years to recover.

What we are now experiencing bears a distinct relationship to these earlier developments. The present government is now involved in a clear, overt attempt to capitalise immediately on the 1979 election success and not only to halt the swing to potentially democratic forms, but to impart a new direction to policy by deliberately strengthening and stabilising the most divisive features in the present system. It is not commonly realised that some 800,000 students of secondary school age – that is, 26.7 per cent of the total number of pupils in secondary schools – are still in 1980 in selective schools of one kind or another (selected either on wealth or 'merit'). 410,000 are in independent schools (already subsidised out of public moneys to the tune of some £130 millions in various ways), while 128,000 more are in the old direct grant (now independent) schools, with 256,000 still in selective 'grammar' schools in the maintained sector. There is still a long way to go, and many battles to be fought, before all these are brought fully into locally controlled and financed systems of education.

What is becoming clear as an aggressive class policy in education is being carried through by a government (or Cabinet) with quite appropriate educational qualifications for such measures. The Cabinet (Thatcher excluded) consists 80 per cent of public school products (30 per cent from one school alone – Eton). The overwhelming majority of Tory MPs were themselves educated at public schools. No doubt they all (including the Education Minister) send their own children to independent schools to be educated. Until recently, Tory governments at least went through the motions of showing some concern for the system of education they administered. Not so in this case. Not only is their contempt for the publicly maintained system self-evident; their determination to strengthen their own base within the independent system is also clear and blatant. This implies that their room for manoeuvre has narrowed – and points to clear weaknesses and dangers to themselves in the policy being pursued.

3

Tory policy in education, as in other areas, represents a very definite challenge to the Left. One advantage of the aggressive policy now being pursued is that the issues are becoming clear for all to see. The challenge is now to formulate an equally definite policy and strategy, covering the whole field of education, relating strategic and tactical proposals to the issue of popular control and democratisation in the struggle for socialism. The aim must be the transformation of education in the direct interests of the mass of the people, working class and middle strata alike. What is required is a popular programme, taking up the real issues which have been highlighted, and transforming them into a programme of action both on a national and (equally important) on a local basis. This involves action in four main areas.

Already a mass movement of great potential power and force is building up in the struggle against the cuts which, in education, will directly affect a high proportion of the population. In this campaign, organisations of the labour movement must initiate, and support mass, popular, local actions of protest – explaining the significance of the cuts and, in co-operation with other democratic organisations of all kinds, leading local community and neighbourhood actions in defence of the schools and schooling. The immediate issues here are the new transport fees imposed by the 1980 Education Act, the break-up and actual sabotage of the school meals service (on which much might be said), teacher and other cuts and redundancies, reductions in finance available for capitation grants, as well as increased charges for adult education and recreational activities, cuts in the Youth Opportunities Programme, and so on. Teachers, students, ancillary workers, parents and indeed the labour movement as a whole need to and are already finding new and appropriate organisational forms by which mass joint struggles may be carried through both locally and nationally demanding the reversal of policies that strike directly at the quality and value of schooling.

Through activities of this kind broad, popular alliances can be built up which, with effective leadership, should have the permanently valuable result of bringing about a much closer popular involvement in the schools and their work. Such an involvement – or alliance – between different organisations or sections of the people in defence of local systems of education and even of particular schools threatened by cuts and closure, opens out the perspective of the creation of local groupings or organisations having the knowledge and the power potentially to exercise control, in co-operation with local authorities, over local systems of education. To achieve this is an essential condition for bringing about a transformation of the schools and of education as an aspect of the transition to socialism.

This implies utilising, activating or mobilising existing democratic organisations, as well as influencing local government machinery *in support of* local systems of education, and in the process achieving the transformation of what some refer to as the 'local state' – so that it is responsive to the people's will. In this connection it is of the highest importance to the Left and the labour movement generally to defend and extend local democracy and to oppose centralising tendencies, symptomatic of Tory and Labour government policies alike.

Secondly, the challenge of contemporary Tory measures highlights the need to fight consciously and deliberately to extend the scope of the publicly provided system and to prevent the deliberate shift of resources towards the independent sector. Since the Tories have thrown down a challenge on this specific issue (with the APS), the Left are now in a strong position in terms of logic to formulate a counter challenge, and to adopt it as policy. This involves the declared and open objective of bringing about a decisive shift, in the allocation of resources, from the independent to the public sector. The following could each form points of policy: (i) cease state subsidies to independent schools now running at some £60 to £80 millions a year, in the form of school fees paid to diplomats, military personnel and others, and instead provide boarding places within the maintained sector (many are already available); (ii) remove charitable status to endowed schools (as most independent schools are, especially the most prestigious such as Eton and Harrow), by which such schools are not subject to taxation; (iii) connected with this, remove the de-rating measures on independent schools, ensuring that they pay full rates; (iv) by Act of Parliament remove the power from local authorities to set up trust funds to finance pupils at independent schools.

Each of these actions can be justified on grounds of equity (or equitable treatment) alone. But the perspective which is now raised by the Tories themselves goes further than this; it is to bring all such schools in the publicly maintained sector, and so under local and national democratic control. This would, of course, require a Parliamentary measure; but the whole issue was subject to enquiry in the 1960s by the Donnison Commission, and in any case there are powerful historical precedents for legislative action along these lines (most of the upper secondary schools in my county, Leicestershire, for instance, were originally independent – endowed – foundations. With one exception they all now form part of the local system of comprehensive schools).

Thirdly, the Left needs to agree on, and formulate, a clear and immediate policy concerning the development of comprehensive education. As a contribution to this, the education sub-committee of the Communist Party published a discussion statement in 1980, *The Comprehensive School*, which contains the outlines of such a policy, and which can become the property (modified if necessary) of the broad democratic movement. The main issues raised include the need to establish genuinely comprehensive local systems of education, based on the neighbourhood principle – whereby each school acts as a centre for those living locally – and the extirpation of covert systems of selection through the operation of 'parental choice', as well as of systems which embody selective processes by retaining parallel systems of schools for students aged 13 or 14, the division being made by what is euphemistically called '*guided* parental choice'. The neighbourhood school system implies the provision of equal resources across the board, but with some discrimination in favour of schools disadvantageously situated. This involves a continuing fight against the implications for the 'choice' clauses in the 1980 Education Act.

Of great importance are the policy proposals concerning the internal organisation and functioning of comprehensive schools. There is first the question of the actual democratisation of the schools themselves – a step long overdue. The formation of school councils, consisting of representatives of the teachers, students and ancillary workers, with clearly defined powers over the inner organisation and policy of the school, both in terms of its academic and pastoral functions, is proposed to replace the current authoritarian role of the Head (a situation peculiar to Britain), whereby he or she alone is responsible to the governors for the functioning of the school. A few schools already operate on these lines, as do schools in many European countries (both East and West). Such a step, giving those who work in the schools responsibility for their functioning, is fully in line with contemporary proposals for industrial democracy, and would release a considerable amount of creative energy on the part of teachers and students. In connection with this, support for the foundation of student unions within the schools is also advocated, as also certain democratic reforms of governing bodies, including the involvement of parents and representatives of local community organisations in school government.

Of key importance for the Left is the neglected area of the curriculum. The single examination at 16 plus is, of course, strongly advocated, the central importance of which has already been discussed. This would enable all students to be kept together without differentiation to experience a common curriculum, or 'common core'. But as regards the curriculum itself there are, perhaps, two main principles which should govern labour movement policy. First, schooling must be so designed as to provide effectively, for the mass of the people, access to knowledge, science and culture. It has never done so in the past, nor had this objective; nor does it do so now. Objectively, therefore, this demand (or policy) inevitably has revolutionary overtones. A content of education, appropriate for all at this particular moment in history needs to be identified, and determined. Teachers and the labour movement generally need to work together on this and to sort out the basic principles and components of such an education.

Secondly, that content of education must, so far as possible, reflect reality, both in terms of science and society, and be so designed as to promote positive social attitudes and knowledge. Much work going on now in the schools is beginning to reflect this approach. There is now a more conscious and deliberate effort in the schools, for instance, to combat both racist and sexist ideas widely prevalent in society at large. In this sense a transformation of the content of education is already beginning to take place. But in addition, in the fields of history, the social sciences, literature, and science itself deliberate moves are needed to transform the content of education to bring it into line with the interests, history and aspirations of ordinary people. This is central to the conception of the transformation of education in line with the struggle for a socialist perspective.

Finally there are a number of ideological questions, relating particularly to the concepts of 'progressive' and/or 'child-centred' education on which, as mentioned earlier, the Left is confused and divided, so giving space to the 'New Right' backlash. In my view, Marxists have a very definite contribution to make here provided that they base themselves on the thinking and analysis of thinkers like Lenin and Gramsci, both of whom tangled with these issues in one way or another, both proceeding from the classic Marxist position on the relation between being and consciousness.[8] The work of Soviet psychologists in particular, for instance the late Professor Luria, Leontiev and others, is also particularly helpful here, since these have focused specifically on the elaboration of a Marxist approach to learning, and conducted a massive amount of relevant experimental work in this field. There is a lot of interest in their contribution among progressive circles both in Britain and the United States. In fact the basic principles of a Marxist approach to the whole business of learning, teaching and education generally is becoming clear, and this experience should be drawn on in developing our own approach which must be specific to the particular situation, and historical traditions, of this country.

While stressing the educability of the normal child, and therefore opposing all fatalistic theories such as those embodied in intelligence testing, Marxism points to the need for the systematisation of education – to the need for structure and for the promotion of carefully designed activities on the part of the child in the process of learning. The role of the adult, and particularly of the teacher, is seen as all-important and a critique needs to be made of those ideas (theories or ideologies) which propose that the child's spontaneous activities and interests should form the ground base of education – a proposal that explicitly denies the need for systematisation and structure (and whose ideological roots lie in anarcho-liberalism). Such ideas, developed early in this century as a reaction from the rigid, arid practices of the past, certainly contain positive aspects, particularly in their espousal of more humanist relations between teacher and child. But when taken up by some on the Left, they lead to a kind of romantic revolutionism that denies the need for political action and sees the isolated classroom as the focus and lever for social change.

Schools have the function of deliberately promoting not only the skills of numeracy and literacy, but, through a progressively deepening grasp of knowledge and culture, the autonomy of the student able to function effectively within society, and to use his or her abilities to change that society according to developing aspirations. Such a formation cannot happen by chance; nor by relying on supposed inborn or innate tendencies and abilities. It requires recognition of the formative power of education, the consequent definition of objectives, and identification of the means by which these objectives may be realised. It is in this whole area that there needs to be discussion among the left democratic forces both among teachers and among the public at large, with the aim of clarifying both general principles, and appropriate procedures.

This is a tall order, but we neglect it at our peril. Far too little attention has been devoted to it in the past. It is important now to recognise this, to make up for lost time, and institute a widespread discussion on these issues, drawing in as broad a spectrum of people as possible.

4

The general direction of policy, then, must be to work towards the transformation of education at all levels in line with the struggle for socialism – the two go hand in hand. A viable policy for the Left in the current situation involves not only a fight against the cuts (though this is essential), not only a fight in defence of the gains made in comprehensive education (though this also is essential), but to go further and work for the implementation of fully comprehensive schooling embodying the independent sector and putting an end to all proposals as to its continued existence. And, alongside this, to work for the transformation of the school, its control and government, inner organisation, as well as its activities in terms of the content of education and methodology. It is argued here that mass, popular support can be won for a broad policy along these lines, holding out the perspective of popular involvement in the transformation of the school.

The conditions are ripe for such developments. The reduction in the number of school pupils over the next few years presents new possibilities to the teachers, provided that the government's efforts to decimate the teaching force can be resisted (as experience shows they can). The micro-processor revolution, already under way, underlines the need for the development of new abilities and skills among the mass of the people and enhances the importance of education. In the process of struggle over the coming years, Tory pretensions can and will be exposed for what they are – a last ditch attempt to consolidate, even extend, existing privileges, and vested interests, and to strengthen the educational power base of their rule. Much patient and hard work will be needed; but a new perspective for the Left is becoming clear. If we can seize this opportunity, the gains could be great.

Notes

1. *Marxism Today*, October 1979. See also Stuart Hall and Martin Jacques (eds.) *The Politics of Thatcherism*, London, 1983, pp. 40–62.
2. *Marxism Today*, November 1979.
3. Neville Bennett *et al., Teaching Styles and Pupil Progress*, London, 1976.
4. But see 'Breaking School Rules', pp. 225-28, for later developments.
5. *Education*, 24 August 1979.
6. *Education*, 2 November 1979.
7. See *Forum*, Vol. 22, No. 2, Spring 1980.
8. Harold Entwistle's *Antonio Gramsci, Conservative Schooling for Radical Politics*, London, 1979, is very relevant to this discussion. See also Donald Cave's forthcoming *Gramsci and Education*.

10

Breaking School Rules: Keith Joseph and the Politics of Education

1

I n the spring of 1984 the government sustained a resounding defeat in the field of education. The events here were quite unusual and, to many, unexpected. It may be worth rehearsing these briefly at the start, since these set the scene against which an increasingly *dirigiste* policy is clearly emerging in an energetic attempt to strengthen centralised control over the shape, content and character of the educational system as a whole, as a crucial aspect of Thatcherite social policy.

The defeat occurred in the field of comprehensive secondary education. For many years in the mid and late 1970s and early 1980s, comprehensive schools (and their teachers) had come under sustained media attack, both in the popular press and on television. Yet (and this may appear contradictory) precisely while this was going on more and more schools were being transformed as comprehensives, so that the latest (1983) figures show that 90 per cent of all students of secondary school age in the maintained sector in England are in these schools, 95 per cent in Wales, and nearly 100 per cent in Scotland. These schools have been operating in particularly different circumstances over the last ten years, especially in urban areas. Drastically falling rolls have compelled further reorganisation; mass youth unemployment creates all sorts of problems relating particularly to motivation for both students and teachers; official (Ministerial) denigration of the work of the schools has been persistent and depressing. There have been,

---

Reprinted (with slight additions) from *Marxism Today*, September 1984.

of course, other factors as well – severe cut-backs in
educational expenditure; the position as regards teachers' pay.
It may be that these factors encouraged the new government-
inspired initiative in the autumn of 1983 to strike at the roots
of the comprehensive system and make a serious attempt to
turn the clock right back.

A public opinion poll, reported at this time, seemed to
indicate that a majority of those questioned supported the
selective grammar/modern school set-up in preference to
comprehensives. This was given very wide publicity, as was to
be expected of any news critical of comprehensive education.
The outcome was predictable. Some 60 Tory MPs, seeing
perhaps electoral advantage, signed a Parliamentary motion
favouring return to selective education. In addition, one of the
Ministers at the Department of Education and Science (Robert
Dunn), made a series of weekend speeches advocating a return
to grammar schools.

Solihull was among a number of Tory controlled local
authorities which leapt on the band-wagon, proposing the
transformation of two successful comprehensives as grammar
schools. The fact that all the other schools would, in effect, be
downgraded as secondary moderns was not mentioned. What
immediately became clear was that those in control had totally
failed to evaluate the feeling among the local population in
support of their schools. There was a massive outcry – large
meetings took place at which enormous majorities voted
clearly against the Council's proposals; in particular very
effective joint activity by parents (who set up a defence
association) and teachers' associations, especially the NUT, was
a feature of the campaign.

In face of this opposition, the original scheme was
withdrawn, but, in an attempt to save face, a second scheme
was then officially presented, now proposing that one school
only should be so transformed. But this again met with a
further massive outcry, together with a very effective campaign
launched by the local NUT association in co-operation with
parents and the local communities. So this scheme also had to
be abandoned.

Solihull had opted, and in a very clear manner, to retain its
comprehensives, and now no more is heard of the original

project. Targets have been lowered to supporting differentiation within schools, an issue to which I will return. But here was a clear and precise public test as to the degree of support that exists for local comprehensive systems – the first on this scale. Whatever people may say to public opinion pollsters, whose questions relate to abstract issues and are carefully worded, when the matter comes down to earth in an attempt to destroy local systems, comprehensive education, it seems, can call on a really massive degree of support. This is the lesson from the Solihull adventure.

But recent developments have gone further than this. The concurrent attempts in Berkshire and Wiltshire to extend existing selective procedures met with an equally unyielding opposition from local populations, again involving mass meetings and consistent pressure on Tory councillors. In both cases local populations have opted to retain non-selective procedures and, in effect, to defend existing comprehensive schools and system. At Redbridge also an overt attempt to turn back the clock and reintroduce (or extend) selective schooling was again met with a public outcry, and a clear rejection by the majority of the people living in this area.

Evidently, then, those who set out to disrupt and, in effect, to sabotage existing comprehensive systems, have been forced to retire with bloody noses. Comprehensive education has defeated a concerted and powerful challenge to its popularity and emerged with flying colours. Those who support, and those who teach in these schools cannot fail to take heart from these developments which transformed the scene over the winter and early spring of 1984, and certainly put a stop to further adventurist policies of this order.

2

It may be worth asking why this recent attack failed so completely and so dismally, and why support for comprehensive systems, in spite of the very real problems mentioned earlier, has built up in this way? The fact is that the mass of these schools are working well – or as well as can be expected given the severe cut-backs they are experiencing. Recently the

Wiltshire secondary heads have told their authority that they simply do not have enough money 'to satisfy even the basic educational needs of their pupils'.[1] Schools are increasingly being supported by voluntary fund-raising on a large scale – a procedure which, the heads rightly say, is inconsistent with the 1944 Education Act. This position reflects that in the country as a whole. Yet in spite of all this, comprehensive schools have many successes to their credit.

Examination results are admittedly a narrow criterion, and open to considerable criticism from many points of view. But these are often appealed to by those who claim that comprehensive education leads to a decline in 'standards'. What is the position here?

Comparing the position in 1981–82 to that eleven years earlier (1970–71, when less than half of secondary students were in comprehensive schools in England) we find that:

1. The percentage of the age cohort gaining five or more O Levels GCE (or their equivalent) – often used as the basic measure as regards trends in standards – has increased by over 30 per cent (from 7.1 to 9.4 per cent). This is a very substantial advance which coincides with a rapid swing to comprehensive education.
2. The percentage gaining from 1 to 4 O Levels GCE (or their equivalent) has increased by over 50 per cent (from 16.8 to 25.6 per cent).
3. The percentage gaining one or more grades D?E I levels or CSE grades 2 to 5 has increased by over 300 per cent (from 9.8 to 31.27 per cent).
4. Conversely, the percentage gaining no passes at whatever level in GCE or CSE has dramatically declined – from 44 per cent (or almost half) in 1970–71 to 12.9 per cent eleven years later.[2]

The fact that no qualifications whatever are offered to over a tenth of the students, and the inappropriateness of some of the actual qualifications mentioned above is another issue altogether. At this point what is worth stressing is the very positive achievements of the schools over what has been a very difficult and in many ways demoralising period. The credit for this must go to the schools – to the students themselves and above all to the teachers whose achievement it is. This success is also reflected in A Level results, which have improved by 7 per cent over the period examined, so that now 17.7 per cent of school leavers gain one or more A levels.

In the light of this overall achievement, investigations such as those conducted by Cox and Marks, which purport to show the superiority of the selective over the non-selective set-up in examination results, seem supremely irrelevant (quite apart from their flawed research procedures), and certainly not worth the enormous publicity the mass media afforded them – true to type.[3] Indeed it was, no doubt, partly the publication of these statistics, which coincided with the débâcle at Solihull (and elsewhere), that may have drawn from the Secretary of State, Sir Keith Joseph, a first, if still grudging, word of appreciation of the teachers in the nation's schools. 'Our schools', said Sir Keith, 'are offering more pupils a broader education and a larger proportion of pupils are successful in examinations at 16 plus.'[4] Not much of an accolade, perhaps, but at least an admission that education was no longer seen, in government circles, as a 'disaster', as Thatcher is reported as characterising it. Indeed the position has been well summarised by Barry Taylor, Somerset's Chief Education Officer, in a talk to the Secondary Heads Association. The achievements of secondary schools, he is reported as saying, 'were remarkable, despite the upheaval caused by the switch to comprehensive education and a background of unemployment, rapid technological and social change, shortage of resources and social instability'.[5] 'Those of us with responsibility for secondary education', he went on, 'need not feel defensive. Secondary schools are currently meeting the daunting challenges which our society represents in a way which is a major success story, not a catalogue of failure.'

3

It may be that the very success of comprehensive secondary schooling – as opposed to the myth of its 'failure' – has contributed to accelerating the clear and energetic thrust of both the present government and DES officials to greatly enhanced central control. Comprehensive secondary education, by its very form and structure, is potentially a great deal more open-ended than the functionally-designed school system of the past to which, it is now clear, there can be no return. It is not only that a whole series of actions (and statements) by Keith Joseph reflect this new centralist thrust (particularly *vis-à-vis* the local authorities and teachers); it is also that there are clear indications of a firm resolve, on the part of high DES officials, to gain a tight control over schools and local school systems with the object of bringing about a basic restructuring of education and so ensure that things do not get out of hand in terms of the preservation of the status quo and particularly of ensuring social stability.

On this latter issue, a recent study based on research casts an unusually revealing light on the thinking of senior officials at the DES – relating, in this case, to new policies seeking to impose sharp forms of differentiation on students at and before the age of 16, both within comprehensive schools and the system of further education.[6] The determination to achieve fully centralised power and control comes across very clearly. A senior DES official is, for instance, quoted as insisting that

> There is a need especially in the 16–19 areas, for a centrally formulated approach to education: we need what the Germans call 'instrumenterium' through which Ministers can implement and operate policy.[7]

Again, on the curriculum and assessment procedures for this grouping:

> I see a return to centralisation of a different kind *with the centre seeking to determine what goes on in institutions*: this is a more fundamental centralisation than we have seen before.[8] (My italics, B.S.)

Further statements by DES officials relate to the current attempt to restructure the curriculum within the school system as a whole, on lines which will be referred to below. As one official is quoted as saying:

> Our focus must be on the strategic questions of the content, shape and purpose of the whole educational system and absolutely central to that is the curriculum. *We would like legislative powers over*

the curriculum and the powers to control the exam system by ending all those independent charters of the examination bodies.[9] (My italics, B.S.)

The argument for centralising powers is based on the need for explicit social engineering to cope with the dangers arising from over-education in a contracting labour market. 'There has to be selection', another (anonymous) official is quoted as saying, 'because we are beginning to create aspirations which society cannot match.' There follows an interesting admission:

In some ways this points to the success of education in contrast to the public mythology which has been created. When young people drop off the education production line and cannot find work at all, or work which meets their abilities and expectations, then we are only creating frustration with perhaps disturbing social consequences. We have to select: to ration the educational opportunities so that society can cope with the output of education.[10] (My italics, B.S.)

The arrogation of centralised powers, in defiance of traditional 'partnership' systems, has a clear social purpose:

We are in a period of considerable social change. There may be social unrest, but we can cope with the Toxteths. But if we have a highly educated and idle population we may possibly anticipate more serious social conflict. *People must be educated once more to know their place.*[11] (My italics, B.S.)

The conclusion the study's author (Stewart Ranson) derives from this (and other) evidence is this, that 'the state is developing modes of control in education which permit closer scrutiny and direction of the social order'.[12]

This, of course, is no new thing in the history of education; indeed involvement by the state in the restructuring and control of education for social/political purposes has been apparent at least from the middle of the last century and earlier. What is new are the modes of control now being developed and brought into play. Significantly, the state, instead of working through and with other social organisations (specifically local authorities and teachers' organisations) is now very clearly seeking a more direct and unitary system of control than has ever been thought politic – or even politically possible – in the past. It is this that requires attention.

However one assesses the move to comprehensive education – and there has been a leftist tendency to denigrate or underestimate its significance – one thing is clear. The unified, single school, accompanied by a definite swing towards a common curriculum and the decline, or at least modification, of rigid forms of streaming, has opened up educational opportunities in a new, and perhaps unpredictable way. The Left – communists, socialists, radical educationists and teachers, sometimes aided by Labour controlled authorities – has fought tenaciously for many years specifically against the introduction of divisive procedures within these schools; a standpoint, incidentally, well reflected in the report of the Hargreaves Committee for the ILEA, where unitary or solidary procedures are recommended for all London's schools.[13] As this battle was proceeding within the schools, the world economic recession together with the Thatcher government's de-industrialisation policies resulted in a sharp contraction of employment possibilities for young people. The thinking of the DES officials, just quoted, reflects a vivid realisation of the contradiction between the skills, abilities and aspirations of young people as developed through home and school, and the actual perspectives offered by present circumstances. The solution, in their view, is the deliberate restructuring of the system embodying processes of continuous differentiation and selection, with each level in the age cohort assimilated to acceptance of its fore-ordained lot both on the labour market and in the social order.

This policy requires that early differentiation between groups of pupils or students be embodied in differentiated curricula (or courses) leading to differentiated objectives – the whole package culminating in a set of carefully designed examinations (or other forms of 'assessment') which set the seal on the structure as a whole.

The present government's policies point clearly in this direction and have done during their five years of office. First, as the parental choice clauses of the 1980 Education Act were designed, through forcing schools to compete with each other for students on the market, to lead to the enhancement of differentiation *within comprehensive systems*. Favoured schools, with good exam results, flourish, while less favoured schools, inevitably with less good results, tend to lose their students, become unviable as schools, and face closure. Alert local authorities, assisted by alert teachers, can and have succeeded in countering these developments, which are assisted by falling school rolls. But the objective is clearly to introduce and firm up a basic division between schools within comprehensive systems. This is one form of differentiation; though one should here recall the major division still existing between the private system (encouraged and supported by the government) and the maintained system as a whole, as a further, and perhaps more basic differentiation.

But of course it is *within* individual comprehensive schools that children must be subjected to different educational routines and procedures having widely differing objectives. Queried by Brian Walden on ITV about the events at Solihull and elsewhere, Keith Joseph stressed this very precisely. 'If it be so, as it is, that selection between schools is largely out,' he said, apparently realistically accepting defeat on this issue, 'then I emphasise that *there must be differentiation within schools.*'[14] This is a clear statement of the tactic to negate the move towards the unification of secondary education – the main objective of the comprehensive reform – and substitute, within the single school, the restructured system the DES officials, quoted earlier, have in mind.

What are the lineaments of that 'ideal' system which will ensure that each are 'educated once more to know their place'? It is clear enough and here Keith Joseph's decisions about the 'single' exam at 16 plus are crucial.

For 15 years or more, comprehensive school teachers and many others have fought a long battle for the fusion of GCE O Level (originally designed for the grammar schools) with the Certificate of Secondary Education (CSE), brought in in 1963 for secondary modern school pupils. The objective was the creation of a single exam which could provide an attainable perspective for *all* students and which would therefore obviate the need to differentiate between students for the two exams (and those not offered any exam) at the age of 13 or 14. Succeeding Secretaries of State, both Tory and Labour, have consistently delayed implementation of this though support for the single exam escalated greatly during the 1970s and early 1980s. A final set of decisions on this was announced by Joseph late in June 1984.

What has happened is that this originally radical reform (in conception) has been turned into its opposite, and developed into a clear and precise instrument for social engineering under central, or state bureaucracy, control. First, it is quite clear that this will not be a single exam at all, nor anything like it. Instead it will be a system embodying differentiation and grading of Byzantine complexity (as Gramsci once described aspects of the Italian system). The new General Certificate of Secondary Education (GCSE), Joseph announced, '*will be a system of examinations*, not a single examination'.[15] There will be 'differentiated papers and questions in every subject'. The present (university dominated) GCE boards are to be retained and made responsible for examining the top grades, A to C. These 'will be clearly distinguished from grades D to G' (there are to be seven grades in each subject). These lower grades will be the responsibility of the present CSE boards. Thus a clear and sharp differentiation between those candidates entering for the higher grades and those entering for the lower is built into the system as a whole. A new, more precisely rationalised system of differentiation now covering *all* students is to take the place of the old.

Further, the measure proposed embodies a clear bid for centralised control not only over the curriculum in general, but over each of its differentiated levels. This is achieved by the definition of 'national criteria' covering examinations in every subject. These 'criteria' are designed as 'instruments' by which control is shifted to the centre, since the Secretary of State must approve them.

Nor is it only a question of *general* criteria governing overall examining (and therefore teaching) objectives. In addition there are to be 'grade-related criteria' which, Joseph announced, 'will specify the knowledge, understanding and skills expected for the award of particular grades'. This implies that for each and every subject, seven sets of 'grade-related criteria' are to be established, in the attempt to define precisely what should be taught (or rather, learned) at *each* level. This surely implies the imposition of a differentiated system *par excellence*.

These decisions make it quite clear that the winnowing out of an élite will remain a primary function of comprehensive schools; the strongly-guarded route through GCE O and A Levels to the universities, higher education generally and the professions is to be retained and probably made even more selective.

This, then, is envisaged as one differentiated 'stream' within comprehensive schools. But the second route, now being erected, is perhaps the most significant in terms of government plans for restructuring. This is the technical/vocational route whose lineaments are not yet entirely clear, though becoming clearer. The way this route is being imposed on the schools contains new features characteristic of the more radical aspects of Thatcherism, involving the use of new state organisations or bureaucracies to act decisively and with speed against traditional procedures and the existing traditional state apparatus (the DES).

This is the use of the Manpower Services Commission, with its generous sources of funds, to initiate the Technical and Vocational Education Initiative (TVEI). Local authorities and schools, starved of resources, were offered additional cash for the specific purpose of providing new technical and vocational courses for named groups of students aged 14 to 18. £15 million of 'extra' money was allotted for this purpose in 1982–83, and the whole scheme expanded greatly in 1983–84, a majority of local authorities now being involved, though many Labour authorities have refused to participate.

Such courses will be provided with a terminal examination, the so-called '17 plus' (Certificate of Pre-Vocational Education), announced by Sir Keith Joseph a year or two ago – to take the place of the Certificate of Extended Education (CEE) supported by teachers and the (now defunct) Schools Council, but regarded by DES officials as too broad, or 'liberal', in its scope. The politics of this whole development are extremely complex, but the outcome is that a clear technical/vocational stream is being established alongside the academic stream within comprehensive schools. Indeed it is likely that the intention is that this stream should bifurcate into a higher and lower level, the majority focusing on more strictly vocational activities in the latter. New techniques of assessment (involving 'profiling', which has ominous implications from the social control angle) are likely to be used here.

Finally, for what Keith Joseph likes to call 'the bottom 40 per cent', plans are still unclear. But in January 1984, in a well-publicised speech at Sheffield to local authorities, Joseph developed ideas for short-term, 'criterion referenced' testing as a means of motivating and holding the interest of this large group of students, whose very real educational needs seem otherwise disregarded. Even the helots must be literate.

In the course of attempting to carry through a drastic restructuring of this kind, Keith Joseph has attempted to exert his authority, as Secretary of State, on the system as a whole, utilising in particular his powers of control and decision over examinations. Joseph's interventions in this sphere have been characteristic of his personal approach and ideology; but several of these interventions have been strongly resented since they appear to involve interference in the curriculum which has certainly not normally been within the Secretary of State's responsibilities.

However, basing himself on his powers over examinations and their criteria, Joseph has specifically refused to allow questions relating to the social functions and relations of science to be included in exam criteria for science (leading to strong protests from the prestigious Association of Science Education), has given his view as to what aspects of history should be studied (emphasising the need for a focus on national and patriotic values), and in various other ways made his preferences very clear. Other government members have ridiculed the growing move for peace studies in the schools, and so on. Perhaps such statements and decisions are straws in the wind, indicating the intention to exert a firmer direct control over the curriculum from the centre than has been attempted for a very long time – including a clear ideological (and Thatcherite) component. A whole series of further DES, or Ministerial, statements on the curriculum are promised, and these, no doubt, will take centralising measures further. Such *dirigiste* initiatives relating to the schools are, of course, in line with the powerful onslaught against university autonomy, their curricula (in the case of the Open University) and their financial position, the immediate manifestation of which is the determination to transform existing conditions relating to academic tenure, where legislation is now threatened. 'The

present government seems hell-bent on centralisation,'
commented *The Times Higher Education Supplement* in a major
leader in June 1984. 'No previous government has so
successfully aggrandised the power of the state while
simultaneously and loudly proclaiming its deepest wish to roll
back its frontiers.'[16]

4

A main characteristic of the recent period has been a quite
fundamental change in the balance of power between those
organisations concerned with education. Traditionally, this has
been conceived as a 'partnership' between the state on the one
hand, local authorities and the main teachers' organisations on
the other. This 'partnership' has been deliberately and
progressively disrupted over the recent period, a process
hastened since the Thatcher government took office in 1979.

First, there has been a concerted attempt to ignore,
downgrade and progressively to devalue the role of teachers'
organisations in determining policy – specifically in terms of
the curriculum, but in other fields as well. This reached its
culmination with the summary abolition of the Schools
Council by Keith Joseph. There is not space to go into the
history and significance of all this here, but the action, and its
results, were characteristic of the government's arbitrary and
undemocratic style. The Schools Council, on which teachers'
organisations were fully represented (and others of course),
was allotted responsibility for examinations policy, and given
the brief of researching and advising on the curriculum, in
1962. It carried out this brief for nearly two decades. The
primacy of the teaching profession on the Council was,
however, clearly resented by the DES in particular. During the
first Thatcher government, Joseph appointed a Committee of
one (Treneman) to investigate the Council and report. This
report, though critical, was favourable, and supported its
continuance.

A few months later Joseph announced the summary
abolition of the Schools Council and its replacement by two
quangos consisting largely of his own nominees – one to

oversee examinations, the other the curriculum. The NUT has refused to co-operate with either of these organisations (or rather, refused to submit lists of possible members from which Joseph would make his nomination). Neither of these organisations has as yet made any serious impact on the educational scene but the main objective has been achieved – that of reducing teachers' influence and, symbolically, explicitly rejecting their primary responsibility for the curriculum, i.e. what goes on in schools.

Second, by various means, some very harsh, local authorities have also been downgraded and, as we have seen in the rate-capping bill and in other ways, severely weakened *vis-à-vis* the central government (the determination to abolish the GLC and other metropolitan boroughs is symptomatic). There is now no organisation equivalent to the Association of Education Committees which in the past (particularly the 1920s and 30s), courageously defied the government when necessary and fought its policy proposals with energy and often with success. Local authorities, especially since reorganisation following the 1972 Act, no longer speak with a united voice in the area of education, and this has left the field open for central government or state initiatives to achieve primacy. The Green Paper of May 1984 which argued for a parental majority on school governing bodies and, if implemented, will create a mass of local parental élites with quite extensive powers, is only the latest in a long line of actions having the intention of reducing the powers of local authorities and confusing the issue with the clear objective of further strengthening state initiatives.[17]

There is, of course, always the possibility of resistance. Indeed, some Labour councils have agreed to defy the government over rate-capping. Equally important, for the first time both the Tory-controlled Association of County Councils and the Labour-controlled Association of Municipal Authorities are united in an outright confrontation with the government specifically over education. The issue is the highly 'radical' decision to divert rate support grant money covering a substantial proportion of the cost of further education courses and colleges from the authorities directly to the Manpower Services Commission, announced in the White Paper *Training for Jobs* (February 1984).

This would effectively remove control over a substantial sector of further education from local authorities and hand it to the MSC so that, as *The Times Educational Supplement* put it, 'it can specify what colleges do'.[18] Both local government associations have expressed their total opposition to this move and threaten to refuse to operate it. Both are demanding that the government's intention to divert the money be rescinded. There could hardly have been a more direct – some would say foolhardy – challenge to local authorities than this; an action which again brings out very clearly the lengths to which the present government is prepared to go to achieve new centralised powers. Over recent years, local authorities have tended to abdicate from their traditional stance in defence of education. Hopefully this new, direct challenge may lay the basis for a more energetic policy in the future.[19]

5

Two issues remain. First, how should the significance of these developments be assessed, and second, what should be the response of the progressive forces and the labour movement?

The ideology and approach of Thatcherism, acutely analysed in a series of articles in *Marxism Today*, seems only a partial explanation. Emphasis on the 'strong state', together with monetarist policies and reliance on the primary of market forces in determining economic development certainly underlies the deliberate policy of shoring up the private and downgrading the public sector. But the clear élitist policy imposing new systems of differentiation across the whole field of education, overtly pursued by the present government, has deeper roots than this. It is clearly linked with the scientific-technological revolution – in particular the rapid application of electronics, automation and robotics, combined with a determined policy of de-industrialisation.

These developments offer what are basically two options. The first involves reliance on market forces for the application and development of the new technology, and, in relation to this, confines access to the knowledge and essential new languages and skills to an élite selected through a carefully structured and hierarchic educational system. On this option, the mass of the people are excluded from access to this knowledge and related skills, and given instead a low level of education in 'the basics' together with what is now known as 'social and life skills', measures now dressed up in the rhetoric of the new vocationalism.

This is the option that has, not surprisingly, been chosen by the present government – one that ties in very precisely with its ideology. The 'policy' embodies a lack of planning in terms of economic development, the creation of mass unemployment, and, as the essential concomitant, close attention to the restructuring of education as a crucial instrument for gaining consent.

But there is a second option, the democratic option. This is based on the standpoint that the scientific-technological revolution gives the conditions for, and even necessitates, raising the educational level of the whole population, with the clear aim of ensuring that *all* are capable of mastering the scientific principles underlying the new technology, of operating it, and of ensuring that it be directed to realising its full potential for human and social development. This option implies that the introduction of the new technology proceeds on the basis of social planning determined by democratic decision-making; that hours of labour are reduced in a planned way while employment in the highly labour-intensive tertiary (or service) sector is largely increased, so contributing to the enhancement of life for all.[20]

This latter option requires greatly increased social control over industrial and work processes and development. It looks forward to socialism as the socio-economic formation most appropriate to the revolutionary developments in science and technology now being experienced.

If this is a socialist perspective, what of the immediate struggle to counter the increasingly clear objectives of the present government? First, all those countervailing forces in society, deeply rooted, and with long traditions of involvement, need to be encouraged not only to resist governmental and bureaucratic measures, but also to take the offensive in a more aggressive and clearly defined manner than has been the case in the recent past. This refers particularly to the local authorities, sometimes defined as the local state, but clearly responsive to local and democratic pressures (as we have seen, for instance, in the case of Solihull and elsewhere). These of course vary in their political complexion, but all have clear statutory duties relating to their own systems of education, by far the greatest of their responsibilities. Their standing with the electorate depends in part at least on their ability to maintain systems that have the confidence of their electors. In their resistance to the manifold encroachments by central government of the kind, discussed earlier, for instance, local authorities clearly have an important part to play.

Second, teachers' organisations, as has been made clear recently, can also act as a force of resistance, and a very important one. Unification of the teaching profession must surely remain a primary aim, since present divisions weaken their power and influence. But the teachers are those in the closest touch with the schools and colleges; potentially they can have the most direct say in what goes on within them, particularly if they act in an organised way. The profession has suffered an understandable drop in morale as a result of the rapid deterioration of their conditions of work and of the hammering they have taken over the last ten years or so. But there are signs of a new militancy and of a professional determination to defend educational values – and so the conditions necessary for their preservation. To strengthen teachers' morale, to encourage here also a more aggressive stance in defence of education and their own professional interests must remain a primary objective.

Finally there is the position of the labour movement as a whole. Educational policy on the Left lost its way to some extent in the 1970s – particularly during the Callaghan government – partly as a result of weak leadership but also because the Labour Party's educational policy was caught up in the ideological confusion caused by the last Labour government's lack of direction and clear abandonment of socialist perspectives. The situation here is now changing. Both the Labour and the Communist parties have formulated clear policy statements covering the whole field of education (and especially the controversial 16 to 19 area). The trade union movement is also now becoming increasingly involved in educational issues. What is needed now is an alliance between the labour movement, progressive local authorities and the teachers around the positive programmes formulated by the left political parties. Important here also is the whole issue of transforming education in such a way as to encourage genuine *community* involvement in local schooling. At Croxteth in Liverpool a highly successful battle has been fought by the community to preserve a comprehensive school serving the locality and to transform it as a centre of community activities.[21]

This article started by referring to a specific set-back suffered by the government in education. The attempt to deliver a further (perhaps mortal?) blow to comprehensive systems by transforming these to selective systems was roundly defeated by mass movements involving parents, teachers and the local community. If it can be done once it can be done again. But the issues are seldom so overt as they were in this case. Often the measures carried through by government are covert, subtle, long-term – for instance, those relating to examinations policy. An effective counter-strategy requires the consistent monitoring of every move, in whatever area, by today's authorities – the deliberate seeking out of information, and the fullest publicity and explanation.

The present government is mounting a carefully designed and relentless struggle to strengthen centralised control over all areas of education, clearly realising the crucial role education plays, both ideological and structural, in the maintenance of existing class and social relations. But the contradiction between human abilities and aspirations and the reality of a rapidly contracting labour market is sharpening. Hence the urgent need for energetic action on the part of the bureaucracy which aims to establish the tight central control thought necessary to cope with developing circumstances. The logic of these events, now unfolding with unprecedented rapidity, is the intensification of contradictions and the sharpening of antagonisms. This provides the conditions for a unified and clear-sighted opposition which, directed by educational and human values (and so the interests of the great majority of the population) can halt the slide towards total central control, restore democratic approaches and measures, and point towards the socialist transformation of education and society as the social form required to realise the potentialities of the third industrial revolution.

Notes

1. *The Times Educational Supplement*, 23 March 1984.
2. DES, *Statistical Bulletin* 2/84, February 1984.
3. Marks, Cox and Pomian-Srzednicki, *Standards in English Schools*, Esher, 1983.
4. *The Times Educational Supplement*, 13 January 1984.
5. *Guardian*, 9 April 1984.
6. Stewart Ranson, 'Towards a Tertiary Tripartism: New Codes of Social Control and the 17+', in Patricia Broadfoot (ed.), *Selection, Certification and Control*, London, 1984.
7. Ibid., 238.
8. Ibid.
9. Ibid., 224.
10. Ibid., 241.
11. Ibid.
12. Ibid.
13. *Improving Secondary Schools*, Report of the Hargreaves Committee, ILEA, March, 1983.
14. *The Times Educational Supplement*, 17 February 1984.
15. For this and succeeding quotations on the proposed GCSE, *The Times*, 21 June 1984.
16. *The Times Higher Education Supplement*, 8 June 1984.
17. *Parental Influence at School: a new framework for school government in England and Wales* (Green Paper); Cmnd 9242, HMSO, 1984. In the event, due to the almost unanimous opposition of bodies consulted, this proposition has been dropped.
18. *The Times Educational Supplement*, 29 June 1984.
19. Unfortunately, divisions within the local authority organisations finally allowed a compromise favourable to the government's intentions early in 1985.
20. The implications of the scientific-technological revolution for education are discussed in more detail in 'Why No Pedagogy in England?', pp. 89ff.
21. Phil Carspecken and Henry Miller, 'Community Education in Croxteth', *Forum*, Vol. 27, No. 1, Autumn 1984.

Index

28. Gramsci praises the elem. sch — but nowadays sch is not the ~~sole~~ counter to superstition etc. as it was then. And also — yes, essential pre-cond for socialism, but not itself anti-cap.

37. Ed in 1880s/90s — idea of 'all can be educated' — not modelled on gram. schs.

42. 1920-40 — IQism + progressivism

51. Must move away from what differentiates chn. to what they have in common.

63 + 8. The right power-holders in ed, for BS, ag. the govt., are these heroic local 'cadres' — not the w/c directly.

72 Marx on state & control. — & see pp 180+

85. Elem schs of late 1800s had a _pedagogy_ — lack of